BUSINESS/SCIENCE/TECHNOLOGY DIV.
CHICAGO PUBLIC LIBRARY
400 SOUTH STATE STREET
CHICAGO, IL 60605

D1204446

Dew of Death

JOEL A. VILENSKY

With the assistance of Pandy R. Sinish
Foreword by Richard Butler

Dew of Death

The Story of Lewisite, America's World War I Weapon of Mass Destruction

INDIANA UNIVERSITY PRESS

Bloomington and Indianapolis

This book is a publication of

Indiana University Press
601 North Morton Street
Bloomington, IN 47404-3797 USA
http://iupress.indiana.edu
Telephone orders 800-842-6796
Fax orders 812-855-7931
Orders by e-mail iuorder@indiana.edu
© 2005 by Joel A. Vilensky
All rights reserved

No part of this book may be reproduced or utilized in any form or by any means, electronic or mechanical, including photocopying and recording, or by any information storage and retrieval system, without permission in writing from the publisher. The Association of American University Presses' Resolution on Permissions constitutes the only exception to this prohibition.

The paper used in this publication meets the minimum requirements of American National Standard for Information Sciences—Permanence of Paper for Printed Library Materials, ANSI Z39.48-1984.

Manufactured in the United States of America

Library of Congress Cataloging-in-Publication Data

Vilensky, Joel A., date-

   Dew of death : the story of lewisite, America's World War I weapon of mass destruction / Joel A. Vilensky ; with the assistance of Pandy R. Sinish; foreword by Richard Butler.

   p. cm.

   Includes bibliographical references and index.

   ISBN 0-253-34612-6 (cloth : alk. paper)

   1. Lewisite (Poison gas)—History. 2. Organoarsenic compounds—Toxicology. I. Sinish, Pandy R. II. Title.

   UG447.5.L48V35 2005

   358'.3482—dc22   2005001678

1 2 3 4 5   10 09 08 07 06 05

R040727067b

CHICAGO PUBLIC LIBRARY

This book is dedicated to my father, Abe Vilensky,
who is always there when I need him.

CHICAGO PUBLIC LIBRARY

Grandma smelled geranium,
Started feeling kind of bum.
Sure you guessed the trouble, right—
Grandma whiffed some Lewisite.

From *How to Tell the Gases,* by Major Fairfax Downey,
United States Field Artillery Branch

Contents

Foreword

A little more than a century ago, international law was made seeking to prevent the use of "asphyxiating gases" in warfare. Less than twenty years later those weapons—chemical weapons—were used during the First World War. That use, first by the Germans but later by the Allies, broke international law. More dramatically, it appalled people throughout the world. The stories of the choking, blistering, pain, and convulsions suffered by victims were heard with horror. So the community of nations went back to the legal drawing board and made further law—the 1925 Geneva Convention. This Convention sought to strengthen the prohibition on any use of chemical weapons. Whereas it is difficult to define very precisely what constitutes a weapon of mass destruction, chemical weapons have been seen as such for the past one hundred years, and they are unique in the extent to which they have attracted international consensus that they should be outlawed. But chemical weapons have also had a seductive history. Simultaneously with efforts to outlaw them, they have repeatedly been the subject of research, manufacture, weaponization, deployment, and use.

The story of lewisite encapsulates the key elements of the history of chemical weapons and their continuing seductive power. That power, at its simplest, has been the notion that rather than suffer the rigors and losses of direct combat, an army could vanquish adversaries by spraying them with substances from the air or blowing a cloud of poison in their direction.

From the First World War to the present time, in countries and situations across the globe, attempts have been made to produce the droplets or gases that would grant this power. Throughout this period, lewisite has always been involved.

The fantasy of chemical weapons has never approached reality. From the beginning there have always been problems of use and safe disposal of chemical agents. This book records the repeated instances of injury and accident associated with lewisite use, and the decisions taken against using lewisite, partly because there was uncertainty whether its use would also, in fact, harm the user.

In addition to such complications, ethical and legal issues needed to be addressed. As is typical in arguments about war, there were always those voices advocating that any means that would help our side win were justifiable. Early in the history of lewisite, arguments were advanced to the effect that it was actually a humane weapon. Death or injury from a good dose of lewisite was presumed to be less agonizing than that from bullets and bayonets. There were, of course, also arguments that any weapon that brought a war to its end sooner rather than later should be viewed as beneficial and admissible. In this context, Winford Lee Lewis argued that knowledge of the planned use of lewisite by the Allies was an important factor promoting Germany's sudden agreement to an armistice.

Joel Vilensky's book, *Dew of Death*, is a detailed and immensely useful account of the development and history of one of the major chemical weapons of our time. It contains both the required scientific detail, and historic and political perspectives. It also identifies principles and issues that apply to weapons of mass destruction generally.

The first and most important of the latter is what I would call the axiom of proliferation. This asserts that as long as any state possesses weapons of mass destruction, others will seek to acquire them. This assertion does not simply derive from logic or some alleged principle of human behavior, although both of these means of analysis do support the axiom. Rather, it is a statement of fact based on experience. The history of chemical weapons —and certainly of lewisite, as recorded in this book—is a perfect example. Every use of chemical weapons has been met with a like response. More particularly, as states have acquired chemical weapons capability, others, especially those who deem themselves in an adversarial relationship with such a state, then act to acquire a similar capability.

The axiom of proliferation has been fulfilled in vastly greater measure for chemical weapons than for any other comparable weapon of mass destruction. Nuclear weapons have constituted a slightly different, more restricted case, but there is great anxiety today that this will not remain so. I shall return to this concept later.

The central meaning of this mechanism of proliferation is that the only way to be safe in the face of the existence of weapons of mass destruction technology is to establish a situation in which there is widespread agreement that no state should have any such weapons, and to create the mechanisms to ensure compliance with such an agreement. The history of attempts to establish such a situation with respect to chemical weapons is one of growing strength and a commitment to a chemical weapons free world. This history is illustrated in a very relevant way in this book.

In the period following the 1925 Geneva Convention, utilization of chemical weapons, in situations where their use was contemplated, greatly diminished. There can be arguments about utilization of chemicals during the Second World War, and in other theatres of conflict during the last fifty years. Of course, there is no dispute about Nazi Germany's use of chemicals in its program to exterminate Europe's Jews and other designated undesirable persons. But it is important to recognize, as Professor Vilensky does, that although very substantial quantities of chemical weapons were produced and stockpiled in the latter half of the twentieth century, there was no large-scale use of them. It seemed that the putative norm that chemical weapons were not admissible was taking hold.

There were two notable exceptions. Chemical weapons were widely deployed by the United States in Vietnam as defoliants and to debilitate enemy combatants. Whereas there has been continuing official prevarication about such use, one of the ways we are able to verify their use is through observation of their enduring effects on the United States and Allied combatants.

The second instance was use of chemical weapons by Iraq in the 1980s, first on Kurdish populations within Iraq, and then on Iran during the Iraq-Iran War. Saddam Hussein's attack on Halabja is thoroughly documented. It is established that Saddam used a range of chemical agents at that time. Iraq also used chemical weapons against Iran in 1984 when it feared being overrun by Iranian troops on its southern border. As Professor Vilensky notes, this use was examined by the United Nations and verified. By coincidence, at that time, it was my turn, as Australian representative, to serve as President of the United Nations Conference on Disarmament in Geneva. On instructions from the Conference, I summoned the representatives of Iran and Iraq separately to express grave concern at the reported use of chemical weapons. The Iranian representative confirmed that chemical weapons had been used against Iranian forces. The Iraqi representative would neither confirm nor deny this. Inconveniently for him, however, an Iraqi general in the field at about the same time publicly remarked, "Of course, when you've got an insect problem, you use insecticide."

A dozen years later, when I was Executive Chairman of the United Nations Special Commission to disarm Iraq, I referred to the same issue in one of my many private conversations in Baghdad with then Iraqi Deputy Prime Minister Tariq Aziz. He readily confirmed to me Iraq's use of chemical weapons against Iran. Indeed, he said that their use, together with the missile-based "war of the cities," had saved Iraq. Aziz and Saddam Hussein were clearly men who believed in the saving power of weapons of mass destruction. This belief ignored then, as it continues to ignore today, that a fundamental driver of Iran's weapons of mass destruction program was Iraq's program, just as Israel's program helped drive both.

A compelling part of this book is its compilation of the chemical weapons arsenals developed by a range of countries around the world and its account of the ubiquitous presence of lewisite in those arsenals. Possibly the most depressing part of this compendium, in addition to the raw fact of its existence, is that in so many cases the weapons manufactured have been produced in vast quantities, which then predictably led to problems of their safe storage and disposal.

The case of the former Soviet Union stands out in this context. Lakes, waterways, fields, and buildings in the former Soviet Union have been poisoned by the vast quantity of chemical weapons, including lewisite, produced there. Securing and cleaning up all of this should be a major international priority.

At an earlier point I mentioned the issue of the proliferation of nuclear weapons. Their vertical proliferation during the Cold War is well established. The four nuclear weapons produced in 1945, detonated first in New Mexico and then over Japan, grew into an arsenal of some eighty thousand weapons, held principally by the United States and the Soviet Union, by the time the nuclear arms race was halted in the mid-1980s. That number of weapons has now been reduced by more than half; in that sense, the trend line is pointing in the right direction.

But the axiom of proliferation remains accurate with respect to so-called horizontal proliferation—the emergence of new nuclear weapons states. Israel is the prime such state, and it has never remotely been brought to account. India and Pakistan have followed; others, including Sweden, South Africa, and Iraq have tried over the years. Today, it seems well established that North Korea and Iran are well launched into acquiring a nuclear weapons capability. One of the claims of these new nuclear weapons states is that the bargain made in the 1968 Nuclear Non-Proliferation Treaty has never been kept; that those with nuclear weapons should eliminate them and those without should never acquire them. As the former has never happened, so the argument goes, there is no reason why the latter should be fulfilled. It is clear with respect to both chemical and nuclear weapons that the only way in which the international community's stated goal can be achieved is for those states that have them to get rid of them.

In many respects chemical weapons led the way into the modern period of weapons of mass destruction. Perhaps, fittingly, they are leading the way out. The 1993 Chemical Weapons Convention, now adhered to by virtually all states, completes the lawmaking process begun in the Hague Conventions at the end of the nineteenth century that extended to the 1925 Geneva Convention. The 1993 Convention provides that no state should ever hold, make, deploy, or use chemical weapons or provide any other state assistance to do so. The prohibition is complete and it does involve the destruction of existing stockpiles. It holds the best possibility of a world free of chemical weapons, including prevention of their acquisition by terrorists.

As Professor Vilensky points out, we will always know how to make lewisite, the "Dew of Death," but that does not mean that we should be compelled to accept such weapons in our lives.

Richard Butler
Former Head of United Nations
Special Commission to Disarm Iraq
November 2004

Acknowledgments

Archivists, librarians, and historians deserve their own resort in heaven. It never ceased to amaze me that I could call or e-mail a librarian in the next state or across the world with a question and 98 percent of the time receive an answer—often with the following question: "Where can I fax you a copy of the relevant documents?" I thus begin by thanking the librarians and archivists without whose help this book would not have been possible: Ellen Alers, Smithsonian Institution, Washington, D.C.; Ellie Arguimbau, Montana Historical Society, Helena, Montana; William Baldwin, United States Army Corps of Engineers, Washington, D.C.; Daniel Barbiero, National Academies Archives, Washington, D.C.; Judy Brimmer, Churchill College, Cambridge, United Kingdom; Gradon Carter, Porton Down, Salisbury, Wiltshire, United Kingdom; Holly Comben, Royal Naval Museum, Portsmouth, United Kingdom; Jacqueline Dougherty, Congregation of the Holy Cross, Notre Dame, Indiana; Marisa Duarte and Heather Morgan, Catholic University of America, Washington, D.C.; Richard Durack, Stratford Library, London, United Kingdom; John Frisk, Purdue University, West Lafayette, Indiana; John Gonzales, California State Library, Sacramento, California; Amira Hamdy, Rocky Mountain Arsenal, Denver, Colorado; Nancy Hanson and Peter Lysy, Notre Dame University, Notre Dame, Indiana; Alan Hawk, National Museum of Health and Medicine, Bethesda, Maryland; Judy Hermann, Chemical and Biological Information Analysis Center, Aberdeen, Maryland; Christopher Hunter, Schenectady Museum, Schenectady, New York; Jodi Iverson, Bernard Schermetzler and Micaela Sullivan-Fowler, University of Wisconsin, Madison, Wisconsin; Raymond Jorgeson, Indiana University, South Bend, Indiana; Mitzi Kanbara, San Francisco Public Library, San Francisco, California; Deborah Kenworthy, Carnegie Public Library, Washington, Indiana; Lesley Martin, Chicago Historical Society, Chicago, Illinois; Robert Michaelson and Patrick Quinn, Northwestern University, Evanston, Illinois; Jan Miller, Willoughby Public Library, Willoughby, Ohio; Martin Mumaw, Davies County, Washington, Indiana; Ann Salsich, Western Reserve Historical Society, Cleveland, Ohio; Jeffrey Smart, Research Development and Engineering Command, United States Army, Aberdeen, Maryland; John Swann, Food and Drug Administration, Washington, D.C.; Kathy Thomas, Post Street Archive, Midland, Michigan; Karen Thomelson, Lake County Historical Society, Kirtland Hills, Ohio; Michael Wilkinson and Rick Ralston, Ruth Lilly Medical Library, Indianapolis, Indiana; Mitchell Yockelson, National Archives and Records Administration, Washington, D.C.; and Renee Ziemer, Mayo Clinic, Rochester, Minnesota.

Many individuals kindly responded to my questions (and sometimes provided documents) about chemistry, chemical warfare, and other topics: Abu Alam, Jo Beckerich, Lucas Berresford, John Blandamer, Robert Boyle, William Brankowitz, William Brooks, Mark Brown, John Bryden, Bonnie Buthker, Chip Carson, Jeanette Clausen, Mac Coffman, Dianne Dehaseth, Ronald Duchovic, Ginny Durrin, John Ecklund, Patrick Eddington, Robert Edson, Michael Forgy, Richard Gibson, Donna Gordon, Marty Gray, Jody Hamm, James Hershberg, Cas Heuer, Harold Jaffe, David Jardy, Kevin Jasper, Daniel Jones, George Kajtsa, Reid Kirby, Michael Koredoski, Jim Lewis, Edmund Libby, John Lindsay-Poland, Iain MacKenzie, Vincent Maloney, Milt and Kathy McClung, Arend Meerburg, Pamela Miller, James Moore, Kevin Morrissey, John Mountcastle, Barbara Nabors, Erik Olsen, Kent Redman, Robert Reese, John Rentschler, Jr., Robert Ritter, Edmund Russell, Todd Sedmak, Kenneth Shuster, Joshua Sinai, Kent Slowinski, William Smith, Paula Schnurr, Tara Sweeney, Elmer Turner, Anthony Trozzolo, Cheryl Truesdell, Michael Wartell, David Wedepohl, Steve Wood, and Jane and Will Wuichet.

Before Indiana University Press accepted this book for publication, I received thoughtful and helpful advice pertaining to publishing it from Julie Barer, Barbara Freese, Tad Floridis, Elizabeth Nagle, Neil Olson, and Robert Shepard.

This book would not have been possible without the patient, and in many cases long-term, assistance of others. The living descendants of Winford Lee Lewis were highly supportive of this project and provided many documents and insights about him: Philip Reiss, Lee and Wilson Harwood, and Wendy and Rich George. Philip Reiss also provided valuable editorial advice. Dr. David Hall, a former Army chemist, spent countless hours explaining lewisite chemistry to me via e-mail. Jeffery L. Frischkorn, a reporter for the *Willoughby News-Herald*, provided me with copies of all of his documents pertaining to the Willoughby plant and took me on a tour of Willoughby and the plant site. Richard Albright, a toxic waste specialist with the Washington, D.C., Department of Health, provided many documents and information pertaining to Spring Valley. Charles Bermpohl, a reporter for the *Northwest Current,* also provided much information about Spring Valley and introduced me to many individuals in Washington who were investigating Spring Valley issues. Mark Baker, historian for the United States Army Corps of Engineers in Baltimore, kept me abreast of the Corps' efforts in Spring Valley and provided me with copies of his records. Dr. Leopold May, Emeritus Professor of Chemistry at Catholic University of America, greatly assisted me by providing information and documents on the history of that institution. Theodore Conant, James Bryant Conant's son, met with me on a cold day in December 2002 in New York City and provided me with insight into his father. I want to thank Dr. Margery Ord for breakfast in Oxford and for arranging the interview with Dr. Lloyd Stocken, to whom I am also very grateful for sharing his memories of the development of BAL. Ellis T. Baggs, who was employed at the lewisite plant at Huntsville during World War II, graciously agreed to allow me to interview him. Deborah Dennis, FOIA officer at the Research, Development, and Engineering Command, United States Army, processed my endless requests as expeditiously as she could. Ed Cohen, Associate Editor of *Notre Dame Alumni Magazine,* encouraged my first article about lewisite that appeared in that magazine. Similarly, John Limpert and Drew Lindsay of *Washingtonian Magazine* greatly encouraged the writing of this book when they accepted my story for their magazine. Linda Rothstein, Editor of the *Bulletin of the Atomic Scientists,* was a joy to work with on an article about lewisite that I wrote for that magazine. Lauren Bryant, editor of the Indiana University magazine, *Research and Creative Activity,* was a wonderful resource for me, answering an untold number of questions about writing and publishing, and Karen Grooms, a writer for that magazine, wrote an encouraging article about my work on this project. Dr. Pamela Sandstrom, head of reference and library information services at Indiana University—Purdue University, Fort Wayne, is thanked for teaching Pandy and me how to search relevant databases for information. I am thankful to Roberta Shadle and Elmer Denman for providing assistance with the illustrations and photographs. Both Jane Quinet and Robert Sloan championed my project with Indiana University Press, and they and Jane Lyle graciously guided me through the publishing process. I am grateful to Candace McNulty for the marked improvement in the book her copyediting provided.

My wife, Deborah Meyer-Vilensky, and children, Sarah and Rachel, encouraged this project; Brian L. O'Connor devoted countless hours to improving the book's readability; Jennifer Cook, Meg Mettler, Philip Reiss, and Steve Sarratore each read drafts of this book and provided detailed editorial comments. Many friends generously gave of their time to provide encouragement and editorial advice: E. Brian Carsten, Joseph Fortin, David Nichols, Jeffrey Strayer, Glenn Merkel, Sid Gilman, Susan Stoddard, Stephen Carmichael, and Ed Weber. Dr. Barth Ragatz, Assistant Dean at Indiana University School of Medicine, Fort Wayne, and my boss, and Dr. Ora Pescovitz, Director of Research for Indiana University School of Medicine, supported my efforts in every way they could. Linda Adams helped greatly by making all the financial aspects associated with this project easy. Douglas and Suzanne Schiffman are thanked for providing me a place to stay while conducting research at the National Archives and Records Administration in Washington, D.C.

Lastly, my research assistant, Pandy Sinish, assisted in all aspects of this book, but most importantly made sure that I was true to my sources. I am very fortunate to have had her help.

Introduction

My grandfather served in the United States Army during World War I and after being discharged became a pushcart peddler on the Lower East Side of New York City. While serving in France he saw the victims of German mustard gas attacks, and these images remained vividly etched in his memory as he described to me the pain and blindness experienced by some of these soldiers. Thus, I imagine that when he began reading the *New York Times* on Sunday, April 20, 1919 (something he did each day), he was immediately attracted to a story headlined "Our Super-Poison Gas: First Story of Compound 72 Times Deadlier Than 'Mustard,' Manufactured Secretly by the Thousands of Tons." The first paragraph began:

> It had the fragrance of geranium blossoms. It was an oily amber liquid, highly explosive and bursting into flame with water. It was the American super-poison gas, deadly by contact or by inhalation of the smallest detectable portion. A drop on the hand would cause intolerable agony and death after a few hours. It was called methyl (partly because that name did not describe it) and it was the climax of this country's achievements in the lethal arts.

My grandfather would have been very proud and pleased to learn that the United States was prepared to beat the Germans at their own game.

"Methyl" was an alias devised by the Chemical Warfare Service (CWS) for "lewisite." Lewisite was initially synthesized in 1903 by a Catholic priest, Father Julius Aloysius Nieuwland. It was later named after Winford Lee Lewis, a chemist who in 1918 rediscovered and purified the compound and characterized its structure. Lewisite achieved its "72 Times" greater toxicity than mustard by incorporating deadly arsenic in a form that could be absorbed by the skin or breathed in through the lungs. After World War I, it became known among the general public as the Dew of Death, because World War I military strategists envisioned it being sprayed from airplanes as tiny droplets of death gently descending to the ground and sticking to everything like the morning dew.

One hundred years after its initial synthesis, on Monday, April 7, 2003, during Operation Iraqi Freedom, Major Michael Hamlet of the United

States 101st Airborne Division reported finding fourteen barrels of the chemical agents lewisite, tabun, and sarin buried in the sand. Later these barrels were determined not to contain chemical agents, but the initial alarm demonstrated that lewisite was among the agents the army expected to find in Saddam Hussein's chemical arsenal. Lewisite, like tabun and sarin, is classified as a "weapon of mass destruction." A one-hundred-year-old chemical weapon still caused Major Hamlet to be fearful for himself and his men. Why?

Just as Father Nieuwland had not intended to discover a chemical warfare agent, I stumbled across lewisite's story quite by accident. I am not a chemist, nor do I have a particular interest in military history. I am a professor of anatomy and cell biology at Indiana University School of Medicine with a research specialty in the history of neurology. There is a very rare neurological disease called Wilson's disease that causes strange, involuntary bird-like movements in its victims. The disease is fatal and until 1951 was untreatable. In that year, a Harvard University neurologist, Derek Denny-Brown, used a compound called British Anti-Lewisite (BAL) to markedly reduce the abnormal movements associated with the disease. This was a spectacular achievement because it was the first instance in which a drug reduced such movements by correcting a chemical imbalance in the brain. Accordingly, it had a profound effect on the whole discipline of neurology, paving the way for many such curative drugs in the future.

In 2001 I was asked to give a presentation at the American Academy of Neurology convention in Philadelphia on this first successful treatment of Wilson's disease. As I prepared for this presentation, I began to worry that someone in the audience might ask me what "lewisite" was, and I had no idea how I would answer. Thus began my journey into the amazing history of this chemical compound. It is actually quite ironic that despite the tens of thousands of tons of lewisite that have been produced since 1903, BAL has probably saved more lives than the number killed by the agent itself.

I was particularly intrigued by the lewisite story because of the irony pertaining to its antidote and the many other ironies that continually appeared in its history. I was also astonished to learn that the Department of Defense still would not release 1918 documents pertaining to its initial research into the compound. Further, lewisite's discovery by a priest was a twist that piqued my interest. Similarly, the fact that much of the work on lewisite during World War I was done at a Catholic institution, the Catholic University of America in Washington, D.C., struck me as unusual. Why would chemical warfare research be done at a religious institution?

Following lewisite's rediscovery in 1918, the CWS secretly ordered the construction of a plant devoted solely to its production. The plant was located in Willoughby, Ohio, a small city outside Cleveland. I toured the Willoughby plant site in 2001 with Jeffery L. Frischkorn, a reporter for the *Willoughby News-Herald*. Jeff had written two stories about the plant for the paper, raising concerns that residues from the 1918 operation might be polluting the area around the plant. Was this true?

World War I ended before any lewisite was used on the Western Front. Was there any evidence that the Willoughby plant had actually produced any lewisite? If so, how much, and what happened to it? When I tried to find answers to these questions, the information was often highly ambiguous and contradictory. Why?

As my research continued, I learned that the chemist who directed the Willoughby plant was a man by the name of James Bryant Conant. That name seemed familiar. I remembered that the same Harvard neurologist, Derek Denny-Brown, who had first used BAL had been hired away from his position in London by the president of Harvard University, a James Bryant Conant. Could it be the same person? I verified that it was indeed.

Conant had additional connections to lewisite. During World War II Conant was appointed chairman of the National Defense Research Committee. In that role he oversaw additional lewisite research and was also the de facto administrative head of the Manhattan Project, which built the atomic bombs that were used against Japan. In the atomic bomb project Conant had to manage delicately the egos of the scientists involved in the project as well as its military overseers. How was he able to do this? He had performed the same role at the Willoughby plant. Thus there was a direct connection between lewisite, the atomic bombs, and winning the Second World War. There were even some hints that German fear of American use of lewisite had led to the Allied victory in the First World War. Was this true?

All of the belligerents in the First World War defied the 1899 and 1907 Hague Treaties and used chemical weapons. Similarly, Germany, Italy, England, France, and the United States were prepared to use lewisite during the Second World War, but toxic chemical agents were only used on the battlefield by Japan in China (however, Germany did use poison gas, hydrocyanic acid [Zyklon], to murder prisoners in the concentration camps). Why? Remarkably, the United States and its Allies, after spending millions of dollars during the early phases of World War II refining and producing lewisite, concluded in 1943 that it would not work very well under combat conditions. Furthermore, the allies tested thousands of their own unsuspecting soldiers with lewisite and mustard gas during the World War II years, producing detrimental health effects that still plague these men today. Why did they do this? And what happened to all the lewisite that was produced during the war?

What is a country to do when it has not yet been able to develop the most modern weapon possessed by its enemy? This was the situation confronting the Soviet Union immediately after World War II. The United States had atomic weapons and the Soviet Union did not. The Soviet Union's response was to develop huge arsenals of chemical and biological weapons, including lewisite. Today Russia has the largest lewisite stockpiles of any country in the world, and it has sought and received millions of dollars of Western aid to develop technologies to destroy its chemical munitions safely. The Soviet production of lewisite has left a trail of arsenic-polluted lakes, rivers, and dump sites surrounding the now defunct lewisite plants.

Currently North Korea is in a similar situation to that of the Soviet Union after World War II. It is developing nuclear weapons but also considers chemical weapons, including lewisite, to be an important part of its military strategy. How much lewisite North Korea possesses is unknown, but factories are believed to be producing it in quantity. Sudan may also be still producing lewisite, and Libya just recently announced that it would discontinue its chemical weapons program, which probably included lewisite.

The issue of arsenic residues from lewisite production is not confined to Russia. Zachary Wilnowski grew up in an area of Washington, D.C., adjacent to the campus of American University (AU). During World War I, the campus and the surrounding area, now known as Spring Valley, was the primary site for developing and testing chemical munitions. Zachary has had great difficulty staying employed because of headaches and chronic fatigue, which he believes are due to arsenic toxicity. Others in the area have had similar symptoms. They believe that these conditions result partly from buried lewisite munitions in this region. Is this true? After initial denials that the AU area had a problem with lewisite and other chemical agent residues, the Army Corps of Engineers has now committed over $100 million to clean up this area. In some cases the Corps is removing the top layers of soil from the front and back yards of residents' homes. Debates (and lawsuits) continue between residents and the Corps as to how much more needs to be done. One Environmental Protection Agency official declared the situation in Spring Valley to be worse than that of Love Canal (a residential area of Niagara Falls, New York, that was evacuated in 1978 because of hazardous chemical wastes). The weapon designed to win World War I may be causing much more damage in 2004 than it did during that war.

Finally, whereas the vast consensus among military strategists is that lewisite is an antiquated weapon of no real relevance to the modern world (save perhaps for North Korea), it nevertheless seems to be having a rebirth. Since the attack against the United States on September 11, 2001, fear of chemical weapon use by terrorists has become a real concern for the Western World. Mock terrorist attacks across the United States have been conducted to test the readiness of communities to effectively combat the danger. Lewisite has been the presumed agent that the imaginary extremists used in some of these tests.

Lewisite, a chemical agent rarely used in any conflict, continues to influence the modern world. We live in fear of its use and its arsenic residue. It has a life, which may or may not be ending. Regardless, its tale reflects the history of technological and political strategies and military conflicts during the twentieth century.

A note on sources: To enhance the readability of this book, source information via superscripted reference numbers is confined to direct quotations. Other chapter source information is provided via a listing of thematic topics covered in each chapter. All of these chapter source lists, which are presented in the notes, contain abbreviated source information except for letters and e-mails, for which the provided information is complete. Full citation information for all other sources is available in the bibliography.

Dew of Death

1   1878: Two Stars Are Born

In 1878 two men of science who would become unpredictably linked to the development of what some consider the world's first weapons of mass destruction (WMD) were born eighty-five hundred miles apart—Julius Aloysius Nieuwland in Belgium and Winford Lee Lewis in California.

Nieuwland is by far the better known of the two, though not specifically for his role in the discovery of lewisite. Nieuwland's primary fame, which culminated in his induction into the National Inventors Hall of Fame in Akron, Ohio, is for his role in the development of synthetic rubber in 1931. This acetylene-based product, initially called Neoprene and, later, Duprene, was marketed by DuPont beginning in 1932. Duprene was superior to natural rubber because it was more resistant to sunlight, abrasion, and extremes in temperature. Royalties from this discovery greatly enriched Nieuwland's employer, the University of Notre Dame, and were used in 1952 to fund the construction of Nieuwland Science Hall on its campus.

Julius Aloysius Nieuwland was born to Flemish parents, John Baptist and Philomena, on the morning of February 14, 1878, in Hansbeke, Belgium. When he was two years old, his family immigrated to the established Flemish community in South Bend, Indiana. On his first day at St. Mary's parochial school in South Bend, six-year-old Julius quietly mumbled his name to his teacher in his native Flemish. The sister could not understand his quick recitation of "Julius Aloysius" and announced that, henceforth, Julius's middle name would be Arthur. Apparently his parents did not object, as his baptismal name was never again used. Nieuwland excelled in and loved his studies in science, but when he graduated from St. Mary's in 1892 his first calling was to the priesthood. His fascination with science, especially botany, was his way of seeing God's work in the world.

Nieuwland chose to become a *religious* priest, that is, a member of a religious order, as opposed to a *diocesan* priest, who is associated with a local parish and serves the local bishop. He was influenced by the strong presence in the South Bend area of the Congregation of the Holy Cross, which is headquartered at Notre Dame. This Roman Catholic community at the time owned the University of Notre Dame and the high school-

1. Julius Arthur Nieuwland, 1899.
Courtesy Congregation of Holy Cross, Notre Dame, Indiana.

college seminary on its grounds, in which young Julius enrolled. The Congregation strongly emphasized teaching as its mission to serve God. Even at the young age of fourteen Julius knew he wanted to serve God by teaching science.

Nieuwland completed a bachelor's degree in philosophy in 1899 at the University of Notre Dame. He then spent time in study and prayer as a novitiate to evaluate whether to take his first vows (and whether the superiors in the Congregation would accept him), which would help confirm his desire to become a priest–scholar. He decided that he did indeed want to pursue this vocation. In August 1900, he traveled with his seminary class to Washington, D.C., to enter the graduate seminary at Holy Cross College on the campus of the Catholic University of America (CUA; at the time Notre Dame did not have a graduate seminary). One year later he took vows of poverty, chastity, and obedience and received his habit (shoulder cape, cord, and cross). He then began a standard trial period to prepare himself for his final vows and ordination as a priest of the Congregation of Holy Cross. Nieuwland became Father Nieuwland on December 19, 1903, and began to fulfill his destiny by enrolling in a doctoral program in botany at CUA.

At CUA Nieuwland chose for his mentor Dr. Edward Lee Greene, a man who had compiled an unrivaled botanical library and herbarium. But just as Nieuwland began studying under Greene, his mentor accepted a new position at the Smithsonian Institution and was unable to supervise Nieuwland's graduate studies. If Greene had remained at CUA, Nieuwland never would have become interested in acetylene chemistry and the chemical processes underlying the discoveries of lewisite and synthetic rubber.

Nieuwland was disappointed in Greene's departure but did not hold any animosity toward him. Years later, in 1914, Nieuwland arranged for him to teach at Notre Dame, where Greene became a professor of graduate botany, bringing to the university his extensive collection of plants and books and ultimately bequeathing it over a hundred thousand specimens and twenty-five hundred rare and valuable botany books.

With Greene's departure from CUA and with the blessings of his Holy Cross superiors, Nieuwland decided to switch majors from botany to chemistry and study under professor of chemistry Father John Griffin. Botany became his graduate minor.

Griffin was interested in the chemistry of the gas acetylene, which has a simple chemical formula, C_2H_2 (two atoms of carbon combined with two atoms of hydrogen). His interest was contagious and Nieuwland quickly became infected. At this time in the early twentieth century, acetylene was a very important compound. First discovered in 1836, it did not become commercially important until 1892, when, upon burning coal tar with lime a Canadian electrical engineer named T. L. Willson obtained a hard black crystalline mass. Serendipity then intervened; Willson accidentally dropped some of the hot black mass into water, producing acetylene. The black material, calcium carbide, afforded an inexpensive way to produce large quantities of acetylene, which burns with a pure white light, providing an easily generated source of illumination. Acetylene was also combined with oxygen for use in welding. In contrast to its use in welding, the popularity of acetylene as a lighting source was short-lived because incandescent electric lights improved and came into common use in the early 1900s.

Nieuwland and Griffin decided to try to understand acetylene chemistry by studying its interactions with other compounds. The result was Nieuwland's doctoral thesis, simply titled "Some Reactions of Acetylene." And the thesis was true to its title. It is a collection of short sections describing the reactions between acetylene and seventy-five other compounds under various conditions. Nieuwland's Ph.D. was the first awarded in chemistry by CUA.

One of the compounds Nieuwland combined with acetylene was an oily, odorous, highly poisonous liquid called arsenic trichloride, ironically referred to as arsenic butter. When Nieuwland first bubbled acetylene gas through arsenic trichloride, nothing happened. Nieuwland, undeterred, decided to perform the experiment a second time, using aluminum chloride as a catalyst. (A catalyst is a chemical agent that acts as an intermediary in a reaction, thus enabling it to occur. The catalyst, however, remains unchanged when the reaction is completed.)

Nieuwland described the reaction that ensued:

> The contents of the flask turned black. When decomposed by pouring the substance into cold water, a black gummy mass separated out, and on standing for some time crystals appeared in the aqueous solution. The tarry substance possessed a most nauseating odor, and was extremely poisonous. Inhalation of the fumes, even in small quantity caused nervous depression.[1]

Nieuwland did not mention in the thesis that his exposure to this toxic mixture caused him to become so sick that he was hospitalized for several days. He did state that because of its poisonous nature he would not pursue further work on the compound. In a 1922 newspaper interview Nieuwland emphasized that, at the time he discovered lewisite, there was no particular use for the toxic mixture formed.

When acetylene and arsenic trichloride combine under the correct conditions, several compounds are formed, one of which is composed of carbon, hydrogen, arsenic, and chlorine ($C_2H_2AsCl_3$). This particular compound has various chemical names, including: dichloro-(2-chlorovinyl) arsine; arsine, (2-chlorovinyl) dichloro-; chlorovinylarsine dichloride; 2-chlorovinyldichloroarsine; 2-chlorovinylarsonous dichloride; and beta-chlorovinyldichloroarsine. Its generic name is lewisite.

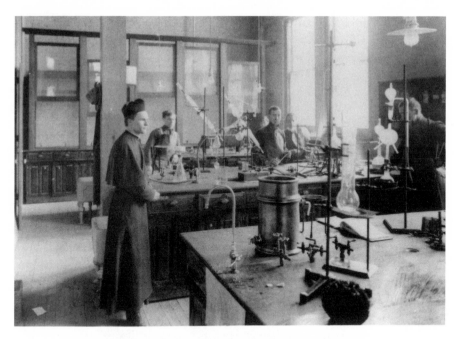

2. Father Julius Arthur Nieuwland, ca. 1920.
Courtesy Congregation of Holy Cross, Notre Dame, Indiana.

Were the conditions in Nieuwland's flask correct for the formation of lewisite? Later in life Nieuwland expressed confidence that he had in fact synthesized lewisite. But lewisite is not tarry and does not precipitate crystals. Perhaps, though, lewisite did form in the flask—at least enough to make Nieuwland ill.

Upon completion of his doctoral research, Nieuwland followed his plan and returned to Notre Dame to become a professor and, later, (1920–23) dean of the College of Sciences. He taught in the departments of botany and chemistry, conducting highly regarded research in both disciplines. At Dr. Greene's suggestion, in 1909 Nieuwland founded a journal devoted to the natural history of the country's Midwestern states called the *Midland Naturalist,* later renaming it the *American Midland Naturalist.* Nieuwland remained the editor for twenty-five years and often contributed articles to the journal.

Nieuwland was awarded the Morehead Medal of the International Acetylene Association in 1932 and then, in 1934, received the Gold Medal of the American Institute of the City of New York. In 1935, Nieuwland was awarded the William H. Nichols Medal from the American Chemical Society (ACS). All three of these honors were for his discovery of synthetic rubber. Nieuwland was also awarded the Mendel Medal of Villanova College in 1936, which was the only honor he received for his work in botany.

During his tenure at Notre Dame, Nieuwland displayed his spirituality in his counseling of students and celebrating daily mass. However, most of his spirituality was probably directed inwardly, nurtured by the joy he felt exploring God's natural world and in teaching. An excellent professor at the graduate level and for motivated and hardworking undergraduates, Nieuwland was not, however, well regarded by mediocre students at the undergraduate level.

Nieuwland's reputation attracted a Notre Dame student named Knute Rockne, who began studying for a master's degree in chemistry under his guidance in 1914. After graduating, Rockne was hired by Nieuwland as his assistant. They worked together for three years and became close friends. One day Rockne noticed an advertisement for football coach and applied for the position. He was offered the job and became one of the most famous college football coaches in history. Nieuwland believed Rockne would have prospered as a chemist, but because Nieuwland also loved football he was only mildly disappointed when Rockne switched careers.

Beginning in about 1933 Nieuwland began suffering from an "acidic stomach." Surprisingly, for a man of science, he had little confidence in the medical doctors of his day and sought medical treatment only when absolutely necessary. His lack of faith in physicians was attributable to a belief that too many physicians were mediocre in their work. Instead of seeking medical treatment he often experimented with self-made remedies, including ingesting dilute hydrochloric acid for his acidic stomach, which would intuitively seem only to have exacerbated his discomfort.

Despite his illness, Nieuwland continued to travel and on June 11, 1936, was in Washington visiting the institution that meant nearly as much to him as Notre Dame. On that day he was sitting in a comfortable chair in room 218 of CUA's chemistry department in Maloney Hall, talking to Professor Henry Ward, when he felt a sharp pain in his chest and had difficulty breathing. He died from a heart attack a few minutes later, which was apparently unrelated to his stomach condition. Obituaries appeared in newspapers throughout the country, including the *New York Times*, and in magazines such as *Science, Commonweal,* and *Catholic World.* His body was returned to Notre Dame and laid to rest in the Community Cemetery (located near Saint Mary's Lake and Moreau Seminary) while *In Paradisum* (*May the Angels Lead You into Paradise*) was sung.

Nieuwland occasionally mentioned his role in the discovery of lewisite in post–World War I interviews. He considered it to be a humane weapon because he believed a smaller percentage of soldiers would be killed by poison gas than by more conventional weapons. Furthermore, many enemy soldiers would be required to care for the gassed men and thus be unavailable for combat. Nieuwland's lack of any misgivings about his role in the discovery of lewisite probably reflected a view that it was simply another part of God's natural world. In any case, if he did discover lewisite, the discovery was accidental. Winford Lee Lewis, however, was looking for just what the good Father had found.

Lewis was born to George Madison and Sara Adeline Lewis on May 29, 1878, in Gridley, California. When Lewis was about four years old, his mother and two of his five brothers died (Sara and one brother from tuberculosis, the other brother possibly from bone cancer). In a semiautobiographical essay published in 1924, Lewis described the Gridley of his childhood as consisting of eighteen saloons, a post office, a grocery store, a blacksmith's shop, and several small churches. He noted that the "men patronized the saloons, the women the churches and the horses the blacksmith's shop."[2] He wondered whether his early exposure to this very alcoholic environment unconsciously directed him toward a career in organic chemistry.

Lewis attended grammar school in Gridley and high school in nearby Oroville. He then enrolled in Stanford University, where he intended to study law but, much to the displeasure of his father, graduated in 1902 with a degree in chemistry. Eager to continue his education, he immediately traveled to Seattle to pursue a master's degree in chemistry from the University of Washington. While there he was employed first as an assistant instructor in chemistry and then as the head instructor in chemistry. Although Lewis's post–high school education centered on chemistry, he had very eclectic interests, commenting later in life that at Stanford he "browsed in many things."

Upon receiving his master's degree from the University of Washington in 1904, Lewis moved to Sioux City, Iowa, to become a chemistry professor at Morningside College. Here Lewis met his future wife, Myrtilla Mae Cook, who was one of his chemistry students. Lewis was drawn to Myrtilla because of her drive and knowledge. When Lewis received a fellowship offer from the University of Chicago, Myrtilla and Lewis abruptly decided to get married. They were married on September 27, 1906, at the Chicago home of her uncle, T. P. Cook, and would later have two daughters, Miriam and Winifred Lee.

Lewis studied carbohydrate chemistry at the University of Chicago under the guidance of Professor John Ulric Nef. At this time, Nef was the most renowned organic chemist in the country and was known to accept only a few graduate students and demand much of them. To earn money, Lewis also accepted a position as an assistant chemist at the United States Department of Agriculture, in the Food and Drug Division. As a respite from chemistry, he also became an extra at the Chicago Opera. Music continued to be a diversion from his professional duties for the rest of his life.

Lewis was awarded a Ph.D. from the University of Chicago in 1909 (five years later than Nieuwland), having majored in chemistry and minored in bacteriology. Lewis's thesis, "On the Action of Fehling's Solution on Malt Sugar," was accepted for publication by the *American Chemical Journal* in its October 1909 issue.

With degree in hand and a bright future ahead, Lewis accepted a position as a chemistry instructor at nearby Northwestern University in Evanston, Illinois, where he was promoted in 1912 to assistant professor and to associate professor in 1916. Lewis was an inspiring teacher of chemistry. One year he taught a course in household chemistry that was designed for young women, but almost two-thirds of the class consisted of men who had been enrolled in previous courses taught by him. In contrast to his later work on poison gases, Lewis pursued very tame research at this time, such as continuing his work on carbohydrate chemistry and investigating how to maintain the water quality of public swimming pools.

In 1917, with the United States now an active participant in the First World War, Lewis decided to apply his chemistry skills for the good of the country. He traveled to Washington, D.C., in the fall of that year to discuss his participation in the war effort with representatives of the War Department. Because of his prior work, Lewis was initially offered a position in the Food Division of the Sanitary Corps. However, "with visions of meat cleavers in the hands of irate camp cooks,"[3] he decided that this was too hazardous an undertaking and volunteered instead for the Gas Service (later the Chemical Warfare Service, or CWS), then under the Bureau of Mines. Lewis was granted a captain's commission in the Ordnance Department on December 22, 1917, and began pursuing poison gas research.

After accepting the position with the Gas Service, Lewis told his wife

3. Winford Lee Lewis, ca. 1917.
Courtesy Philip Reiss.

that they would have to live on "prunes and beans" (lyrics from a popular song of the time), referring to a drop in income resulting from his leave of absence from Northwestern University. Apparently, and incorrectly, Lewis expected the war to last a few more years, because he sold his Evanston house at 726 Milburn Street after his wife and two daughters moved to Washington in January 1918.

The war ended in November 1918, and in 1919 Lewis returned to Northwestern as a full professor of chemistry and head of the Chemistry Department, but he also continued his association with the CWS. In June 1919 Lewis was promoted to major in the CWS Reserves, in 1922 to lieutenant colonel, and in 1933 to colonel. He clearly enjoyed his rise through the ranks and preferred being called "Colonel" by family members, mostly grandchildren, for the rest of his life. Before returning to Northwestern, Lewis had rejected a position as chief research chemist at the Goodrich Chemical Company in Akron, Ohio. The company had offered him a salary of $5,000 per year plus a 25 percent initial bonus. Northwestern offered him $3,500. Apparently, Lewis valued basic (as opposed to applied) research and teaching substantially more than the additional money. Similarly, he counseled his son-in-law, Wilson Harwood, never to allow money to get in the way of his career.

In an article published in the *Chemical Bulletin* immediately after the war ended, Lewis displayed remarkable prescience about Germany and World War II. He wrote, "Who can say that Germany, if there is Germany, is defeated and penitent? The memory of that 'forty miles from Paris' will fire her military brain with a gambler's mania to try again for decades to come."[4] Lewis believed that it was the threat of massive Allied retaliation, presumably with gas, that caused "Fritz" to "faint" on Armistice Day.

Unlike his prewar research, which had focused mainly on carbohydrate chemistry, Lewis's postwar research at Northwestern initially continued his lewisite-related work on arsenic-based compounds. Later publications, however, again pertained to carbohydrate and food chemistry. In June 1920 Lewis became chair of the Chicago section of the ACS.

Lewis accepted a position as director of the Department of Scientific Research for the Institute of American Meat Packers in 1924. Here he studied food waste and spoilage problems and devised procedures for better utilization of waste products, while remaining on the faculty at Northwestern until 1930. He retired in 1941 from his directorship at the Meat Packers due to health problems, possibly associated with Parkinson's disease.

During his postwar career Lewis received a patent for one invention. The Lewis-Hughes Police Grenade was a round, hollow, copper shell about the size of a baseball that contained three chemicals in glass vials. Upon impact the glass vials would break, causing the chemicals to mix. This, in turn, caused the copper shell to open and release tear gas. These grenades were widely used to quell mobs and to displace holed-up criminals. They were better than previous grenades because they did not require explosive materials to detonate, just a hard throw.

Throughout his post–World War I career Lewis expressed pride in the work he and his group did on the development of lewisite. The whole country first learned of his role in lewisite development through the publication, on May 25, 1919, of articles in the *New York Times* and the *Washington Post*. Many articles followed in newspapers and magazines across the country. Lewis was not only proud of his work on lewisite, but also advocated for the use of poison gas in war, believing it to be a step up in the evolution of weapons and a more effective offensive weapon than high explosives.

On June 7, 1923, a celebration was organized in Lewis's honor by the Pioneer Historic Association of his hometown of Gridley. Among the many people in attendance was the governor of California, Friend Richardson. At the celebration Lewis argued for a national policy of "rational pacifism." This he described as the ability to "fight like hell when the cause demands."[5] Lewis's achievement was recorded on a bronze tablet that was affixed to a six-hundred-year-old oak tree on the family farm. The inscription on the tablet read:

> The Lewis Oak
> Tribute to
> Major Winford Lee Lewis
> Originator of "Lewisite" Gas
> Born on this property
> May 29, 1878
> and
> To Those of the Community
> Who Served in
> The World War[6]

The plaque currently is affixed to the outside wall of the Veterans' Hall in Gridley. The plaque was moved to this location in 1944 after the Lewis Oak toppled during a windstorm.

Although Lewis's professional life was dominated by chemistry, his home life centered around devotion to his family and other interests, including reading the classics, music, and writing poetry for his daughters, one of whom (Lee Harwood) remarked that he wrote for "the pure joy of writing." A sample of Lewis's poetry was published in the *Washington Alumnus*:

> The turkey is a noble bird,
> His is our country's greatest pride.
> His neck is ragged, sunburned, shirred
> He wears his tonsils all outside.[7]

This sample suggests that although Lewis may have enjoyed writing poetry, he was a better chemist than a poet!

Lewis was not a pompous man and did not dwell on his accomplishments. When listing his degrees for an article he was asked to write on "How I Became a Chemist," he concluded the list with M.V.F.D. A perplexed editor telephoned him asking what degree those letters represented. Lewis responded, "Member Volunteer Fire Department."

On the morning of January 20, 1943, Lewis asked Myrtilla if she would like to go for a ride. She agreed, but said she had to finish something at her desk first. Lewis went upstairs to his study to wait. Myrtilla became anxious after a few minutes when he failed to return. She ran upstairs and saw footprints in the snow on the flat deck overlying the garage that extended from Lewis's study. Making her way to the railing at its edge, she saw Lewis's body motionless on the driveway below. Lewis is believed to have had a heart attack, which caused him to stumble and fall while cooling off on the deck (his skin often had a strong burning sensation). He was dead when the ambulance arrived. Funeral services were held at St. Mark's Church in Evanston, and his ashes were scattered on a hill in back of Stanford University by the Chairman of the Chemistry Department.

An obituary on Lewis by Otto Eisenschmil appeared in the *Chemical Bulletin* in 1943. Eisenschmil, who was Lewis's friend and colleague, stated that in his later years Lewis preferred to dwell on his work on the chemistry of sugars and organic arsenicals, rather than on lewisite. Lewis's daughter, Winifred Lee Harwood, also remembers her father wishing that his work on sugar chemistry was better known than that of his development of lewisite. Lewis considered chemistry "a sport as well as a profession and therein lies the lure." Lewis knew he could have earned more money outside the university, but he "would rather live outside Eden with Eve than inside without her."[8]

2   The Poisonous Yellow Cloud and the American Response

By early 1915, less than one year after World War I began, it had become a stalemated, defensive war. Both sides realized that high-explosive artillery shells were ineffective at dislodging men from defensive trenches. And blankets of machine-gun fire prevented successful offensive actions without associated devastating losses—Germany alone had suffered over 2.5 million casualties. Both sides thus believed that *something* else was needed to drive enemy soldiers from the relative safety of their trenches, and poison gas became that *something*, despite the international agreements of 1899 and 1907 banning the use of asphyxiating gases as weapons (interestingly, the one major country that did not sign these agreements was the United States). France initiated plans to use tear gas, but Germany introduced chlorine gas, a strong lung irritant, first.

Delivery was the main problem confronting the German generals in their planned use of chlorine. How were they to get the agent to the enemy's trenches? Later in the war, gas artillery shells would be used, but initially no such gas shells existed. Fritz Haber, director of the Kaiser-Wilhelm Institut für Physikalische Chemie at Dahlem, proposed a simple but feasible solution—release a poisonous cloud of chlorine gas from cylinders. German gas troops were organized and trained accordingly.

April 22, 1915, was a charming spring day with a slight northeast breeze whispering along the trenches near Ypres, Belgium, a Flemish market town just beyond the French border. The breeze was unusual; on most days the European winds blow from west to east. The Germans had been waiting for this unusual breeze; they began heavy shelling of the opposing Algerian and French forces at 4:00 P.M. The gas troops then opened the nozzles on about 6,000 previously positioned metal cylinders containing chlorine gas, releasing approximately 160 tons of it.

"[T]wo strange yellow wraiths of fog crept forward, spread, drew together, took on the blue-white tint of water-mists, and drifted before the gentle wind, down upon the rather puzzled but unsuspecting (Allied) lines."[1] The clouds reached perplexed Algerian troops first and shortly thereafter French troops. What was it? Perhaps merely some smoke from a new type of explosive powder? Then, as the heavier-than-air gas seeped into the crevasses that protected them from artillery shells and gunfire, the Allied troops began breathing the poisonous vapors. Some of the victims ran, pointing to their throats as they struggled to breathe. The less fortunate ones writhed on the ground, struggling to use their now water-logged lungs. These victims were drowning as plasma from their pulmonary blood vessels invaded the air spaces of their lungs. Their bodies turned green. Five thousand men died of gas that day.

The not-yet-incapacitated French and Algerian soldiers retreated, leaving a gap of 4.5 miles between the Allied and German forces. The Germans advanced, capturing the small towns of Langemarck and Pilkem, plus some two thousand prisoners and fifty artillery guns. At nightfall the Germans erred, deciding to consolidate their positions rather than pursue the retreating troops. This allowed the latter to regroup and counterattack the next day.

The successful Allied counterattack on April 23 prevented the Germans from advancing further. The German command ordered another gas attack, this time against a Canadian-held position near Saint Julien. The Canadians initially resisted but eventually lost Saint Julien and a small tract of land, although they were not forced into a full retreat.

Despite their lack of preparedness for a chlorine gas attack, the Allies almost immediately developed an effective gas mask, rendering subsequent German chlorine attacks less devastating. And the Allies began using the same gas in return. On December 19, 1915, the Germans upgraded to a more toxic gas, phosgene (phosgene reacts with the normal moisture in the upper airways to form carbon dioxide and hydrochloric acid that immediately irritates the cells lining the trachea; additionally, phosgene that reaches the lower airways attacks the surface of alveolar capillaries causing membrane damage and pulmonary swelling). Effective gas masks were again quickly developed by the Allies to protect their soldiers from this agent. This pattern continued—the Germans would develop a new offensive agent and the Allies would respond with an effective defense (gas masks). Then, within about six months, the Allies would start manufacturing the same agent, and use it against the Germans. Both sides also developed gas artillery shells, eliminating dependence on the wind for agent delivery. Chemical warfare thus became a contest between the development of effective offensive gases and defensive gas masks. Because of this seesaw battle between offensive and defensive developments, gas was not proving to be the decisive weapon the German High Command had envisioned it to be. But then came mustard.

Beginning in July 1917, the Germans filled their gas shells with a liquid poison that when vaporized stuck to anything and everything. Further, these mustard vapors were able to penetrate clothing, including rubber boots and leather gloves. Chemically, mustard gas is 2,2'-dichlorodiethyl sulfide, $(ClCH_2CH_2)_2S$. Although unrelated to mustard seed, it typically is described as having a characteristic mustard-like odor, although the unpleasant odor has also been described as resembling rubber, dead horses, rotten vegetables, gasoline, garlic, and lamp oil. When inhaled, mustard is five times more toxic than phosgene. Mustard is also insidious; upon first exposure it does little more than induce sneezing. When the first British soldiers were exposed to mustard gas they removed their gas masks, because they thought the Germans were trying to deceive them into falsely believing a poison gas attack was occurring. However, within a few hours, their eyes became inflamed and swollen, they developed painful blisters wherever the agent touched the skin, and they began to vomit. Their throats burned, they developed severe coughs, some became blind, and some died by the third or fourth day. Within three weeks of the introduction of mustard, it had caused fourteen thousand British casualties—more gas casualties than had occurred in the entire previous year. The British named this new gas "HS" for "Hun Stuff."

Mustard is a very persistent chemical agent. It remains active for weeks, even on the ground or bushes. Allied soldiers had to fear every step they took. They often felt helpless, because neither gas masks nor clothing provided effective protection. Morale problems became paramount.

In contrast to the previous chemical agents pioneered by the Germans, the Allies were unable to readily retaliate with mustard. The British did not produce mustard until April 1918 and did not use it in battle until September of that year. And their version was 30 percent weaker than the German compound. The French used it a little earlier, in June 1918. Thus, for almost a year Allied soldiers were bombarded with a chemical agent for which they lacked a good defense and to which they could not respond in kind. In terms of the gas war, Germany had scored a very decisive victory.

The United States did not enter World War I until April 6, 1917. For almost three years prior to this the United States had debated its course of action, yet it remained basically unprepared for war. This was especially true for gas warfare. When the United States finally declared war, it had no

4. Gas mask drill during World War I.
From Dorsey, "Contributions."

gas masks or plans to make them or any plans for large-scale gas production. This lack of foresight may have reflected the prevailing view that gas warfare was barbaric, unbecoming of the American soldier, and it undoubtedly cost American lives.

Reluctantly, with the begrudging realization that the United States would have to become involved in the chemical war, the government turned to the agency most experienced with asphyxiating gases, the Bureau of Mines. This organization, with the cooperation of the American Chemical Society (ACS) and the Chemistry Committee of the National Research Council, began to recruit university chemists for gas warfare research. By July 1917, fifteen thousand chemists had responded to a survey asking whether they would be willing to help in the war effort. Because at this time there was no mechanism to pay civilians working for the military, the hired chemists were simply granted military commissions as an expediency enabling them to be paid.

The chemists needed laboratories to conduct their research, and by the end of May 1917 the Bureau of Mines had been authorized to utilize laboratories at twenty-one universities. By September, additional laboratories were operating at many other academic institutions, including the Catholic University of America (CUA) and American University (AU) in Washington, D.C.

CUA had not waited to be asked to serve its country. "In view of the present emergency the Catholic University of America has the honor to offer itself to you for such services as the Government of the United States may desire from it," wrote Rector Thomas Shahan to President Wilson on March 28, 1917. Wilson responded two days later, "Let me thank you warmly for your generous letter of March 28. I am very grateful to you for your pledge of cooperation and support."[2] This exchange led to the establishment on January 15, 1918, of a chemical weapons research unit there. Surprisingly, the establishment of this unit did not appear to pose any ethical dilemma for the university. This absence probably reflected the media-portrayed view that the enemy soldiers were little better than barbarians, and the belief that CUA's scientific resources were needed to defeat them. Accordingly, Shahan said in a notice to university students on May 26, 1917, "This war itself is a scientific war; and before it ends we shall need, as other nations have already found, to continue unremittingly at the task of research and preparation."[3]

Shahan's offer may have reflected more than a willingness to help in the war effort. Catholics comprised a significant percentage of the enemy's soldiers and civilians, and Protestant America was wary about whether or not American Catholics would fight their religious brethren. Protestant America also questioned whether Catholics' ultimate loyalty was to Washington or the Vatican. Thus, Shahan's offer was perhaps a symbolic as well as a practical one—it demonstrated Catholic patriotism.

The chemical weapons laboratory established at CUA was designated Organic Unit No. 3 of the Offense Research Section and was under the direction of newly commissioned and former Northwestern University associate professor of chemistry Captain Winford Lee Lewis. Lewis's immediate supervisor, the director of Organic Unit No. 1, at AU, was Captain James Bryant Conant. AU and Conant also play important roles in the lewisite story.

When the United States entered World War I in 1917, AU was just establishing itself as a university; it would graduate its first class that year. In April 1917, shortly after the United States entered the war, AU's board of trustees offered President Wilson the use of the university campus in support of the war effort. The offer was accepted. The Bureau of Mines began building offices, laboratories, and testing facilities on the campus to study all aspects of gas warfare (chemical, physiological, pharmacological, and mechanical). The campus, with only a single complete building before the United States entered the war, contained 153 buildings when the war ended. Similarly, by the end of the war approximately twelve hundred scientists were stationed there. The Army Corps of Engineers also trained at AU, initially calling their base Camp American University, and later, Camp Leach, whereas the facilities of the Bureau of Mines became known as the American University Experimental Station (AUES). The total station, including AU and surrounding land tracts, consisted of 509 acres.

Although the Bureau of Mines performed well in directing the country's chemical warfare efforts, the army wanted control of all weapons-related research. Thus, in September 1917 the army began lobbying to have the work placed under its jurisdiction. The Bureau of Mines protested, arguing that nothing was to be gained by such a transfer. The Advisory Board of the ACS agreed, stating, "The efficiency, success, fine spirit, and enthusiasm under the leadership of the Bureau of Mines is a matter upon which we wish to congratulate the bureau, as well as upon the splendid group of unselfish, self-sacrificing men who carried on this arduous and dangerous work."[4] However, President Wilson signed an executive order transferring the chemical warfare resources and personnel from the Bureau of Mines to the army on June 26, 1918. The Chemical Warfare Service— CWS—was born under the direction of Major General William L. Sibert.

Sibert was an engineer who had built bridges in the Midwest, served in the Philippines, and helped build the Panama Canal. Sibert believed in gas as a weapon of war. He also believed that no weapon had a greater possibility for surprising an enemy than gas. As he took command of the CWS, Captains Lewis and Conant were busily at work at CUA and the AUES laboring to perfect a gas that would deliver the ultimate surprise to the Germans.

3 The Hunt for a New King

Lewis's first military assignment was at the AUES, where he was ordered to study the corrosive action of gases on artillery shells so that more effective gas shells could be designed and built. However, he found the working conditions there so hazardous that he considered them intolerable. In an act illustrating that the scientists' military commissions were more a convenient tool for the government to pay them than a true indication of their incorporation into the military, Lewis effectively went on strike: he simply refused to pursue any additional research until he and his men were given a safer working environment. Colonel James F. Norris, who directed both offensive and defensive chemical research at the AUES, responded not with a reprimand, but by telling him to have a "colored" truck driver take him, a load of chemicals, and his men to nearby CUA, where Organic Unit No. 3 had been established. Norris also made Lewis head of that unit.

Lewis had no idea which chemicals he would need at CUA, so he took a little bit of everything in stock, including bottles of hydrochloric acid and ammonia, and a cage full of rats for testing the toxicity of any newly developed compounds. En route to CUA, the truck hit a rut; several bottles of the acid and ammonia broke, producing a cloud of nontoxic ammonium chloride. The driver, upon seeing the cloud, feared for his life and ran from the truck. He had to be caught and reassured that the gas was not dangerous before he would return. Eventually Lewis's unit arrived at CUA and began analyzing the purity of mustard gas, perfecting a colorized detector for this gas (that is, a device that turns a specific color when exposed to it), producing ricin (a toxin refined from the castor bean plant seed) for possible use as a chemical warfare agent, and developing other new chemical agents.

Lewis was painfully aware of the German successes with mustard gas, but he also knew of mustard's deficiencies, such as the delay in its effects (which made mustard a better defensive than offensive weapon) and that it was not typically deadly. The Allies wanted a gas similar to mustard, but better for offense, and they wanted to develop a useful toxic gas before the Germans. Lewis was specifically asked to develop a gas that would be

5. Organic Unit No. 3 chemists in uniform performing a drill in front of
Maloney Hall at Catholic University of America, ca. 1918.
Courtesy Philip Reiss.

(1) effective in small concentrations; (2) difficult to protect against; (3) capable of injuring all parts of the body; (4) easily manufactured in large
quantities; (5) cheap to produce; (6) composed of raw materials that were
readily available in the United States; (7) easy and safe to transport; (8)
stable and hard to detect; and, most importantly, (9) deadly.

These nine attributes led Lewis and his group to examine the ancient
poison arsenic as the base for a new agent. They were not the first to consider using arsenic as a chemical warfare agent in World War I. Both sides
had previously experimented with arsenical agents, both as tiny particu-
lates designed to cause sneezing and as a toxic liquid. But neither approach
had proven particularly useful. The liquid arsenic compound tested (only
by the British) was arsenic trichloride. However, arsenic trichloride has severe drawbacks, primarily that it is reactive and corrosive. Thus, it was
almost as dangerous to the men handling it offensively as those on the
receiving end. Furthermore, although very toxic when inhaled, it is not
readily absorbed through the skin. Thus, gas masks and clothing offered
good protection.

Lewis and his crew needed to find something better. They thought and
experimented and spent time in CUA's extensive chemistry library on the

6. Catholic University of America chemistry laboratory, ca. 1918.
Courtesy Catholic University of America, Washington, D.C.

second floor of Martin Maloney Hall, which was then a new and beautiful granite masonry building. The building still houses CUA's chemistry department, and the ceilings of the basement laboratories (above the suspended ceilings of today) continue to shed even freshly applied paint because of the vapors absorbed from the work done there in 1918. On a shelf in the hall's library stood Nieuwland's thesis, "Some Reactions of Acetylene." But none of Organic Unit No. 3's staff looked at it, because its title provided no clues to the gem inside.

However, Father John Griffin, Nieuwland's thesis advisor, was still on the CUA faculty in 1918 and remembered Nieuwland's hospitalization while working on his thesis. Griffin reviewed the dissertation and showed Lewis the section of Nieuwland's thesis describing the reaction of arsenic trichloride and acetylene in the presence of the catalyst, aluminum chloride.

Lewis was interested. Griffin's role in bringing Nieuwland's work to Lewis's attention was acknowledged in a postwar article by the head of the Chemical Warfare Service's Research Division, Colonel George A. Burrell: "Too much credit cannot be given to Dr. J. J. Griffin, head of the chemical department at that place (CUA) for his work, interest, and cooperation."[1]

Griffin's involvement with the lewisite story did not end with his conversation with Lewis. By the time Griffin died in 1921 he had amassed a considerable estate (Griffin was a diocesan priest and therefore was not required to take a vow of poverty). His will stipulated that his property be given to a religious organization in Baltimore rather than to his sister. Griffin's sister tried to invalidate the will, alleging that Griffin was mentally unstable during the last years of life. She said that Griffin often told stories about his work during the war, claiming that he had a personal letter from the president commending him for his work on lewisite, which had resulted in Germany's surrender. Griffin apparently never allowed anyone to see this mysterious letter. Eventually, Brigadier General Amos A. Fries, director of the CWS at the time, testified at the estate trial in 1923 that Griffin did not directly participate in the development of lewisite. Whether this was enough to allow his sister to invalidate the will is not known.

After reviewing Nieuwland's description of the poisonous compound, Lewis wondered whether it actually might be able to supplant mustard as the "king of war gasses." He knew that acetylene, arsenic trichloride, and aluminum chloride were easy to manufacture and that the raw materials for those compounds were plentiful within the United States. Later, lewisite was found to be easy to transport and store because it is stable in steel barrels (or bombs) kept below 122°F.

It would seem likely that at this point Lewis would have contacted Nieuwland, who was a professor at the University of Notre Dame. There is no evidence that he did so, although an exchange of letters between them in the early 1920s suggests that they were at least professional acquaintances. Perhaps Lewis could not contact Nieuwland because of security issues.

Lewis described his initial work on lewisite by saying that the compound "took on a nauseating odor and [caused] marked irritation effect to the mucous surfaces. The headache resulting persists several hours and the material seems to be quite toxic."[2] Presumably, Lewis was encouraged by these characteristics. In order to further evaluate the poisonous mixture in his flask, Lewis needed to know exactly what the compound was chemically. He and his team began trying to purify the mixture by distillation, a process in which the material is heated and the vapors emitted at

7. Apparatus first used to produce lewisite at Catholic University of America, ca. 1918. Note the washbasin, which probably served as a cooling bath. Also note the air tanks, which were probably filled with acetylene.
Courtesy Philip Reiss.

various temperatures are cooled, separating the mixture into its constituents. However, each time the mixture was heated, it exploded. It was only after Lewis's superior, Captain James Conant, director of organic research for the CWS, suggested using a 20 percent HCl wash to "desensitize" the mixture by removing the aluminum chloride catalyst, that the explosions stopped, allowing Lewis to proceed with purification of the compound.

Lewis's successful distillation resulted in three arsenic-containing compounds that came to be known as lewisite 1, 2, and 3 (L1, L2, L3), the differences corresponding to the number of acetylene molecules that combine with a single arsenic trichloride molecule. These three compounds have different chemical properties and different physiological actions. L1 and L2 are highly toxic vesicants (blister-forming agents) and respiratory irritants, with L1 being the more virulent. L3 is neither a powerful vesicant nor respiratory irritant, although it does induce violent sneezing. Because L1 is the most toxic of the three and therefore the most desirable from a military viewpoint, it has generally been considered synonymous with the term lewisite. Further, because initial experiments produced almost three

$$HC\equiv CH \;+\; \underset{Cl\quad\;\;Cl}{\overset{Cl}{As}} \;\xrightarrow{AlCl_3}\; \underset{Cl\quad HC=CH}{\overset{Cl}{As}}\!\!\!\!\searrow_{Cl} \qquad (L1)$$

$$2\,HC\equiv CH \;+\; \underset{Cl\quad\;\;Cl}{\overset{Cl}{As}} \;\xrightarrow{AlCl_3}\; \underset{\underset{Cl}{HC=CH}\quad \underset{Cl}{HC=CH}}{\overset{Cl}{As}} \qquad (L2)$$

$$3\,HC\equiv CH \;+\; \underset{Cl\quad\;\;Cl}{\overset{Cl}{As}} \;\xrightarrow{AlCl_3}\; \underset{\underset{Cl}{HC=CH}\quad \underset{Cl}{HC=CH}}{\overset{\overset{Cl}{HC=CH}}{As}} \qquad (L3)$$

8. Lewisite chemistry.

times as much L3 as L1, much effort during the development of lewisite as a weapon was directed at changing the relative percentages of the lewisite forms produced. Thus, it was found that further heating of L2 and L3 under pressure and with excess arsenic trichloride available converted them to the more deadly L1.

Following the success of Lewis's unit at purifying lewisite, it tested the three varieties on donkeys, monkeys, and men. Lewis even tested it on himself. In a postwar 1919 lecture to a current events class, he described placing a tiny drop on his hand, which immediately swelled and became painful. He also lectured that the agent was far more powerful than mustard. Mustard, he said, has a body, whereas lewisite also has "two arms."

After two weeks of promising tests with lewisite, the chief of the CWS Research Division ordered that the entire unit concentrate its efforts on this compound and increased the number of men under Lewis's command from fifteen to about thirty-five. A postwar CWS "Summary of Achievements" praised the labors of Lewis's men, noting the hazards under which they worked, especially the lack of proper ventilation. This was sadly true—Lewis's unit had a higher casualty rate than any other within the CWS; at one time nearly 50 percent of the unit was ill from chemical exposure, and another 30 percent was on leave for up to two weeks recovering from the effects of the fumes. In a 1919 newspaper article, Lewis stated that the casualty rate suffered by the people working in his unit was as high as that at the front. Thus, it does not appear that Lewis's move from the AUES to CUA actually resulted in a safer working environment for him and his men, although it did result in the development of lewisite.

Who should receive credit for discovering lewisite? Nieuwland would seem the apparent choice, but in postwar letters Lewis voiced doubt as to whether any lewisite had actually formed in Nieuwland's flask in 1903. Further, Nieuwland, in contrast to Lewis, did not describe the chemical properties of the compound that he had created or try to purify it.

Nevertheless, each man believed he deserved the credit for the discovery. Nieuwland, in a November 14, 1922, letter to General Fries, wrote, "W. L. Lewis . . . worked out the Lewisite discovered by *me* [my italics] in 1903."[3] Some popular articles of the time also gave Nieuwland credit for its discovery. For example, the January 17, 1922 issue of the *South Bend (Indiana) Tribune* reported, "Discovery of 'Lewisite,' the most deadly poisonous gas the world has ever known, is credited today to the Rev. Julius A. Nieuwland."[4] The *Notre Dame Scholastic* in 1922 also credited Nieuwland as the discoverer of lewisite, as did the *New York Times* when in 1936 it stated that Nieuwland won "international renown for his discovery of Lewisite gas."[5]

Lewis, in a December 11, 1928, letter, also to General Fries, criticized an article by Major Cyrus B. Wood in the March 1928 issue of *Military Surgeon* that gave the impression that Nieuwland had discovered lewisite. Major Wood wrote:

> It is, chemically, b-chlorvinyl dichloroarsine. Its use was proposed by Dr. W. Lee Lewis, organic chemist, formerly with Northwestern University, who did *not* [my italics] as some may say, discover this compound, but who did work out to a certain extent the process of its manufacture.[6]

Lewis wrote in a later letter to Fries about Wood's "loose treatment of the facts,"[7] stating:

> I think you know me well enough to know that I am not much personally exercised over refinements of credit in scientific work. I do think, however, that we should all strive to keep a historical record of any developments on a fact basis.[8]

Nevertheless, clearly Lewis was sufficiently proud of his namesake to chastise Wood for not having attributed the discovery of lewisite to him.

Lewis justified his criticism of Major Wood's article by stating that in 1918 he had asked his subordinate, Second Lieutenant Roy Ginter, to replicate Nieuwland's initial work, but that Nieuwland's description did not provide sufficient information for that to be accomplished (Ginter had tried to purify Nieuwland's compound by distillation, but was unable to do so). Thus, Lewis surmised that Nieuwland's product was actually a complex chemical mixture of arsenic trichloride, aluminum chloride, and acetylene, but that the mixture had not chemically combined to form lewisite. Lewis also pointed to Nieuwland's description of the crystals and the black, gummy mass that formed when the mixture was poured into water. Because lewisite is a liquid and does not crystallize, Lewis concluded that lewisite had not been present in Nieuwland's flask. Interestingly, Lewis did not comment on the strong smell Nieuwland described in his thesis. Impure lewisite (mainly L3) has a powerful geranium-like odor. Nieuwland had not mentioned any resemblance to the smell of the compound to geraniums, which would have meant lewisite had formed. And because Nieuwland was a renowned botanist, he would surely not have overlooked a strong odor of geraniums. On the other hand, some vapor associated with the mixture made Nieuwland very sick. Further, the fact that a black gummy mass and crystals formed does not preclude that one or more of the lewisite variants were also present in Nieuwland's flask.

General Fries responded very sympathetically to Lewis on December 26, saying that he would ensure that Nieuwland was not credited with discovering lewisite and that Lewis was recognized not only for accomplishing the first separation of its components, but also for its discovery. Fries also suggested that German knowledge of the United States development of lewisite contributed to an early armistice. In other words, Fries credited the threat of using lewisite with helping to end the war. There is no direct evidence in support of Fries's remarkable opinion, which would be hard to document in any case because of the top secret security surrounding lewisite's development. However, on June 22, 1918, Colonel Raymond Bacon of the army's Ordnance Department, in a speech to the American Institute of Mining Engineers that was described in the *Washington (D.C.) Star,* stated that the United States was developing a gas more deadly than any currently being used. Perhaps this was meant as a warning to the Germans that lewisite was coming. Interestingly, future President Herbert Hoover also spoke to the engineers on this date, discussing the supply of food both in the United States and abroad.

In a later letter to Fries (dated January 15, 1929) Lewis again asked for the correction, insisting that his request was on behalf of the many men under his command at CUA and was being made only in the interest of preserving an accurate historical record. And in a still later (January 22) letter, Lewis stated that he raised this issue in a "constructive spirit."

Lewis described the details of the process he pioneered for making lewisite in a 1923 article in *Industrial and Engineering Chemistry* and in a 1925 article in the *Journal of the American Chemical Society.* In the acknowledgment accompanying the 1923 article, Lewis remarked:

> The present paper is a partial report of an investigation carried out between April 13 and August 23, 1918, in Organic Unit No. 3, Offense Research Section, United States Chemical Warfare Service, stationed at the Chemical Laboratory of the Catholic University of America, Washington, D.C.[9]

Lewis continued with a list of all the men who participated in the work at CUA. In the section "Previous Work," Lewis credits Conant with the later stages of lewisite development.

Surprisingly, even if Lewis was correct in his assertion that Nieuwland did not truly discover lewisite, the credit for discovery should probably be attributed to German scientists. Johannes Thiele investigated the reaction of acetylene and arsenic trichloride in 1916–17, and at the same time, but independently, two other German scientists, H. Wieland and A. Bloemer, also studied the compound. Accordingly, in his 1941 book *Chemical Warfare,* Curt Wachtel stated that he worked in the pharmacological section of the Kaiser-Wilhelm Institut für Physikalische Chemie during World War I (where the Germans developed their chemical agents) and supervised the testing of over three hundred toxic gases, including lewisite. His evaluation indicated that lewisite would not be a reliable war gas because its toxic effects were less lasting than those of mustard and the irritant effects were so strong that men would be warned immediately of its presence. Julius Meyer, in his 1926 book *Der Gaskampf und Die Chemischen Kampstoffe* (Combat gases and chemical combat materials), said of the development of poison gases, "Gegenüber den Ergebnissen der deutschen Forscher haben sie kaum etwas Neues gebracht" (Opposite the results of the German researchers, they [British and American investigators] have brought hardly anything new).[10] Meyer continued by saying that even once purified, lewisite will discolor and hydrolyze (react with moisture) very quickly, rendering it ineffective for military use.

Interestingly, the German view that lewisite would have been much less effective than envisioned by the CWS was shared by the British, whose scientists received samples of lewisite for evaluation in 1918 and concluded that it was not equal to mustard. They also believed that German gas masks would provide adequate protection.

When the war ended Lewis described the operation of the CWS during the war as "stupendous" and "overwhelming." He said that he had been provided with every resource money could buy, including couriers, mechanics, glassblowers, and transportation agents. The CWS used these resources, he said, to express the outrage of an "ingenious people" in the development of novel weapons, of which lewisite would have been a primary example.

The three letters Lewis wrote to Fries insisting that he and his men receive proper recognition for the discovery and development of lewisite seem out of character. Both his friend, Otto Eisenschiml, and daughter, Winifred Lee Harwood, described Lewis as being more concerned that he be remembered for his basic scientific work than for discovering lewisite. Similarly, the letters he wrote in response to requests for his photograph or autograph were very humble and usually humorous, as were his speeches and articles. Nevertheless, the letters to the CWS probably indicate that being remembered as the discoverer of lewisite did matter to Lewis personally. And it is certainly not incorrect that he be credited with the discovery of lewisite. Even if Nieuwland and the Germans had synthesized the compound, Lewis was the first to accurately describe its chemistry.

After Lewis and his unit had finished determining lewisite's basic chemical and physical properties, further development was transferred to Conant at the AUES. There Conant supervised additional animal testing and investigated processes for small- and large-scale manufacturing. Lewis's unit then turned to other research, his name having by then become attached to the compound forever.

4 The American University Experimental Station

Captain James Conant received the baton for lewisite's development from Lewis. Although Conant did not participate in the discovery of lewisite, he eventually had as much to do with its becoming a weapon as Nieuwland and Lewis.

Conant was born to Jennett and James Scott Conant on March 26, 1893, in Boston. He was a precocious child with a great interest in chemistry. His high school yearbook said, "This year he has practically lived in the laboratory, concocting every kind of condition of smell. We sincerely hope he will not blow up the laboratory at Harvard."[1] Conant graduated from Harvard in 1913, in 1916 received his doctoral degree from that institution, and became a chemistry instructor there.

Although he enjoyed teaching, Conant, like Lewis, wished to contribute to the war effort. He decided to enlist in the army as a noncommissioned officer in 1917 to work on the development of gas masks at the front lines. But his friend Colonel James Norris, who directed the Bureau of Mines chemical warfare research unit at the American University Experimental Station, told him "You're crazy," because he believed Conant could do much more for the war effort by synthesizing new offensive poisons than by working on gas masks. Norris convinced Conant to accept the position of Chief of Organic Research for the Chemical Warfare Service, with his laboratory at the AUES.

One of Conant's first tasks in his new position was to create a CWS code for lewisite. Some of the codes that already existed were HS and G-34 for mustard gas, CG for phosgene and PS for chloropicrin. As part of their effort to maintain secrecy about lewisite, Conant and his superiors decided to use one of the mustard codes, G-34, for lewisite. Thus, beginning about July 1918 G-34 referred to lewisite, whereas all references to G-34 before that time referred to mustard. As further confusion, sometimes M-1 (or MI [mustard imitator]) was also used to refer to lewisite, although this desig-

9. James Bryant Conant, ca. 1918.
Courtesy Cleveland Public Library.

nation did not become common until the 1920s, and L became lewisite's symbol during World War II.

Conant's next task was to shepherd lewisite through the various "sections" within the Research Division of the CWS. These sections investigated various methods of preparation, chemical properties, and physiological actions on animals and humans (as studied by the Pharmacological Section) of new agents. Unfortunately, partly because of the secrecy surrounding the lewisite research (both then and now), few details of these investigations are available. However, some information on both human and animal testing is known, thanks partly to the memory of Sergeant George Temple.

Sergeant Temple was in charge of maintenance for the fifteen hundred electric motors at the AUES. According to a 1965 interview that Sergeant

10. Building at AUES where volunteers (presumably including George Temple) were subjected to lewisite skin tests, 1918.
Courtesy Addie Ruth Maurer Olson.

Temple granted the American University student newspaper, the *Eagle*, he and the other AUES soldiers assembled each morning in front of Hurst Hall for roll call. On some mornings the officers asked for volunteers to be tested with the experimental gases, and the obliging Temple volunteered seven times to be tested with lewisite.

When a small drop of lewisite was applied to Temple's left forearm, his skin turned deep red and one-inch-high blisters developed that did not heal for eight weeks. The scars on his forearm were still recognizable in 1965, and he recalled that the silver colored blisters were excruciatingly painful. Because he successfully refrained from breaking his blisters (some of the other volunteers were not so stoic), his forearm was photographed, and an artist drew it to capture the color of the blisters. The scientists also made a plaster cast of his forearm, which caused him great pain.

Temple said that once, while he was maintaining a motor, a pipe broke, and he accidentally breathed in the vapors of a gas (not lewisite) designed to kill its victims by causing bleeding in the lungs. Temple barely escaped with his life. He told of some of his friends who were less lucky, saying that he believed more American men were killed by gas at the AUES station than were killed by gas in battle. As in coal mines, canaries were used throughout the AUES to warn the workers when gas levels were not safe.

In a 1919 article in the *Journal of Industrial and Chemical Engineering* the director of the Research Division, Colonel George A. Burrell, stated that the percentage of casualties in the Research Division was undoubtedly greater than in any other unit in the army except the actual gas manufacturing unit at Edgewood Arsenal (EA). A profile of Conant in the *New Yorker* in 1936 also referred to the accidents that occurred at the AUES: "Pipes would frequently leak or vats would boil over. A vast tub of soapsuds awaited the frenzied plunges of men on whom the horrid stuff [lewisite] had settled."[2]

In addition to the tests on people, Temple described how "hundreds and hundreds" of stray dogs were gassed, as well as some monkeys. Temple did not mention the other species of animals that were also used for testing at the AUES: goats, cats, rabbits, guinea pigs, rats, mice, snails, slugs, and canaries. The smaller animals were generally used for laboratory tests, whereas the larger animals (dogs and goats) were used for field tests. The field experiments were conducted on leased farmlands surrounding the campus. Soldiers tied the animals to stakes, exposed them to chemical bombs, and watched them struggle and usually die. The carcasses were then shaved and dissected to determine exactly how the gases affected the animals' physiology.

The lewisite animal tests conducted by the Pharmacological Section revealed that the first symptoms were blinking and tearing of the eyes, followed by nasal secretion, retching, and vomiting. These symptoms resulted from severe irritation and swelling of the mucous lining of the nose, throat, and respiratory tract. Next, the animals (generally dogs) began to salivate excessively and their eyes became inflamed. Their nostrils clogged and they coughed excessively. Many died at this stage. If the dogs continued to live, they sneezed violently with a continuous flow of watery fluid from their nostrils. More dogs died during this period. If an animal survived past the fifth day, recovery usually ensued and was complete within seven to ten days.

Postmortem examination of the dogs showed the development of an extra membrane in the nostrils and throat, varying degrees of swelling in these structures, and the collapse of lung tissue. Lung infection (pneumonia) was typically the cause of death. The liver and kidney were also often congested.

Tests using direct application of liquid lewisite to the skin of dogs caused immediate irritation, which was very different from the delay that occurred with the application of liquid mustard. Redness appeared in four to six hours and blisters in sixteen to forty-eight hours, depending on the concentration. Sublethal doses of liquid lewisite caused deep burns and death of skin cells. Infections sometimes also occurred, accompanied by sloughing of the skin and exposure of the underlying muscle. Healing then occurred. High doses caused death in one to twelve days. Until their deaths the dogs excreted arsenic in their urine.

The pharmacologists concluded, based on the dog tests, that a man of average weight (70 kilograms or 154 pounds) would be killed by about one-third teaspoon of lewisite applied to his skin.

The lewisite evaluation process at the AUES caused a political incident involving a former United States senator. Nathan Bay Scott had retired in 1910 after twelve years as a senator from West Virginia. Prior to that he had been West Virginia's representative to the Republican National Committee, and after retirement he remained a dominant force in Republican politics. Scott resided in a home on Ridge Road, about four hundred yards from the AUES. On the morning of August 3, 1918, the senator and his wife and sister were seated on the back porch enjoying the cool breeze that was blowing across the experimental field toward their home. The senator noticed a dense cloud of yellowish gas slowly advancing toward the house. He thought at first that the cloud resulted from burning brush. Shortly after, however, all three smelled a faint odor and felt intense pain in their eyes. They immediately entered the house, summoned help by phone, and closed all the windows. Physicians arrived from the Experimental Station with respirators, and later the senator and his family traveled into the city for treatment by his personal physician. The senator's throat and eyes were burned and his face was blistered. His quick action of entering the house and closing the windows probably saved his family's life. When Scott and his family ventured outside after the gas cloud had dissipated, they found dead chickens, wild birds, and small animals. In addition to the Scotts, some soldiers from the camp were affected by the gas and hospitalized.

The senator complained vigorously, prompting an investigation by senior CWS officers. The investigation found that one of the pipes attached to a still in "Shack #8" had become obstructed, resulting in an explosion and the release of eight to ten pounds of lewisite.

The gas was described as "German mustard gas" in a *Washington Post* story about the incident. An official press release from the War Department downplayed the danger, saying that the Scott family's injuries were more "imagined" than real. Nonetheless, eventually General Sibert, director of the CWS, became involved, saying in a letter that additional precautions

11. **Some temporary buildings at the AUES, ca. 1918.**
Courtesy U.S. Army Corps of Engineers.

would be taken to prevent the recurrence of such an incident. The publicity surrounding the lewisite release resulted in the Washington Board of Commissioners on October 30 requesting that such tests be moved from the AUES site. The commissioners cited as evidence both that the senator had been "disagreeably affected" and that some motorists nearby had smelled the gas. The request of the commissioners never had to be implemented, because the war ended two weeks later. Interestingly, Lewis suggested in a 1921 speech that the explosion may have been intentional, although he provided no details as to why such a lewisite release would be deliberate.

Whether the explosion was accidental or deliberate, the War Department took advantage of it by announcing that lewisite (the pseudonym "methyl" was probably used) was too dangerous to be produced. This was a ruse designed to fool Germany. Inadvertently, this announcement depressed Lewis's men, because he had not been permitted to tell them that lewisite production was in fact being continued outside Washington.

The secrecy surrounding the work on lewisite conducted at the AUES is represented by a statement in "Report of the Work Done at Bureau of

Mines Experiment Station American University D. C. on War Gas Investigations During May, 1918" (unfortunately we do not know who wrote the document or who was its audience). "Captain Lewis at the Catholic University, is making no report, as he has instructions to place nothing regarding his work in writing at this time. Captain Conant is also doing certain work with which you are undoubtedly familiar, and concerning which nothing is said."[3]

About nineteen hundred soldiers (twelve hundred of whom were scientists) were assigned to the AUES, although many of the commissioned men were soldiers in name only to facilitate their receiving a salary. Nevertheless, AUES was a military base, and thus, promptly at 4:00 P.M., everyone was required to participate in military drills. Eventually the army rescinded the drill regulation, but while the drills occurred they created personnel problems, because some of the less experienced chemists held higher military ranks than the more experienced ones.

In addition to working and drilling, the soldiers at the AUES also relaxed together. They organized themselves into football, baseball, and basketball teams, and even a glee club. They wrote and published a monthly paper, the *Retort*, which had a heading as follows:

> "ALL TO THE MUSTARD"
> The Retort
> A Newspaper Published by the ENEMIES of GERMANY at American University Experimental Station, Research Division, Chemical Warfare Service, United States Army.

"Retort" refers both to a witty comeback and to a chemical apparatus for boiling a liquid and condensing its vapor. Thus it had meaning to the chemistry professionals working at the AUES, and it also perhaps referred to the soldiers' work at the station as a chemical parry to Germany's thrust of chemical weapons into the war.

The October 6, 1918, edition of the *Retort* survives (ironically this was the first and only issue published, due to the Armistice) and lists the standings of the baseball teams, which were named (in order of standing): Defense, Gas Mask Research, Toxic, Offense, Small Scale Manufacturing, Mechanical Research, Executive, and Pyrotechnic. This edition also described a reception for the Research Division held at the Catholic University of America at which Captain Lewis and his wife were hosts. Additionally, Colonel Burrell wrote an essay on the importance of their work and sympathized with the desire of many of the men to fight the "Hun" in France.

After lewisite passed all of its preliminary evaluations, Conant was ordered to supervise the development of a small-scale manufacturing process, which he did successfully. This was the final step before an agent was referred to the Development Division for large-scale manufacturing. As Conant readied for this final transfer, he received an order from Colonel Burrell that he too was being transferred to the Development Division, which was not headquartered at the AUES. Conant packed his bags and got ready for an eight-hour train ride.

5   Willoughby: The Chemical Warfare Service's Ace in the Hole

Basic research by the CWS had convincingly demonstrated the potential of lewisite as a weapon of war by July 1918, necessitating the transfer of the lewisite project from its Research to its Development Division. The Development Division's responsibility was to transform the small-scale processes for the production of gases devised by the Research Division into large-scale manufacturing ones. The Development Division had previously performed this function for mustard gas, so that by the end of October 1918 the United States was producing more mustard gas than England, Germany, and France combined. The plants that were producing mustard were staffed by soldiers and directed by officers. Originally the CWS had tried to convince private companies to manufacture chemical warfare agents, but the companies refused because of the dangers involved and the lack of a postwar market. As with mustard, it would be a military plant that would manufacture lewisite.

Unlike the American University Experimental Station, which was located in Washington, D.C., the headquarters of the Development Division was located in a suburb of Cleveland called Nela Park. Why was a branch of the CWS located in Cleveland? Because of gas masks. On April 28, 1917, three weeks after the United States declared war on Germany, Dr. Warren K. Lewis of the Bureau of Mines traveled to Cleveland to meet with representatives of the National Carbon Company and the National Lamp Works Company, which was part of the General Electric Company. Warren Lewis's immediate concern was the development of gas masks for American soldiers being sent to France. He knew that charcoal had previously been shown by Russian scientists to effectively absorb poisonous gases when used in the canister attached to the face mask. Warren Lewis met with Mr. Frank Dorsey of the National Lamp Works Company and engineers from the National Carbon Company because they were more knowledgeable about charcoal than anyone else in the country. Together, the two

**12. Colonel Frank M. Dorsey, ca. 1918.
Courtesy Will and Carol Bushek.**

companies energetically began the process of successfully developing an effective American gas mask.

The civilian operation of the two companies was augmented with military men (the first contingent of thirty soldiers arrived on November 7, 1917) and was eventually entirely militarized. The transformation was complete by August 1918, by which time there were 250 officers and men stationed at Nela Park. The facility was named the Development Division of the CWS, and Mr. Dorsey had become Colonel Dorsey to head it.

Colonel Dorsey, a native of Dresden, Ohio, was thirty-eight years old at the time of his appointment to the CWS. He was a tireless worker, often traveling between Cleveland, the gas mask factory in Astoria, New York, the mustard factory at Edgewood Arsenal (EA), Maryland, and the AUES. By mid-1918 Colonel Dorsey had acquired the reputation of a chemical manufacturing genius who could makes things happen.

The research done at the AUES had convinced CWS Director Sibert and his staff that lewisite could be far more effective than any previous agent used in the war, including mustard gas. Use of this agent at a critical time and as a complete surprise was expected to be decisive, perhaps capable of sending the German army into a total retreat and securing a quick Allied victory.

The CWS and the army believed that the planned spring (March) 1919 Allied offensive was the decisive time to bombard the enemy lines with lewisite-loaded artillery shells. General Sibert's staff calculated that 3,000 tons of lewisite would instigate a German retreat. Could such a phenomenal amount be produced in time? Logic suggested it would not be possible to produce and deliver 3,000 tons of lewisite by March: the exact mechanisms for large-scale production of lewisite had yet to be developed; no factory site had been found nor a factory built; no supplies or equipment had been ordered; no workers had been trained; no one had been appointed to direct such a plant; and, 3,000 tons of lewisite would require 7,282 fifty-five-gallon steel drums just to transport it. Furthermore, even if a plant could be constructed and made operational by the planned date of December 1, 1918, virtually all of the lewisite would have to be made in December and January in order for the 3,000 tons to be ready by March 1. The plant would have to be producing almost 50 tons a day.

Despite the seemingly impossible nature of this task, a mood of invincibility prevailed in the United States, a mood that viewed winning the war to be worth any price. In early July 1918, Colonel Dorsey was informed that, as chief of the Development Division, he had overall responsibility for the lewisite plant, and Conant was placed in charge of chemical operations at the plant. These two men were thus given a gigantic goal—win the war with lewisite and get the doughboys home.

Dorsey's first task was to find a site for the plant; one in or near the Nela Park headquarters in Cleveland would be ideal. But there were significant security issues; German spies were well aware of the mustard gas plant located at 340 East 131st Street in Cleveland and would undoubtedly become curious about another government construction project in the city. Dorsey knew that secrecy was of utmost importance to prevent German scientists from developing countermeasures to lewisite.

Cleveland itself was thus not a viable option. But the lewisite plant could not be located too far from Cleveland, because Dorsey needed to be able to visit the plant often. He looked at a map and his eyes were drawn to the small town of Willoughby, about eighteen miles east of Cleveland. Willoughby was far enough away that a government construction project could proceed unnoticed by the Cleveland newspapers and would therefore probably go unnoticed by German agents, but the town was close enough to Cleveland that he could easily supervise the construction of the plant and its production of lewisite.

Willoughby is located on the banks of the Chagrin River, which drains into nearby Lake Erie, and had a population in 1918 of about 2,650. White settlers began occupying the area after the American Revolution when soldiers were compensated for their service with land grants in what was then called Chagrin, after the river. The name Willoughby was adopted in 1835 to honor Dr. Westel Willoughby, who founded a local medical college and willed his estate to the village. In 1895 the Cleveland, Painesville, and Eastern (C.P. & E.) Railroad brought the outside world to this isolated farming community. Later, two trolley lines were built connecting Willoughby to Cleveland, the Shore Line, and the Euclid Avenue Line. In 1918 the economy was based on both agriculture and manufacturing, of which the Standard Tire and Rubber Company was the largest firm. Willoughby had two newspapers, the *Independent* and the *Republican*. Willoughby's business district at the time was all of five blocks long. Today, Willoughby has a population of about twenty thousand.

Colonel Dorsey drove to Willoughby, toured the town, and met with a local attorney, John D. Fackler, who represented many of the major business and landowners of the community. Was there any land available that could be converted into a government manufacturing plant? Fackler pondered the question and made a few suggestions, which Dorsey rejected because of insufficient land area or inadequate access. Then Fackler suggested the abandoned Ben Hur motor plant on Ben Hur Avenue, located about a mile from downtown. Dorsey and Fackler drove to the site and Dorsey liked what he saw. The abandoned automobile factory building was still there, as was an office building. The site had plenty of room for the military base Dorsey envisioned. Most importantly, the plant site was relatively isolated. Eventually the Willoughby military base would occupy thirty acres there.

The July 12, 1918, issue of the *Willoughby Republican* cited a "rumor" that the government was a prospective tenant for the plant, at which "supplies" would be manufactured. Fackler was reported to be traveling to Washington to negotiate the leasing of the plant, which was owned by Mrs. Ana W. Smith. Fackler returned to Willoughby on July 25, having completed negotiations for the plant's lease.

Once Conant was informed that a plant site had been selected, he quickly left Washington to take charge of the research and laboratory setup of the lewisite project, arriving in Cleveland on July 20. He was met at the train station by Colonel Dorsey and the newly appointed plant superintendent, Lieutenant Colonel W. G. Wilcox. All three drove to Willoughby to evaluate the plant site and contemplate how to accomplish their monumental task.

Although Dorsey had briefly toured the Ben Hur plant before committing to the lease, he had not been cognizant of the true state of the two buildings located on the site, neither of which, he now realized, were habitable. The office building was the better of the two, with concrete floors and separated offices. But the building's water and sewer pipes had frozen during the winter and were now cracked. The officers realized that the cracked pipes would all have to be replaced, an unfortunate delay they had not anticipated and one that increased the stress they were already feeling.

The factory's existing dirt floor was unsuitable for a chemical plant. It would have to be leveled and finished with concrete. This building would also need plumbing (it never had been fitted with indoor plumbing) and its electrical system was chaotic, necessitating complete replacement. And the clock kept ticking, with the planned March 1919 offensive looming large in their minds.

Clearly, renovations needed to be done quickly. The first issue was how to pay for the services of the workmen. Establishing government accounts with local firms would take too much time. Colonel Dorsey was able to arrange for his former employer, the National Lamp Works Company, to front the money for renovation and construction, with government reimbursement to be made at some later date.

The two next most immediate problems pertained to security and workmen. Wilcox immediately had twenty-five soldiers from Cleveland reassigned to the Willoughby site. These men arrived on July 26, under the direction of Sergeant (later Lieutenant) Royce, and promptly pitched tents, cleared weeds, and began stringing barbed wire around the plant property. Eventually, guards would walk the perimeter of the fence twenty-four hours a day and an alarm system would be installed to alert the guards to any intruder. At one point, security at the plant was so tight that the soldiers began referring to the plant as the mousetrap: once in, they could never escape (this nickname does however seem somewhat inappropriate, because the men did "escape" for meals).

Securing craftsmen was another unanticipated problem facing Conant and Wilcox, who remained in Willoughby while Dorsey returned to Cleveland. Willoughby tradesmen were all engaged in local projects, and importing workers from Cleveland would necessitate they be paid for transportation time (about three hours a day), which would greatly shorten the workday and entail increased expenses. Similarly, the cost of housing and feeding such workmen in Willoughby would have been excessive, even if adequate facilities could have been found.

Conant and Wilcox were desperate. Their only recourse was to appeal to Willoughby's mayor, W. J. Carmichael, who had been the mayor since 1914 and, because he had overseen the construction of the town's first water filtration plant, had strong connections with the Willoughby tradesmen. Mayor Carmichael was also a strong supporter of the war effort; his campaign poster had been headlined, "FOR PEACE! But not for a peace that compromises Right!"[1]

Mayor Carmichael arranged for the suspension of all other building projects in Willoughby for this urgent need by the government. Local tradesmen—plumbers, carpenters, electricians, and construction workers—were lassoed into the project; building renovations began almost immediately. This initial work cost the life of Anthony Tripping, a contractor from nearby Painesville, who died on August 13 while moving heavy shelving at the plant.

With renovations underway, Conant could finally attend to his primary task—designing the plant and ordering equipment and supplies. Workmen were paving the factory floor by August 1 even while draftsmen were working under Conant to design the plant. At the same time some equipment for initial small-scale manufacturing began arriving, and other equipment for large-scale production was ordered. In particular, Conant needed very large steel chemical reactor units to make the huge quantities of lewisite Sibert had ordered. These units would probably have been glass lined in order to resist the corrosive action of the chemicals. The units were to be connected to each other by pipes conveying the pre-lewisite liquids until the final product was ready for storage. Where do you buy ten thirteen-hundred-gallon steel reactor units with automatic stirrers in the middle of a war? With great difficulty Conant eventually found a Cleveland foundry that could fabricate them.

The man responsible for placing the orders for equipment and supplies was Lieutenant Gracey. He began ordering the reactor units and other equipment on July 23, although the plant did not have a railroad siding or its own trucks to facilitate delivery of the equipment. Gracey worked initially without a staff and with very inadequate telephone and telegraph facilities. He solved the delivery problem by arranging for the soldiers at the plant to pick up the equipment and supplies using their personal vehicles. Eventually, by mid-October, two sidings from the New York Central Railroad were completed. By November 1, Gracey's operations had become so efficient that supplies and equipment were pouring into the plant at the rate necessary to meet the production quota on schedule. By the time the Willoughby plant was completed and equipped, the War Department had invested $5 million (about $60 million in 2004 dollars) in it.

Conant needed men with chemical training to work in the plant. Quickly realizing that his initial estimate of 300 men to operate the plant was grossly insufficient, he had plans drawn up to house 1,100 men. By early November, 22 officers and 542 enlisted men were working at the plant.

Initially, while most of the officers slept in tents on the property, the enlisted men were crowded into and slept on the ground floor of the office building. Surprisingly, despite the plant's prison-like security, some of the officers, presumably Conant and Wilcox and their immediate staff, were permitted to live off the base. The August 2 issue of the *Willoughby Republican* requested Willoughby residents who had rooms to rent to officers to contact the Red Cross. Similarly, the October 4 issue of the *Republican* reported that three houses near the plant on Ben Hur Avenue had been rented by the government for officers' quarters.

For the first month or so, living conditions at the plant were awful for most of the men. In addition to the uncomfortable sleeping quarters, there were no mess facilities, so three times a day the men marched into town to have meals at the Willoughby Inn. This was quite time-consuming, and frustrated both the officers and men. It was not until the middle of August that a noon meal was served at the plant, but breakfast and dinner continued to require marches into town. Finally, in late August, the Cleveland Construction Company was contracted to build barracks and a mess hall for the men. The first barrack was ready for occupancy in early October, but the remainder were not completed until the first of November.

Acetylene, arsenic trichloride, and aluminum chloride, which react to form lewisite, are hazardous materials, and lewisite is very toxic. This produced a potentially dangerous workplace, necessitating the presence of a

13. Barracks at the Ben Hur lewisite plant, 1918.
Courtesy Western Reserve Historical Society, Cleveland.

hospital. On August 3 Captain G. A. Plummer and Lieutenant M. Wolfe, both doctors serving in the Medical Corps, arrived. They examined each soldier and taught all the principles and practices of basic sanitation. The doctors drafted plans for a forty-eight-bed hospital, which was also erected by the Cleveland Construction Company and completed in November. Both doctors were very proud of their record at the plant: no soldier died from exposure to toxic chemicals, although many received painful lewisite burns.

After the war, the editor of the *Journal of Industrial and Engineering Chemistry,* Charles Herty, paid tribute to those who worked in the poison gas plants:

> [these men] were killed, not in the thrill of battle, not under the glory
> of a charge, but back here in the steady grind of preparing material
> for the men at the front. They went into hospitals and they went to the
> grave, serving their country nobly and loyally.[2]

In August a young man by the name of Nate Simpson arrived to work at the Willoughby plant. Simpson was a chemist who expected to be commissioned upon entering the army, but instead became Private Simpson. In a reminiscence he sent to the Lake County (Ohio) Historical Society in 1970, Simpson described traveling from Washington, D.C., to Cleveland and reporting to the YMCA. The private had been told only that he would be working on a secret project at a secret location. Although he was feeling anxious about where he was going and what he would be doing, Simpson felt lucky to be enjoying a few days of traveling and was grateful to be on American soil rather than fighting the enemy in France. After a couple of days in Cleveland, he and two other soldiers boarded a trolley car bound for a place almost twenty miles away that they had never heard of: Willoughby, Ohio. During the trip, the conductor told the boys that he had taken more than a hundred GIs to Willoughby, but had never brought one back. This raised some concern in young Nate's mind.

After arriving at the plant, Wilcox instructed Simpson that he would be court-martialed if he disclosed where he was stationed to anyone, even loved ones. Simpson also was told never to discuss what was being manufactured at the plant. His mail was censored and sent through a mail drawer, #426, in Cleveland (twenty-five years later this security procedure would be repeated when the mail for the Los Alamos, New Mexico, Manhattan Project was funneled through Box 1663, Santa Fe). Simpson was further dismayed to learn that he was not permitted to leave the plant grounds except for meals. Fortunately, General Sibert eventually rescinded this rule. On Saturday, August 10, Sibert visited the plant and, after receiving pledges of loyalty from the soldiers, ordered the plant to be governed in a manner similar to that of a regular army post. Simpson was glad that he and the other men could now obtain short-term passes into Willoughby, although they could not venture farther.

Simpson's day at the Ben Hur plant began at 6:00 A.M. when Conant, who had been promoted to Major, sang "All-Up" into the public address system. Simpson, in common with the other men, often worked until midnight or even later, seven days a week.

At the plant Simpson was assigned to test the purity of the final product, L1. He felt good about this position because it enabled him to take advantage of his chemical training, which he believed was superior to that of the other testers. He was surprised, however, when his analysis of L1 consistently disagreed with those of the other testers. Were they right or was he? Simpson expressed his concern at the many conferences the men and officers attended to discuss progress. These conferences were often argumentative because the men differed on how best to produce lewisite as soon as

**14. Lewisite plant workers (soldiers) in their barracks, 1918.
Courtesy Western Reserve Historical Society, Cleveland.**

possible. But Simpson was consistently alone in his view that the final product was not as pure as was needed. Undeterred by oral rebuttals to his opinions, he wrote a ten-page report for his immediate superior explaining why the analytical method being used by the other testers was unreliable. His superior, rather than considering Simpson's arguments, simply had him transferred out of the testing section and into the research section. Simpson found this humiliating and was glad when he was finally discharged from the army after the war.

The discrepancy between Simpson's results and those of the other testers is indicative of the many technical questions that would continue to surround lewisite throughout its existence, the most important of which was whether it would be effective in battle. Simpson apparently suspected that the product being made at Willoughby would not function as envisioned. Others may have shared Simpson's view but kept silent rather than equally share his humiliation. Indeed, as Conant himself was to write in his 1970 autobiography, "Later, I learned that there had been many doubts as to whether lewisite was, in fact, effective."[3]

Conant's research at the AUES had suggested that lewisite could be

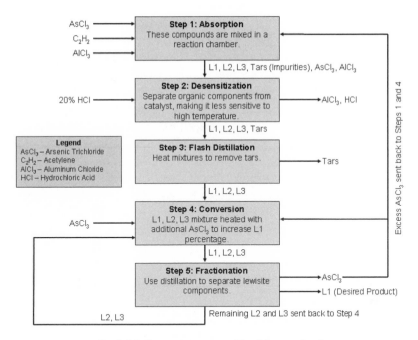

15. Probable five-step process of lewisite production.

manufactured in five steps, and for security reasons most of the soldiers were allowed to know only one of the steps. Even today, the exact five-step process by which lewisite was made at the plant has not been revealed. However, based on information provided in CWS documents and some of Lewis's later articles and speeches, it seems likely that the five steps were: 1. Absorption (mixing of raw materials, arsenic trichloride and acetylene); 2. Desensitization (Conant's contribution; the catalyst is removed by adding hydrochloric acid so that the compound can be heated without exploding); 3. Flash Distillation (removes impurities in the form of tars); 4. Conversion (L2 and L3 are converted to L1 by heating with additional arsenic trichloride); and, 5. Fractionation (separates the three lewisite components, and L1, the final product, is removed).

Dorsey initially assumed the CWS would be able to purchase arsenic trichloride and acetylene for step one. He wrote a letter on September 21 to the Dow Chemical Company in Midland, Michigan, asking whether the company would be able to produce arsenic trichloride for the Willoughby plant. Dr. A. W. Smith replied for Dow on September 27 that Dow would prefer not to supply the material because of the fumes and the problems associated with disposal of refuse containing arsenic. After receiving this letter, Dorsey decided the plant had to manufacture arsenic trichloride on its own, but he apparently never explained how the plant would dispose of the arsenic residues that so concerned Smith. Disturbingly, what happened to those arsenic residues remains an open question to this day.

Undoubtedly acetylene could have been purchased commercially at the time. However, the vast quantities needed, plus the necessity for it to be absolutely free of water, prompted Colonel Dorsey's decision that it too would be produced at the plant. Accordingly, calcium carbide was purchased from the National Carbon Company and reacted with water to produce acetylene. Records indicate that a large sulfuric acid tank was constructed on the site. The sulfuric acid was used to remove any excess water from the acetylene, so that the lewisite reaction could proceed most efficiently.

The large reaction units at the plant had to be heated to different temperatures for steps two to five. The deadly geranium-smelling fumes from the chemical processes that occurred with this heating were vented outside, but occasional accidents occurred causing the fumes to be exhausted inside the plant. Accordingly, gas masks were ordered, arriving on August 25. Captain (Doctor) Plummer mandated that the men always have their masks within easy reach. Frequent drills were conducted to help the men learn to don their masks in seconds. A warning system with an alarm was installed that rang whenever a spill occurred. Some of the men even had to wear airtight suits while working in the plant. Washing machines were ordered in early September so that contaminated clothing did not leave the plant.

Fire was also a constant danger. Fires could occur from explosions or accidents associated with the heating of the reaction chambers. A fire brigade was organized and placed under the direction of Captain Plummer.

How did the town of Willoughby react to this influx of soldiers, which equaled over 25 percent of the town's entire population? The residents watched the soldiers, who marched each day into town to dine but who otherwise remained hidden within this large, odorous, barbed-wire-surrounded enclave. The rumors must have been rampant. What was being made there? To explain the pungent odors, Conant told Mayor Carmichael that a new form of rubber was being produced. However, this did not satisfy all the residents. According to the *Willoughby Independent,* some of the more "nervy" citizens attempted to discover what was transpiring behind the brick walls, but these inquisitive souls were immediately rebuffed by armed guards.

Despite their lack of knowledge of the plant's workings, Willoughby residents were proud to have it in their midst. There were Willoughby sons fighting the Huns, and the townspeople wanted to support the war effort by doing everything they could to help the boys working at the plant. The women of the town, knowing the soldiers would appreciate some home-cooked food, began to bring baked goods and fruit to the plant's entrance. In early August, the Red Cross donated twenty-six bathing suits to the soldiers so they could swim in Lake Erie, although at this time the soldiers were not permitted to leave the plant. Because of high demand on the army's resources, the camp was short of mattresses and blankets, but after a request from Major Conant, these items were donated. Later a record player was also donated, as was a grand piano, a gift from Mrs. Harry A. Everett, so the soldiers could enjoy some music.

After Sibert lifted the restrictions on visiting Willoughby on August 10, social interactions between the town's residents and the plant ensued. On Saturday evening, August 31, the Red Cross held an informal reception for the soldiers in the gymnasium of the Andrews Institute for Girls. Ten officers and 105 enlisted men attended, their drab uniforms a striking contrast to the evening gowns of the ladies. The soldiers were encouraged to smoke and dance, refreshments of ice cream, cake, and punch were served, and live entertainment was provided by a pianist and a drummer from Cleveland. Mr. McMahon sang several patriotic numbers and Mr. Wallace recited a few humorous selections. The soldiers expressed great appreciation for the reception when they left at 10:30 P.M. to return to the base.

A home-cooked supper was provided by the Willoughby Hostess Chapter to half of the soldiers from the plant on September 23. The other half were served on September 30. At both of these receptions, photographs were taken of every soldier and given to them as souvenirs. Nate Simpson described how he and others were given passes to "escape" the plant and have dinner in the beautiful private home of a married couple. He stated that he had a "new heart" by the end of the evening. In October, the Andrews Institute was opened to the soldiers on Tuesday and Thursday evenings. They were allowed to socialize and enjoy some reading materials and games.

Soldiers must have been a common sight on the streets of Willoughby by October. On October 17 an open letter from the Woman's Committee of the Council of National Defense appeared in the *Willoughby Independent* chastising the appearance of girls on the street at night without a proper chaperone. The committee wanted to protect soldiers and civilians alike from unfavorable comments and suggested girls not be allowed on streets after 8:00 P.M. unless chaperoned.

The pleasant social activities were accompanied by frenetic activity at the plant. Work had progressed so fast that Conant was later awarded a special commendation from the CWS; the plant had been ready to produce lewisite a month earlier than expected. Nearly completed by November 1, the plant had sufficient raw materials on site for production to begin. But just as this was occurring, the Armistice was signed (on November 11), an event that was both a blessing and a great disappointment to the soldiers at Willoughby. They had worked for approximately four months under extreme pressure to do the impossible, only to learn suddenly that all of their efforts had been in vain. Lewisite would not be used in this war. The frustration manifested by the surprise ending of the war was felt throughout the CWS. Lewis, in an article that appeared in the *Chemical Bulletin* in January 1919, said, "Who would have wished to waste another copper, or risk one scratch of Sammy's epidermis in pure vindictiveness? Nevertheless, we of the Chemical Warfare Service felt strangely punctured, depressed and irritable next morning after the celebration."[4]

Most of the soldiers remained in Willoughby through November because the work at the plant could not stop immediately—there were batches of lewisite in various stages of completion on November 11. However, the men were now allowed to travel to Cleveland, and mail censorship and Sunday work were both stopped. For Thanksgiving the men enjoyed fresh homemade pies that were donated in response to Mrs. Carmichael's request that Willoughby residents "bake a pie for a soldier." Finally in December, approximately 350 men were discharged, while the remaining 200 men dismantled, inventoried, and disposed of the equipment and materials. Cheers and shouts erupted after the posting of the first hundred names of those soldiers who were to leave.

On November 29, 1918, Willoughby residents felt pride as they read the story under the *Republican's* headline, "Here is the Big Story of the Great Work of the Soldiers who Have Been Stationed in our Midst." The *Independent* ran a similar headline on December 5: "Now We Know What Those Ben Hur Boys Are Doing." The papers related that the most terrible gas ever forged by man was being manufactured in their midst for use against Germany. The *Independent* described how the false name of the product was "Methyl" and that, "a half day's output or less . . . would put Willoughby and adjacent territory out of existence." The compound was reported to have had such potential for devastation that its formula would remain guarded in the future. The *Republican* stated that only five men outside the plant knew what was being made there, and that both the Germans and British had tried but failed to produce a gas similar to "Methyl." The transition from laboratory to large-scale production was described as an example of personal heroism constituting a "wondrous tale."

In early February, some of the remaining soldiers sang in a church program at the Willoughby Church of Christ, and later that month a farewell program was held at the YMCA for those soldiers who were leaving. They enjoyed a motion picture, some vocal solos and piano numbers, and even a boxing match between two of the soldiers. By March 1919, all of the soldiers were gone from the Ben Hur plant in Willoughby. The Development Division of the CWS was subsequently abolished, and Dorsey was honorably discharged from the CWS on May 10, 1919. Dorsey only lived until age fifty-two, dying on February 31, 1931.

After the last of the soldiers departed, the plant remained unoccupied until November 1919, when the Buckeye Rubber Company purchased the property. It became the Ohio Rubber Company in 1926, and in 1953 that company became part of Eagle-Picher Industries, a manufacturer of rubber automotive parts. The plant site is now owned by the DeMilta Iron and Metal Company, a scrap metal company. Some of the original buildings remain, as does the water tower.

Although much is known about the Willoughby operation, some important questions about the operation have not been adequately answered. Had the plant actually produced any pure lewisite by November 11, 1918? If so, how much, and what happened to it? What happened to all the toxic lewisite-tainted equipment, pre-lewisite compounds, and imperfect lewisite batches that must have been produced? And what about the equally toxic equipment containing arsenic trichloride and lewisite production waste products, and even the stockpiles of arsenic oxide (which is used to make arsenic trichloride) that were there when production ceased?

Popular and semiofficial accounts provide somewhat conflicting answers to some of these questions. In its November 29 story, the *Willoughby Republican* reported that the plant was manufacturing twenty tons of lewisite per day and that "several tons" had already been produced when the Armistice was signed. A 1942 newspaper article in the *McNook (Nebraska) Gazette* quoted Lewis as saying that several thousand tons had been produced, whereas Conant in his autobiography says that only "pilot" production had ensued (but it is unclear what constitutes pilot production). On the other hand, Lieutenant Colonel W. D. Bancroft in his 1919 *History of the Chemical Warfare Service of the United States* stated that the plant had achieved "commercial production."

In 1919 *Harper's Magazine* ("War Inventions that Came Too Late") reported that the Willoughby plant had produced a total of 150 tons of lewisite and was manufacturing it at a rate of 10 tons per day when the war ended. Articles from 1919 in the *New York Times* and the *Washington Post* also reported that 10 tons per day were being produced, but they do not cite the total production figure of 150 tons. Later books and articles, many appearing in the popular press after World War I, repeat these numbers. Because some of these books and stories were written partly as propagandistic devices associated with CWS efforts to portray itself favorably after World War I, the information is suspect. For example, the magazine articles (such as the *Harper's* article) also included grossly exaggerated claims about the killing power of lewisite.

If we assume that 150 tons of lewisite were indeed produced at the plant, what happened to them? Some reports indicate that the material was placed in 364 fifty-five-gallon drums and taken by train to Baltimore, a trip that was probably one of the most extraordinary events ever to occur on American railroad tracks. All other train travel on the tracks it used between Cleveland and Baltimore was suspended during the two-day trip. The engineer was the only railway employee on the train, all the other personnel being armed soldiers. Once in Baltimore the barrels were carefully loaded onto barges, taken fifty miles offshore and dumped into waters three miles deep, a procedure that, at the time, was routinely used to discard mustard gas. Some other sources suggest a somewhat different story—that the material was already on a freighter en route to Europe before the Armistice was signed and that, once the signing occurred, the entire ship was sunk because the CWS feared bringing lewisite back into the country.

There are lingering questions pertaining to the disposal of the plant's equipment, unused raw materials, pre-lewisite compounds, and waste products. We do know that during this period in history unwanted hazardous compounds were typically buried. This was certainly the case at the AUES and at the mustard gas plant in Cleveland. That some lewisite or its byproducts were buried on the Willoughby grounds is without dispute. According to a government document, thirty-five laboratory bottles ranging in size from two ounces to one gallon were found in a circular pit on the

16. Collage of newspaper articles about lewisite that
appeared shortly after World War I.

property during excavation for a construction project in July 1957. These
bottles were collected by the army and transported to EA for decontamination, where they were erroneously reported to contain 50 percent lewisite
and 50 percent water (as explained in chapter 7, this is a chemical impossibility because lewisite reacts with water; it is therefore unclear what the
bottles actually contained).

The worrisome notion that tons of toxic lewisite-related materials might
have been buried at an unknown site in Willoughby is consistent with the
recollection of Colonel Dorsey's eldest daughter, who told me in May 2004
that she had a strong recollection of her mother saying, "thank God that
horrible stuff was buried in Willoughby."

There is also an undocumented report by a former manager at the Ohio
Rubber Company, which occupied the site of the former Willoughby lewisite plant, that in the mid-1970s a container filled with lewisite was unearthed at the plant site, and that it was sent to the army Corps of Engineers for disposal. The Corps has no record of this incident. And there is
an anecdotal report by an elderly Willoughby resident who remembers his

father relating a story that shortly after World War I he was hired by the army to dump drums of material from the plant into Lake Erie.

The lack of information pertaining to the amount and disposal of the lewisite produced at the Ben Hur plant reflects the secrecy surrounding this compound. As recently as 1993 a report by the Army Corps of Engineers on the Willoughby plant erroneously reported that it produced mustard gas rather than lewisite (the Corp's investigators did not understand that the designation "G-34" referred to lewisite after July 1918, whereas before then it had designated mustard gas, as noted in chapter 4). It is possible that somewhere classified military documents exist with a full accounting of the amount of lewisite produced, and of the fate of it and the toxic materials associated with this remarkable project. Such documents would be of great interest to historians, the Environmental Protection Agency, and the good people of Willoughby. Thus far, unfortunately, as related in the final chapter, such documents are inaccessible to nonmilitary personnel.

Nate Simpson's reminiscence is not the only surviving record of an individual who worked at the Willoughby plant. On May 24, 1927, C. H. Memory, Jr., another soldier who was assigned to the plant, wrote a letter to the CWS with some suggestions for improving production procedures. He was motivated by the failure of Congress to support an agreement banning the use of chemical agents in future wars. Memory complained that workers had great difficulty controlling the temperature in the reactor within which the arsenic trichloride and acetylene combined because the valves regulating the flow of "brine" (a coolant used to prevent overheating during this phase of the process) were too far from the reactor. Memory worried that this exposed the men to the risk of unnecessary injury and was very concerned because during the production of arsenic trichloride the reactors boiled over, "with dangerous results."

CWS Major J. W. Lyon responded to Memory's letter on May 27, thanking him for his "helpful hints" and replying that "These things will be considered when the Chemical Warfare Service again starts the manufacture of this gas."[5] On June 23, Memory wrote directly to Major Lyon saying that he had neglected to mention an accident that occurred due to excessive pressure during one of the arsenic trichloride runs when the room "quickly filled with fumes." Memory then proceeded to describe how to correct the problem, concluding, "Let us hope no gas will be made for many years. However, with troops in China and Nicaragua, I have felt obliged to offer whatever suggestions seemed to be practical."[6]

Would lewisite have won World War I for the Allies if Germany had not unexpectedly surrendered in November 1918? Perhaps; perhaps not. As mentioned above, even Conant had doubts about lewisite's actual effectiveness, which, as explained later, is much diminished by decomposition when combined with water (hydrolysis). Ulrich Mueller, in his 1932 book *Die Chemische Waffe* (Chemical weapons), was of like mind, suggesting that if lewisite had been used during the war, it would have been a great disappointment to the Allies because of hydrolysis. However, in his 1926 book *The Medical Departments of the United States Army in the World War*, the United States Surgeon General, Major General M. W. Ireland, stated that after some lewisite has been hydrolyzed by moisture on the surface of the skin, successive droplets may then be able to penetrate and produce injury. Similarly, in *Chemicals in War* (1937), Lieutenant Colonel Prentiss stipulated that because the hydrolysis products are themselves toxic, lewisite still could have been effective. Prentiss also stated that the vast majority of conditions under which armies fight are dry. Thus, he continued, hydrolysis would not be a factor in most battles and lewisite could be highly effective. Finally, Prentiss indicated that the hydrolysis of lewisite should be viewed as a process whereby the chemical changes its form, but at the same time retains its toxicity. Colonel Waitt, in his 1942 book *Gas Warfare*, similarly indicated that although rainy weather would hinder the effective use of lewisite, one hydrolysis product, lewisite oxide (also known as chlorovinylarsonous oxide; CVAO), is poisonous and will blister the skin upon contact.

This view that lewisite had a battlefield potential propelled it to become a component of the chemical arsenals of the major belligerents during World War II, to continue in this role during the Cold War, and even today to be part of the chemical arsenal of some countries.

6 The Inter-War Years

Once the "Great War" ended, the feeling in America was that the country had been forced to use inhumane weapons to help win the war. Nevertheless, American science had risen to the occasion by developing new poison gases, especially lewisite. This perspective was fostered by widespread publicity about lewisite beginning in 1919, when articles appeared in large metropolitan newspapers and national magazines. Typically these articles included grossly exaggerated claims of lewisite's toxicity, sometimes referring to it as the "Dew of Death," a name given it by General Fries, who became director of the CWS in March 1920.

The first of the articles appeared in the *New York Times* and the *Washington Post* on May 25, 1919. Both articles described a Department of the Interior exposition being held in Washington that highlighted the Department's wartime activities. (As described earlier, the Department of the Interior's Bureau of Mines had been responsible for the development of lewisite until the CWS became a part of the War Department in June 1918). The exposition featured a number of displays, one of which contained a vial of the "deadliest poison ever known, 'Lewisite,'" resting on a pedestal. The *Times* article boasted that ten airplanes carrying lewisite "would have wiped out . . . every vestige of life—animal and vegetable—in Berlin. A single day's output [of the Willoughby plant] would snuff out the millions of lives on Manhattan Island." The article concluded by reiterating how dangerous the material was; "Everybody at the exposition . . . keeps as far away from it as possible."[1] The *Post* described the history of lewisite similarly, also bragging that one day's output from the Willoughby plant was sufficient to kill all four million inhabitants of Manhattan.

The *New York Times* article angered Van H. Manning of the Bureau of Mines because it implied that the CWS rather than the Bureau was primarily responsible for the development of lewisite. Manning issued a press release stating that Lewis developed lewisite while poison gas research was still under the auspices of the Bureau. This press release was followed by a caustic comment in the *Chemical Bulletin* charging that leaked details about lewisite's potency reflected the inability of CWS chemists to keep a secret. Lieutenant Colonel Bancroft, Director of the Research Division of the CWS, responded to this accusation by insisting that release of information about lewisite is absolutely "barred" among CWS personnel. The "bitter" dispute between the Bureau of Mines and the CWS was also described in a May 4, 1919 *Washington Post* article. Members of Congress were described as being "irritated" over the slighting by the CWS of the very important role played by the Bureau of Mines in preparing the country for gas warfare.

Lewis responded to the *Chemical Bulletin* accusation, saying that he had not contributed to the sensational stories that had been published about lewisite and that details about the compound were still supposed to be confidential. A report of the dispute between the CWS and the Bureau in the July 1919 issue of the *Chemical Bulletin* commended Lewis for his work on lewisite and suggested that he should have been awarded a Distinguished Service Medal. The article also made the interesting comment that "There seems to be a strange mixture of publicity and secrecy on the subject [lewisite]."[2]

On June 15, shortly after the *New York Times* and *Washington Post* articles appeared, the Sunday magazine of the *Cleveland Plain Dealer* published "Gas Intended to Wipe Out Hun Armies Dumped into the Sea," by Harry A. Mount. The article began by describing the armed train ride and dumping at sea of Willoughby's lewisite. Next it asserted that "methyl" would have "wiped out" half of the German army because it was seventy-two times as toxic as mustard gas. Mount continued by stating that lewisite enters the bloodstream immediately and causes an agonizing death in a few hours, and that one ton could "depopulate" Cleveland. He concluded by commending the work of Conant and Wilcox in developing the compound.

Five months after Mount's article was published, Frank Parker Stockbridge authored "War Inventions That Came Too Late," the *Harper's Magazine* article mentioned in chapter 5. The overenthusiastic Stockbridge lauded American ingenuity while claiming that lewisite was "the most powerful weapon of war ever wielded."[3] The author boasted that when the armistice was signed the United States had enough lewisite on hand to eliminate the entire German army, and that the country had in preparation huge guns that could hurl lewisite shells "incredible" distances. Stockbridge also described (accurately) a lewisite delivery weapon, the "Kettering Bug," named after one of its coinventors, Charles Kettering, that was the forerunner of today's cruise missile. This inexpensive pilotless plane was designed to fly approximately fifty miles, fall to the ground, and detonate its two-hundred-pound lewisite bomb in the middle of enemy forces. The plane was never completed during the war, nor during World War II when more research was done on the concept.

The strange mixture of publicity and secrecy surrounding lewisite is reflected in a book, *The Medical Aspects of Mustard Gas Poisoning*, published in 1919 in association with the CWS. Despite the fact that the term lewisite appears in newspapers as early as 1918, the authors withheld its name, stating the following:

> The effect of German poison warfare upon the non-Teutonic world was to excite horror and execration. But reason and necessity demanded retaliation in kind; and such a boomerang the Germans were getting in the last months of the war. Had not a premature armistice intervened this boomerang might have become a veritable agent of annihilation to the German army; as it has been stated on good authority that the American Chemical Warfare Service holds the secret of a gas much more toxic than any used by the Germans.[4]

None of the 1918–19 newspaper articles on the development of lewisite mentioned Nieuwland's role in its discovery. Such information first appeared publicly in a 1922 *South Bend (Indiana) Tribune* article, "Notre Dame Dean is Credited with Great Discovery." This article, which was based on an interview with Nieuwland, related how the priest-chemist initially synthesized the material and described it in his thesis. Nieuwland told the reporter that lewisite would penetrate clothing, corrode the skin, and cause death in a few hours, and was very dangerous to manufacture. Nieuwland also is quoted as saying that he was working on a compound even more toxic than lewisite, although there is no independent confirmation that he ever purposely conducted poison gas research.

Lewisite became the subject not only of popular newspaper and magazine articles, but also of stories, books, and scientific papers in both the United States and Europe. Will Irwin was a war correspondent who, after being wounded, returned to America to direct the foreign propaganda office of the government's Commission on Public Information. He wrote a popular 1921 book, *The Next War: An Appeal to Common Sense*. It described lewisite as follows:

> It was invisible; it was a sinking gas, which could search out the refugees of dugouts and cellars; if breathed, it killed at once and it killed

not only through the lungs. Wherever it settled on the skin, it produced a poison which penetrated the system and brought almost certain death. It was inimical to all life, animal or vegetable. Masks alone were of no use against it. Further, it had *fifty-five* times the "spread" of any poison gas hitherto used in the war. An expert said that a dozen Lewisite bombs . . . might with a favorable wind have eliminated the population of Berlin.[5]

After the war Irwin returned to his career as a journalist and advocated for pacifist causes, including America's entry into the League of Nations.

In a 1922 *Chicago Herald and Examiner* serialized novel, "The Slayer of Souls: A Story of Love and Adventure," by Robert W. Chambers, the lewisite vial displayed at the Department of Interior's exposition is stolen by a sorcerer. Just as the sorcerer is about to fling the vial to the ground and release its deadly contents, a good witch causes the vial to become red hot. This heat melts the sorcerer's body, causing the vial of lewisite to gently fall to the ground and roll into the surrounding swamp, along with the sorcerer's remains. An "enemy of all mankind" thus was eliminated.

Lewisite also was an integral part of "Poisoned Light," a story that appeared in an October 1921 issue of *Detective Story Magazine*. Here the fictionalized discoverer of lewisite is murdered using the same gas he invented. The murderer designed a specialized light bulb that exploded when turned on, releasing the gas. The mystery is solved by the hero, detective Pinklin West, who arrests the villain.

Stories about lewisite's potency also appeared in European publications. *Death From the Skies,* by Heinz Liepmann, was published in England in 1937. It described an "eye-witness" account of a man entering a room that contained an imperceptible amount of lewisite vapor. After a few minutes the man was seized with violent pains and suffered from uncontrollable vomiting. Four days afterwards he began suffering from arsenical dermatitis, and such great "shock" that, despite being tall and muscular, he completely "broke down." At the end of three months, he died from lewisite poisoning.

A more realistic view of lewisite was presented in a 1937 German book, *Der Chemische Krieg* (*Chemical Warfare*). The authors of this book, who were engineers, military officers, and university professors, dismissed the claim that a dozen lewisite bombs could destroy all life in Berlin. They argued that lewisite's effect is too small and its odor too distinctive to be of any use offensively (enemy soldiers would simply leave the area). However, the authors did believe that lewisite might be useful defensively in lieu of an explosive shell barrage to dissuade an ongoing attack.

The first scientific article on lewisite was published in 1921 by two British Royal Navy chemists, Stanley Green and Thomas Price. They, seemingly inappropriately, revealed the formula for lewisite, which the CWS had shared with the British Chemical Warfare Service during the war. Green and Price's article raised the ire of General Amos A. Fries and Major Clarence J. West, who stated in their 1921 book, *Chemical Warfare:*

> Unfortunately or otherwise, the British later decided to release this material for publication, and details may be found in an article by Green and Price in the *Journal of the Chemical Society* for April, 1921. It must be emphasized that the credit for this work belongs, not to these authors, but to Capt. W. Lee Lewis and the men who worked with him at the Catholic University branch of the American University Division (the Research Division of the CWS).[6]

Fries and West's book also stated that lewisite production methodology was considered one of the most valuable secrets of the war. Considering this and their indignation toward Green and Price, it seems peculiar that they also provided the precise Green and Price reference in their book.

The article written by Green and Price had been approved by "the [British] Chemical Warfare Section of the Directorate of Artillery, War Office."[7] To further justify the publication of their article, the authors stated without citation that the American CWS had, prior to the publication of their own paper, "announced" that a highly vesicant compound is formed when acetylene is combined with arsenic trichloride in the presence of aluminum chloride. Their use of the word "announced" is very curious, because there was no previous public disclosure of the formula for lewisite. Green and Price later in their article referred to the American "report," but again provided no details. In a 1921 speech Lewis stated that the Green and Price article was based upon "American *confidential* [my italics] communications." Further, in a 1923 article on lewisite, Lewis indicated that the "report" referred to was a 1918 CWS communication, which undoubtedly was not available to the public. Thus the rationale behind Green and Price's publication of heretofore confidential information is mysterious, especially because the article probably facilitated the subsequent spread of lewisite production to other countries. Perhaps the explanation relates to the "substantial inducements," including the freedom to publish, that the British government offered its top poison gas scientists at the time.

Lewis, in common with Fries and West, was annoyed at the appearance of the Green and Price article. It led him to ask General Fries for permission to write a more complete and factual article on lewisite. Lewis received permission, and in 1923 he and coauthor G. A. Perkins (who worked with Lewis at Catholic University of America) published an article in *Industrial and Chemical Engineering*. In this paper, the authors summarized the work done on lewisite by Lewis's unit at CUA and included a hypothetical description of the chemical processes involved in the reactions. (Although Lewis knew the chemical reactions that led to lewisite, the mechanisms underlying these reactions were poorly understood). Their article included a statement that the CWS had granted permission to publish this paper. The article described the work done by Lewis's CUA unit as follows:

> The authors and their collaborators reduced the reaction to controllable conditions, isolated three pure compounds from the reaction mixture, proved their nature, worked out the methods of laboratory control, and submitted plans for large-scale production. In the later stages of the work J. B. Conant and his laboratory also took up the chemical study of these substances, and to them we are indebted for the hydrochloric acid method of desensitizing original reaction mixtures.[8]

Although the Green and Price article probably did facilitate the spread to other countries of technology necessary to produce lewisite, Fries and West might have been less indignant had they known that German scientists had independently developed and evaluated lewisite during the war. A German physician-scientist, Hermann Büscher, in his 1931 book *Grün- und Gelbkeuz* (*Green and Yellow Cross*, which referred to the colored crosses used to identify the German gas artillery shells during World War I), said of the Green and Price and the Lewis and Perkins articles, "There was nothing in these publications that was essentially new to German scientists."[9]

The popular articles expressing exaggerated claims about the effectiveness of lewisite were published at a time when the future of the CWS was very much in doubt. Surprisingly, the War Department was the primary agency trying to abolish the CWS. Most military officers viewed America's use of chemical weapons during the war as degrading and dishonorable. Further, chemical weapons research brought scientists, who were considered undisciplined, into the military. Public sentiment also supported the elimination of the CWS because of the fear engendered by the exaggerated claims for the effectiveness of chemical weapons. Lewis alluded to this fear when he wrote, "Lewisite, by an accretion of superlatives, has acquired powers compared with which his Satanic Majesty becomes an angel of Mercy."[10]

To rebut the chorus singing the evils of chemical weapons, the directors of the CWS, General Sibert and then General Fries, and the active and reserve CWS officers (including Lewis) became highly vocal defenders of the Service and the use of chemical weapons. They gave lectures and wrote articles in a successful lobbying effort to maintain the existence of the CWS.

Lewis was a particularly dedicated advocate for the CWS. Between 1919 and 1930 he gave public lectures as well as lectures to the military academies with such titles as "A Conversation on Gas," "Some Aspects of Gas Warfare," "Gas Warfare and the Engineer," "The Mechanism of Mustard Gas," "Some General Features of Gas Warfare," "Chemicals in Future Warfare," and "Is the Elimination of Gas Warfare Feasible?" He also wrote popular articles in magazines such as *Atlantic Monthly* with titles that were similar to those of his lectures. In a 1925 article, "Poison Gas and Pacifists," a sidebar said:

> The deadliness and barbarity of new gases capable of annihilating civilian populations and whole armies are never absent from present-day discussions of war. *Lewisite,* most potent of all these agencies of death, is spoken of in hushed terms. Last spring, a protocol was drawn up at Geneva, which Congress will soon be called upon to ratify, prohibiting such inhuman agencies of combat in favor of the more humane triumvirate of bullets, bombs and bayonets. What are the facts? Dr. Lewis, the chemist after whom *Lewisite* is named, tells the story in irrefutable terms. The Editors hope that his article will turn pacifists from the futile idea of controlling methods of warfare to studying its causes.[11]

In this article Lewis described the impossibility of banning gas warfare and countered the public view that lewisite was so powerful that "One drop applied to the tongue of a dog has destroyed cities!"[12] Lewis reasonably argued that if lewisite was that powerful he and all the other scientists who worked with it would have been annihilated. However, Lewis did believe that lewisite was 2.2 times more effective than mustard and that three drops would be sufficient to kill a human, remarking that "The big guns on battleships would be as playful as kittens compared with the destructiveness of lewisite."[13]

In "Is Prohibition of Gas Warfare Feasible?" Lewis likened the use of gas weapons to the use of poisons by snakes and insects. He declared that during World War I the chance of an injured soldier recovering from gas was twelve times greater than that from such "Christian weapons as high explosives, bullets, shrapnel and the like." He noted that every aspect of warfare is an "improper use of science." Lewis concluded by saying, "It [gas] is the most efficient, most economical, and most humane, single weapon known to military science."[14]

In some of his lectures and articles Lewis also made the intriguing suggestion that the scientific use of chemical weapons might be more on the side of "right" than the use of more conventional weapons. In a public address near Chicago on August 18, 1928, he argued that because advancement in the technology of warfare characterizes an intelligent nation, this intelligence will make the nation right more frequently than wrong. In his *Atlantic Monthly* article he emphasized this point: "Thus its [chemical weapons'] introduction into warfare might be presumptive of a faint growth of righteousness in this imperfect world."[15] In a 1925 article in the *Chicago Tribune* he said, "It [gas warfare] offsets mere brute weight and should be regarded as a weapon of civilized defense."[16]

Although Lewis rallied against the exaggerated claims of lewisite's toxicity, he also may have contributed to the view that lewisite was more potent than the facts testified. In a lecture Lewis gave in October 1919 to a current events class, he said that lewisite was not used during the war because England and France considered the gas to be too inhumane. There is no evidence available to substantiate this claim and it does not seem credible, considering that there was really no lewisite that could have been used. Similarly, Lewis said in a speech to the Rockford, Illinois, Elks Club in December 1921 that lewisite sprayed from airplanes would have led to a speedy termination of the war, and that he was glad that the Armistice alleviated the need to use the material.

In addition to its journalistic campaign to save itself from elimination, the CWS promoted peacetime uses for its chemical agents. In collaboration with civilian agencies, the CWS advocated using its agents as tear gases, insecticides, pesticides, and, surprisingly, medicinal aids. The two most widely known World War I poison gases, chlorine and mustard, figured most prominently in this campaign. Chlorine was publicized as a treatment for people suffering from colds, bronchitis, and whooping cough. The *New York Times* reported on May 2, 1923, that inhalation of weak concentrations of chlorine could control epidemics of "grip" and colds almost instantly. It also reported in May 1924 that President Coolidge was treated for a severe cold with chlorine and was cured within three days. Mustard gas was purported to prevent guinea pigs injected with tuberculosis-causing bacteria from succumbing to the disease, suggesting it could also prevent the disease in humans.

Lewisite was similarly touted for peacetime use. A derivative of it (chlorovinyl arsenious oxide) was shown to have the highest toxic value among over a hundred agents tested against marine borers, which destroy docks and other waterfront structures. In writing about the work of the CWS on marine borers, General Fries said:

> During the war and since, the Chemical Warfare Service has been engaged on an intensive study of powerful and poisonous chemicals. The tremendous amount of accumulated knowledge, together with personnel trained in their handling, makes the Chemical Warfare Service supreme in any studies involving their use. No other organization has the knowledge, written or otherwise, or the trained personnel for making, testing and protecting against these chemicals. That is the role of the Chemical Warfare Service in peace.[17]

Lewisite, like chlorine and mustard, was purported to have medicinal value. The May 2 *New York Times* article on chlorine and mustard also stated that Dr. A. S. Loevenhart, a renowned pharmacologist at the University of Wisconsin, exposed forty-two institutionalized persons suffering from "paresis," which referred to the final stages of syphilis, to lewisite (no details of the dosages were given). Of these, half were described as cured of their paresis, discharged from the hospital, and enjoying "lucrative" employment. In other words, lewisite was reported to cure the symptoms of syphilis, presumably by killing the microorganisms (spirochetes) in the brains of the patients. The article doesn't explain how a substance that was often described as deadly in as little amount as a third of a teaspoon could be administered clinically.

None of the three "cures"—chlorine, mustard, or lewisite—was considered valid for very long. Whereas the utilization of chlorine to treat cold symptoms was probably accurately reported in the newspaper accounts, it is unlikely that lewisite was ever actually used to treat paresis. Indeed, there is no reference even within Dr. Loevenhart's own research records, which are archived at the University of Wisconsin in Madison, to treatment of patients with lewisite. Loevenhart, however, was actively involved in chemical weapons research during World War I, including the testing of lewisite at the American University Experimental Station, and he did use arsenic-based water-soluble compounds (some of which he received from Lewis and one of Lewis's students, C. S. Hamilton) to treat patients with syphilis. This collaborative effort between the Department of Chemistry at Northwestern University and the Department of Pharmacology at the University of Wisconsin eventually led to the 1930s discovery of an arsenic-based drug, Mapharsen, which became a very successful antisyphilitic treatment.

In addition to its use against marine borers and syphilis, lewisite, the *New York Times* reported on July 8, 1925, was used in a vault security device that thwarted a bank robbery in tiny Elnora, Indiana. Because of the prevalence of Midwest bank robberies during this decade, the Citizen's Bank in Elnora had taken the unusual and expensive step of contracting with the Anakin Lock and Alarm Company of Chicago to design its vault's security system. On July 7 robbers attempted to break into the vault but were rebuffed when lewisite was released by the security system. The day after the robbery, Theodore Burzlaff and A. I. Montgomery of the Anakin Company returned to Elnora to repair the damage. Mr. Burzlaff told a local reporter, "This gas is the best protection against safe blowers that I know of," claiming that 105 bank robberies had been averted by the system he referred to as the "Anakin Protection."[18] More details about the robbery were provided in the July 9 issue of the *New York Times*: "The gas was placed in a delicate glass container which would shatter at the least disturbance to the vault."[19]

The bank robbery story was also reported, with some slight differences in detail from the *Times* articles, in two articles in the *Washington (Indiana) Democrat,* which is the local county newspaper serving Elnora. The first reported that poison gas prevented the robbery but did not mention the specific gas, whereas the second stated, "The gas is the product of Professor Lewis, head of the chemistry department of Northwestern University."[20]

A story in the *New Orleans Times Picayune* dated August 6, 1925, described how a lewisite protection device manufactured by the Anakin Lock and Alarm Company successfully thwarted an attempted robbery at the Orange Crush Bottling Company in New Orleans. The article, however, referred to lewisite as a "tear gas," which is curious, although lewisite does cause tearing of the eyes.

Was lewisite used as a security device? Lewis categorically denied this allegation, writing in a September 12, 1925, article that the stories reporting the use of lewisite to stop bank robbers belong in the same category as those that contain grossly exaggerated claims of its effectiveness. It also seems rather unlikely that the CWS would provide lewisite for such a purpose, or that it could be employed safely. Furthermore, it is reasonable that the reporters confused lewisite with tear gas, because the tear gas device that Lewis did invent, described in chapter 1, could also be used to protect bank vaults. Nevertheless, additional popular press articles referred to mustard gas being used to protect bank vaults.

Although lewisite use in security devices seems unlikely, an unusual nonmilitary application was apparently conducted in England. A *Chicago Tribune* article dated April 26, 1925, described the research of Professor Maxwell-Lefroy, an entomologist at the Imperial College of Science and Technology in South Kensington, London. Dr. Maxwell-Lefroy was investigating lewisite's fly-killing capabilities. While conducting such an experiment the professor remained in a room filled with the vapor too long and would have died had rescuers not administered oxygen for an hour. The professor had diluted the lewisite in mineral oil, which he admitted probably helped save his life. He also stated that the flies seemed quite content in the lewisite-vapored room. The professor did not indicate how he was able to obtain lewisite, but presumably it was from the British Chemical Warfare Service.

Despite his near demise, Professor Maxwell-LeFroy continued experimenting with lewisite as an insecticide. In October 1925, after he did not return home for dinner, his wife found him in his laboratory unconscious and bleeding from his nose. He had been overcome by lewisite fumes perhaps mixed with some other chemical. Maxwell-LeFroy was very secretive about his work and his assistants were uncertain of the exact combination of agents he had been investigating at the time, although lewisite was believed to be one of them. This time the professor was not so lucky; he died from inhalation of the fumes. Professor Maxwell-Lefroy's insect-killing legacy lives on in the company he started, Rentokil, which is Britain's leading pest control firm.

The publicity about lewisite during the inter-war years placed Lewis in the national spotlight, which brought him many letters and unusual requests. One group of women asked him to develop a compound that could remove superfluous body hair. The group's letter ended, "Some of us in talking over your wonderful discovery of Lewisite, decided if the matter were brought to your attention, that you doubtless could bring relief [to this condition] through your knowledge."[21] Lewis's publicity also brought him some condemnation. He received at least a hundred letters lambasting him for developing a death-producing gas.

Lewisite's exaggerated killing capabilities not only influenced the American citizenry, but also had a dramatic effect on war departments throughout the world. The ministers in charge of these departments felt that, if the United States had this remarkable weapon, so must they. Thus, through cooperation, by espionage, or from the articles written by Green and Price and by Lewis and Perkins, many countries established facilities to test and/or produce lewisite. Britain and France, the World War I allies of the United States, were the first to do so. Britain actively tested lewisite on soldiers at its Porton Down facility during the inter-war years. During the 1930s Italy developed facilities that could produce lewisite at a rate of five tons a day. Italy's dictator, Mussolini, ordered poison gas (mustard and probably lewisite) to be sprayed from airplanes in Italy's 1936 invasion and conquest of Ethiopia. Ethiopian Emperor Haile Selassie described how a series of Italian airplanes led one another across the sky releasing a continuous fog that drenched soldiers, women, children, and cattle with the deadly agents. Italian troops also effectively used "portable spraying units" filled with mustard and probably lewisite that were mounted on soldiers dressed in protective suits.

In 1937 Major Paul Murphy, former Director of Experiments at the British Chemical Defense Station at Porton Down, published an article in the *Chemical Warfare Bulletin* entitled "Gas in the Italo-Ethiopian War." He described two discrepancies between the assumed use of mustard gas by the Italians and the resulting symptoms in the Ethiopian troops. First, the onset of the pain and blisters was more rapid than would be expected based on the experiences of soldiers during World War I. Second, he noted that the virulence of the agent was less than that used during that war. Based on these observations, he hypothesized that the agent used was, in fact, lewisite. He indicated that although he had made enquires, he could not determine for certain whether lewisite was used, either alone or with mustard. Parenthetically, having previously employed poison gas against the helpless Ethiopians, Mussolini again advocated using it to repel United States troops landing in North Africa during World War II.

The Soviet Union became particularly interested in the production of lewisite after World War I. To facilitate the development of its chemical weapons program, it partially relied on covert German assistance. The German military could thus secretly continue chemical weapons research, although this violated the Treaty of Versailles, which the Allies had imposed on Germany upon its surrender in World War I.

In the early 1920s Soviet scientist A. E. Favorskii was asked by his government to develop a process for producing lewisite at the Leningrad Artillery Academy. Later, in 1928, Soviet chemist Vladimir Ipatiev and his assistants, Shapiro and Liberman, apparently working with Favorskii, developed a novel method for producing lewisite. This method used low temperatures and pressures, which resulted in a safer process for producing large quantities of lewisite. The scientists generously gave the secret patent for this process to the Revolutionary War Council.

By 1928 the Soviet Union was ready to produce lewisite at its Berezniki chemical weapons facility, and by 1935 Soviet scientists had perfected an eighteen-hour manufacturing process, which yielded a very pure product. Soviet scientists also developed a thickened form of lewisite, presumably to be sprayed from airplanes.

Although by the mid-1930s the Soviet Union's production technology was relatively advanced, for unknown reasons its scientists desired assistance from Lewis. In January 1937 Lewis received a telegram and a follow-up telephone call requesting that he travel to the Soviet Union to supervise the building of a lewisite plant. Lewis declined formally to the Soviet representative, Mr. William Arsen, in a letter:

> Since then [our phone conversation] I have given the matter rather continuous thought and I am clear that I wouldn't want to further such an activity. I am not trying to make a heroic gesture, and I realize that any attitude I might take is but a feeble factor in any program a foreign nation might adopt looking to the expatriation of the war gas Lewisite. In other words, I know that the essential facts regarding the manufacture of this gas are recorded. I recorded them myself with the full approval of the War Department. I know that it would be a comparatively easy matter for a chemical engineer to build a plant in which to manufacture this gas. Nevertheless, I feel that it would be no source of satisfaction to me personally to be a party to such manufacture by another country.[22]

The Soviet Union not only produced chemical weapons, but also sought optimal ways to use them. Lewisite and mustard were tested on thousands of its citizens involuntarily, including scientists at "*sharashkas*" (Soviet scientific institutions that utilized the forced labor of incarcerated scientists; Alexander Solzhenitsyn's first novel, *The First Circle*, is a vivid account of life in a *sharashka*). Open-air tests were also conducted using lewisite at locations that later became modern housing compounds, which may be negatively effecting the health of today's residents.

Poland too showed a post–World War I interest in lewisite. Research was conducted in 1928–39 at the Anti-Gas Institute, a branch of the Ministry of Military Affairs in Warsaw. At the time a large number of geraniums were grown at the institute to camouflage the odor associated with the work being done there on lewisite.

Finally, post–World War I Japan, in an effort to modernize its military, put particular emphasis on the development of chemical and biological weapons, including lewisite. Of all the countries that began producing lewisite after World War I, Japan was the only one to use it militarily in the Second World War.

Although the CWS during the 1920s survived the efforts to eliminate it, its budget was dramatically reduced. Very little research on lewisite as a military agent was conducted during the inter-war years. This lack of a significant investment in the CWS during this period resulted in World War II beginning with the United States relying on the same agents that had been developed during World War I. In contrast, Gerhard Schrader, a chemist seeking new pesticides for the I. G. Farben Company in Germany during the mid-1930s, discovered tabun and sarin. Both of these compounds are nerve agents that block the activity of a key enzyme within the nervous system, acetylcholinesterase, resulting in death due to paralysis of the muscles used for respiration. Schrader considered sarin to have "astonishing high" potential as a war gas. During World War II Germany produced twelve thousand tons of tabun (only small-scale manufacture of sarin occurred before the Soviets captured the production facility). Germany also produced the more conventional war gases (e.g., lewisite, mustard, and phosgene).

The publicity about lewisite during the inter-war years prompted Hermann Büscher to investigate its toxicity. In his 1931 book, *Grün- und Gelbkreuz* (*Green and Yellow Cross*), he described how after World War I German scientists were debating the best methods to destroy their stockpiles of war gases (as required by the terms of the Armistice) when an accidental explosion at the storage site at Breloh destroyed most of the stockpiled weapons. Büscher then became the physician assigned to care for the workers who performed the dangerous cleanup at the Breloh depot. At the time he knew almost nothing about treating the effects of exposure to war gases, but he became intensely interested in the subject and carefully documented his observations. Then, in 1925, Büscher began to investigate the medical effects of war gases not only clinically but also experimentally, using human subjects. Büscher does not say how he obtained the agents he used in his experiments, although by all indications he made them himself. He noted that he used "technical" lewisite, which is a mixture of all three variants and the one he says that would have been used in the war (this is not correct; lewisite factories were designed to maximize the most toxic, L1, variant). Büscher's book does not reveal who served as the subjects for his experiments. He stated:

> Behind me there stands no scientific institute, no chemical industry, no Ministry of Defense. . . . The only thing that is behind my efforts is a deep desire, an almost insatiable craving, to get at the fundamental facts in the mysterious action which the chemical war materials exert upon the human organism.[23]

In 1944 Büscher's book, which contains the most detailed experimental data on the effects of mustard and lewisite on human skin conducted prior to World War II, was translated into English by Nell Conway, an employee of the Kettering Laboratory of Applied Physiology at the University of Cincinnati, which was under contract to the CWS. Dr. Robert Kehoe, Director of the Kettering Laboratory at the time, said in the Preface:

> [T]he earthy and intensely practical experimental methods employed by Dr. Büscher have yielded certain results that otherwise might not have been so convincing, while his accounts though fulsome demonstrate his acute interest and the high degree of accuracy of his clinical observations.[24]

Büscher provided very detailed descriptions and photographs of the development of mustard and lewisite blisters beginning five minutes after exposure and continuing through complete healing (about twenty-one days). His primary clinical recommendation to promote healing after exposure to lewisite was "retention of the blister." Büscher also found that, contrary to observations made during animal experiments by Edward Vedder (reported in *The Medical Aspects of Chemical Warfare*), the effects of lewisite on human skin were less serious and painful than those of mustard.

Büscher had applied to his experimental subjects more than 1.4 milliliters of lewisite per seventy kilograms of body weight, an amount that Vedder considered fatal, without any serious consequences. Accordingly, he concluded that lewisite lacked significant systemic toxicity. However, Vedder may have been referring primarily to the effect of the L1 variant, whereas Büscher's lewisite was probably mainly L3, the primary constituent of unpurified lewisite, known not to be a significant vesicant. Furthermore, without knowing Büscher's source for lewisite, and considering his

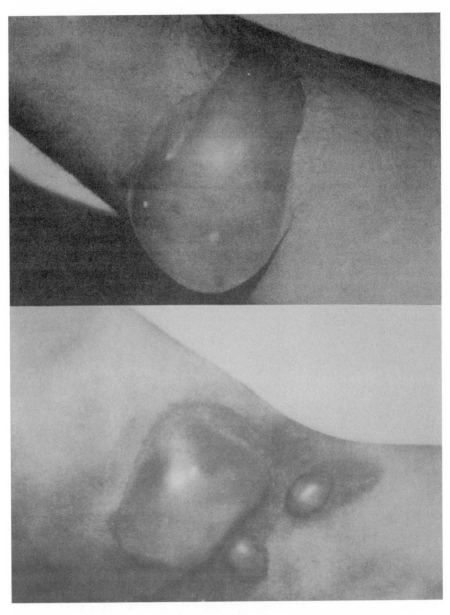

17. Lewisite blisters twenty-four hours after single drop placed on the forearm.
From Büscher, *Green and Yellow Cross*.

lack of formal training in chemistry, it is reasonable to question whether the substance he called lewisite was truly lewisite at all.

All of the inter-war articles and books on lewisite and the other World War I poison gases led to the reasonable belief that chemical weapons would play an integral role in any future war. Thus, the 1939 start of World War II brought great fear among the world's citizens that their skies would soon be filled with enemy airplanes spraying tons of deadly gas, especially the Dew of Death, down upon them. Fortunately, this did not occur. If it had, however, what would lewisite have done to its battlefield victims?

7 Military Biology and BAL

Military Biology

Lewisite's military value lies in its immediate (acute) effects. Exposure causes instantaneous excruciating pain when it enters the eyes, a stinging pain when it contacts the skin, and, when it is inhaled, sneezing, coughing, pain, and tightness in the chest, often accompanied by nausea and vomiting. How does lewisite's composition of carbon, hydrogen, chlorine, and arsenic cause these symptoms?

Most of these effects are based on arsenic, a poison known to be lethal since ancient times, that comprises 36 percent of lewisite (L1). Normally, cells use enzymes (catalysts) to break apart (metabolize) the chemical bonds in carbohydrates, releasing life-sustaining energy. Arsenic binds to and thereby functionally inactivates one or more of the enzymes critical for this process. Unable to produce energy, the affected cells die.

Obviously, for arsenic to be an effective chemical warfare agent, it needs to reach the cells of vital body organs. Because enemy soldiers will not readily drink or eat arsenic-tainted food, the most reasonable routes to enter the body are by way of absorption through exposed skin (and unexposed skin if the agent can penetrate clothing), and by inhalation. From a military perspective, absorption through the skin is the better of the two routes because, whereas gas masks can readily protect against inhalation, it is difficult and very cumbersome to entirely sheath a soldier in protective clothing. Further, if in the process of absorption the arsenic interferes with the metabolism of skin cells and/or irritates the skin, it becomes a vesicant (blister-causing compound) as well as a systemic poison; this gives the agent even greater potential as a battlefield weapon.

Chemically, arsenic is a semimetal (sometimes referred to as a "metalloid"), sharing some characteristics with both metals and nonmetals. It exists in nature chemically combined with other elements (for example, oxygen and iron). Minerals containing arsenic compounds are usually obtained as byproducts of copper and lead smelting. These inorganic arsenic compounds (compounds that do not contain carbon) are toxic if ingested or inhaled and may also be quite irritating to the skin, although systemic absorption through the skin does not occur. A number of inorganic arsenic compounds were tested as chemical warfare agents during World War I, including one of the key elements in lewisite, the liquid arsenic trichloride. This compound was eventually rejected because it is corrosive and highly reactive with water, forming hydrochloric acid (HCl). Most of the other inorganic arsenic compounds were also relatively ineffective, often because it was difficult to deliver toxic dosages.

Lewisite is an organic arsenic compound because it is composed partially of carbon (12 percent), which is derived from acetylene. In contrast to the inorganic arsenic compounds, which tend to be hydrophilic, or soluble in water, it is lipophilic, or soluble in fats. The cell membrane, which is like an electrified security fence surrounding a cell, is easily penetrated by lipophilic compounds, but not by hydrophilic compounds. Lewisite's fat solubility allows it to covertly conduct its arsenic into the cell.

Even before lewisite can penetrate the skin to invade cells, however, it often must first traverse a layer of sweat. Thus, to understand the toxicity of lewisite it is necessary to understand what happens when lewisite reacts with water—that is, undergoes hydrolysis.

Hydrolysis is the reaction of a substance with water that results in the formation of one or more new compounds. In the case of lewisite, hydrolysis primarily produces a water soluble arsenic-containing acid called chlorovinylarsonous acid (CVAA) and some HCl (when water is in limited quantity; see appendix 3). Thus, when lewisite contacts sweaty skin it will undergo hydrolysis, producing the toxic acid compound, CVAA. However, the amount of perspiration on human skin depends on such factors as body temperature, activity level, and an individual's proclivity to sweat. Furthermore, different body parts perspire at different levels, e.g., armpits are sweatier than chests. A large amount of lewisite contacting a non-sweaty soldier or a non-sweaty body part may result in unhydrolyzed (unchanged) lewisite penetrating the outer layer of skin cells and directly invading the body, whereas a small amount of lewisite on a very sweaty body segment may not penetrate this region of skin (it may nevertheless produce irritation, as arsenic in virtually any form is still a skin irritant). Moreover, the hydrolysis of lewisite is dependent on the temperature and humidity of the air, being more rapid as they increase.

The hydrolysis of lewisite has been the central issue pertaining to whether lewisite would be effective under battlefield conditions. Most recently, the military manual on chemical and biological weapons published by the Departments of the Army, Navy, and Air Force in 1990 stated that lewisite rapidly decomposes above 70 percent humidity and that, accordingly, it has a shorter duration of effectiveness than mustard, although the products of lewisite's hydrolysis are described as being toxic themselves. Nevertheless, Sterling Seagrave in his 1981 book *Yellow Rain* wrote, "One previous chemical warfare agent for which the army had great hopes, lewisite, was produced without field tests and proved to be a total failure. It turned out in practice that lewisite was unstable in the presence of moisture."[1]

Lewis and Conant were undoubtedly aware of the problem posed by the hydrolysis of lewisite; a 1918 report summarizing experiments with lewisite stated that it was the toxic "hydrolytic" products that would be effective in contaminating the ground and objects. Thus, at that time the CWS did not consider lewisite hydrolysis to be a significant deficit.

In addition to the confounding effects associated with hydrolysis, lewisite's ability to irritate skin cells is not simple. Its effects on the skin are not derived solely from arsenic's interference with cellular metabolism. Lewisite also directly irritates the outer surface of skin cells causing an "inflammatory reaction" similar to that produced by poison ivy.

Just five to fifteen minutes after exposure to lewisite, human skin has been reported to appear both red and swollen, as in a sunburn, and dull dead-white to gray, as in an acid burn. A fluid-filled separation develops between the superficial and deeper skin layers because fluid and many white blood cells spill out of the affected capillaries. A blister containing the cellular fluid develops six to eight hours after exposure. As it develops, the blister stretches the skin, causing pain. Gradually a crust forms and the lesion dries. The blister requires one to three weeks to heal, a shorter period than that of a similar sized mustard lesion. The scrotum, armpit, and neck seem most sensitive to lewisite, presumably because of the relatively thin skin in these regions. Furthermore, lewisite can flow along the body surfaces and irritate very sensitive areas such as the armpit, elbow and knee joints, and around the buttocks and crotch.

Once lewisite and/or CVAA penetrates the outer layer of skin, they not only invade the surrounding cells but also rapidly enter the bloodstream, where more hydrolysis may occur. Lewisite, or the products of its hydrolysis, are then absorbed by various body organs, especially the lungs, liver, gall bladder, and kidneys. Not only does lewisite kill cells by interfering with their ability to produce energy, but it also appears to increase the permeability of the blood vessels within organs. When this happens, acellular fluid (plasma) escapes from the blood vessels and enters these organs, reducing the volume of blood in the vessels and, accordingly, blood pressure—a phenomenon known as "lewisite shock." Thus, the victim, in cases of intense lewisite intoxication, dies from a loss of blood pressure. Such a death is similar to that which occurs in a severely burned victim.

The lungs appear to be more sensitive to lewisite exposure than any other body organ. When lewisite is inhaled, fluid rapidly escapes from the lung's blood vessels. The fluid occupies the intercellular spaces where air normally resides. The victim has great difficulty breathing and, depending on the amount of lewisite absorbed, may suffocate to death—essentially, drowning in this fluid. Inhalation of large volumes of lewisite vapor may cause death in this manner in as short a period as ten minutes. With lesser volumes, someone who inhales lewisite will initially experience hoarseness and a cough. The cough may become productive, with a "sweet" sputum, and the hoarseness may progress to an inability to speak. These symptoms result from necrosis (death) of the mucosal cells lining the respiratory tract, and pneumonia may complicate inhalation injuries. At high concentrations, inhalation may also result in lewisite shock. As described in chapter 4, animals exposed to lewisite vapor at the AUES suffered severely and died rapidly. Their lungs swelled as fluid flowed into the air spaces from the capillaries, producing a dry-land drowning.

It is not known exactly how lewisite increases the permeability of capillaries in general, or why lung capillaries are more susceptible to lewisite toxicity than the capillaries in other organs. But we do know that these effects, like those on the skin, are not solely due to arsenic. A British study in 1927 found that lewisite was ten times more toxic than arsenic trioxide. Similarly, a 1988 study by three British scientists compared the toxicity of lewisite and a common inorganic arsenic compound (sodium arsenite) by injecting the compounds into rabbits. They found that lewisite was 6.5 times more toxic than the inorganic compound. The authors attributed this increased killing power partly to lewisite's lipid solubility, but also suggested that lewisite possesses some other toxic property not currently understood.

Can a soldier wearing a gas mask still suffer from lewisite inhalation poisoning? Many of the post–World War I articles about lewisite made extraordinary claims about lewisite's ability to penetrate gas masks, and such claims were still present in reputable books as recently as 1940. I have found no CWS data from either war in which lewisite's ability to penetrate the rubber and plastic components of masks was tested, although such tests were likely conducted. However, Büscher, in *Green and Yellow Cross*, presents results of a detailed investigation of lewisite's ability to penetrate cloth, rubber, and leather.

In one study, Büscher placed a drop of lewisite on the nonaffixed side of various materials attached to a subject's leg or forearm and examined the skin ten to thirty minutes later. In the thirty-minute test, Büscher found that lewisite was unable to cause blisters through thick cowhide leather or rubber, whereas it could readily penetrate cloth. However, thinner leather showed less of an ability to block the effects of lewisite than did the thick leather, and Büscher believed that ordinary shoes would provide protection for only about twenty minutes. These findings suggested that a soldier with a mask would have sufficient time to escape from a lewisite-saturated area.

Lewisite can also enter the body through the eyes. In animals, lewisite penetrates each ocular layer by causing the more superficial cell layers to slough off. Permanent blindness can quickly result from relatively small doses. Ocular infiltration is accompanied by severe pain, headache, and eyelids that swell shut.

It is hard to estimate the military value of lewisite's effects on eyes. Eyes would detect lewisite-induced pain before the olfactory system could detect the geranium odor associated with the compound. However, masks would protect against eye damage, and quickly leaving the area would also protect against serious eye damage. Nevertheless, in the absence of masks it would seem that a massive retreat of enemy soldiers suffering excruciating eye pain would be useful in most combat situations!

Soviet sources reported that in addition to the symptoms described above, lewisite causes edema and hemorrhage in the brain, bradycardia (slow heart rate), and dilation of the heart's right side. They also reported that in severe cases, lewisite causes hemorrhage of the blood vessels in the heart. Finally, a Chinese analysis classified lewisite as a vomiting agent. The military value of vomiting is that it forces soldiers to remove protective masks.

How much lewisite would be required to kill a person? The answer to this question varies depending on which sources are consulted. And the answers have generally been based on extrapolations from World War I animal experiments, which are not very meaningful because susceptibility to lewisite varies among species. Further, toxicity is dependent on the purity of the lewisite and how it enters the body. Initially very small doses, such as 1.4 milliliters (about 0.3 teaspoon) were considered fatal; such a small dose was still listed as fatal in a 1957 pharmacology textbook. Even a 2000 report by four British toxicologists stated that 7 grams (1.5 teaspoons) would be lethal in 50 percent of humans, and that as little as 0.000002 teaspoon would cause a blister. In 1937, Prentiss stated that 2.6 grams (0.5 teaspoon) of lewisite would kill an average 150-pound man, whereas a recent military publication claimed that 30 mg/kg (0.4 teaspoon) is fatal in 50 percent of exposed persons. Yet another source—a document provided by the Utah Department of Environmental Quality—claimed that 2.8 grams (0.6 teaspoon) would be fatal. However, Büscher reported that 0.3 teaspoon can be applied repeatedly to a 150-pound man without any symptoms of arsenical poisoning, and a United States government report described an accident in which a worker at a lewisite plant suffered lewisite burns over 20 percent of his body and yet did not die from arsenical poisoning.

If employed under ideal conditions lewisite's military value could be significant, with pain, blisters, and death being inflicted on enemy soldiers in a very short period of time. Whether ideal conditions could ever have been achieved remains questionable. Still, one Chemical Corps officer I recently interviewed about lewisite immediately responded with "That's very nasty stuff."

Could anything prevent the consequences of being exposed to such "nasty stuff"? Fortunately, the answer is yes.

British Anti-Lewisite (BAL)

When World War II began, there was every expectation that the Dew of Death would live up to its namesake. Civilians, especially the British, envisioned enemy airplanes spraying lewisite on their cities, and when Germany invaded Poland in 1939, finding antidotes to lewisite and mustard became imperative for both the United States and British chemical warfare agencies. No antidote to mustard was developed, but for lewisite a remarkable antidote, BAL, was synthesized.

At this time Professor Rudolph Peters was chairman of the Department of Biochemistry at Oxford University. During the First World War he had initially served as an infantryman in France, but he was later recalled to Britain's chemical warfare unit at Porton Down to study phosgene and mustard. In 1939 Peters and his Oxford colleagues, Professors Sinclair, Thompson, Ogston, Holliday, Philpot, and Stocken, in cooperation with the Ministry of Supply, initiated research to find antidotes to chemical warfare agents. Peters, Thompson, and Stocken conducted most of the work on lewisite. Their approach was to determine the cellular enzymes that were most sensitive to arsenic (it was assumed that lewisite's arsenic content was responsible for its toxicity) and develop a compound to reverse arsenic's effects. Previous research had suggested that arsenic primarily inhibited the activity of an enzyme called pyruvate dehyrdogenase, and Peters and his group believed a class of compounds called thiols (compounds containing a sulfhydryl [SH] group) could function as an antidote. However, they became quite frustrated because, despite their belief that they understood the mechanism of arsenic toxicity, the tested thiol compounds failed to block the effects of arsenic on cellular metabolism.

Accordingly, Peters informed the Ministry of Supply that the initial hypothesis to explain arsenic's toxicity might be in error. Nevertheless, Stocken and Thompson decided to pursue the hypothesis further by evaluating a related group of compounds called dithiols (compounds containing two sulfhydryl groups). Due to war-related shortages in chemicals, Stocken and Thompson had to synthesize a dithiol supply by purifying one of the proteins in human hair. These renowned scientists found themselves traversing Oxford from barbershop to barbershop collecting the floor sweepings of hair that the barbers saved for them. But their labors bore fruit; they were able to demonstrate that dithiols had a greater chemical affinity for arsenic than cellular enzymes, offering the potential for an antidote. Next they had to find a dithiol that could be tolerated well by human skin. They synthesized and tested more than forty dithiol compounds, and on July 21, 1940, they were successful, synthesizing a compound that human skin could tolerate relatively well. They had created a compound with the chemical name 2,3-dimercaptopropanol, which was first called simply OX217 (Oxford, 21 July) or DTH (for "dithiol"), but later became known as BAL. Thompson tested the safety of BAL on his own skin, and further tests on volunteers (medical students) in the department demonstrated BAL's effectiveness in counteracting the irritating effects lewisite has on human skin.

I obtained a personal description of the development of BAL from ninety-one-year-old Lloyd Stocken when I interviewed him on July 9, 2003. On that day Dr. Stocken rode his bicycle to his office, as he has done for more than sixty years. He is a gentleman with an athletic build who now spends much of his time tending his garden, but who still comes to his office at Oxford University one day a week. I was surprised to learn from him that in 1941 there was no atmosphere of crisis surrounding the

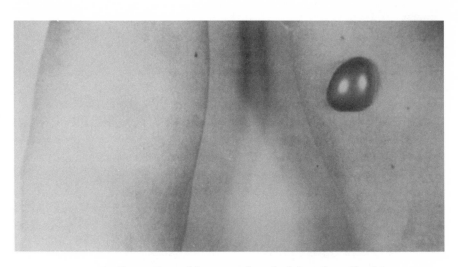

**18. Comparison of forearms after administration of lewisite,
followed by BAL on one side.
Courtesy Lloyd Stocken.**

search for an antidote to lewisite. The scientists worked their normal hours, arriving at 9:00 A.M., taking lunch at about noon and tea at 4:00 P.M., and leaving for home at 7:00 in the evening. However, they were not permitted to discuss the nature of their work with anyone, including their spouses, although everyone knew it was war related. Thus, the local barbers did not question Stocken's request for the daily hair sweepings from their floors. Dr. Stocken also related how some of the work being done used pigeon brain tissue for testing. Once the brains were removed, the scientists happily took the carcasses home for supper!

Following its initial testing at Oxford, BAL was immediately subjected to a series of military tests in both Britain (at Porton Down) and the United States, where various United States government agencies cooperated in studying BAL's preparation, manufacture, biochemistry, toxicology, pharmacology, and clinical applications. When an American CWS Colonel first tested it on himself, he commented that the stinging action of BAL was worse than that of lewisite! However, American research led to improvements in BAL's synthesis and to the development of more tolerable forms of both BAL ointment and an injectable liquid, which could reverse the systemic effects of lewisite.

The British and American testing of BAL revealed how effective it was:

19. Ninety-one-year-old Professor Lloyd Stocken
with original apparatus used to synthesize BAL
and original vials of BAL.
Courtesy Margery Ord.

if treatment was initiated within five minutes of lewisite instillation into the eye of a rabbit, recovery was almost complete. Similar results were obtained on rabbit skin and on the skin of human volunteers. Analysis of the urine of animals revealed that BAL deactivated arsenic by chemically bonding with it, after which the combined BAL-arsenic compound was excreted by the body. Beyond this, the scientists used a novel, visually compelling test to prove that BAL restored the ability of cells to produce energy. They added arsenic to a petri dish containing living, swimming human sperm. Immediately, the sperm stopped swimming. When they then added BAL to the dish, the sperm began swimming again. BAL was also shown in the United States to be effective for reversing the effects of mustard gas on the eyes, and plans were developed by the DuPont Company to manufacture two hundred thousand pounds of it per year.

The Allies considered BAL a secret "weapon." They reasoned they could effectively use lewisite against the Axis powers, but, because of BAL, the use of it by the Axis against them would be of very limited effectiveness (although the British later assumed that German chemists had also synthesized BAL). Accordingly, no public announcement of BAL's development was made until November 1945, approximately three months after World War II ended. At that time, articles describing the compound appeared virtually simultaneously in *Science* and *Nature,* the two most prestigious scientific journals in the United States and Britain, respectively. During the period of secrecy from 1941 to 1945, clinicians with security clearances who were involved in studying BAL's effectiveness against lewisite wondered if it would be equally effective against other forms of arsenic poisoning. Therefore in England it was tested on factory workers who were accidentally exposed to arsenic, and again the compound was found to be remarkably effective.

During much of the early and middle parts of the twentieth century, arsenic compounds were used to treat syphilis. But this "cure" was sometimes worse than the disease, because the patients began suffering the effects of arsenical poisoning. Once BAL was developed and described, physicians began using BAL injections successfully to counteract these effects. In 1946 BAL was also found to be an effective antidote for overdoses of mercury. A study done at Johns Hopkins University in that year found that before BAL, approximately one-third of patients who attempted suicide by swallowing mercury bichloride died. After such patients were injected with BAL, twenty-two out of twenty-three of them survived (presumably to their disappointment). Thus, BAL, developed purely as an antidote for a potentially deadly chemical warfare agent, began saving lives threatened by non–war-related poisoning.

Unfortunately, BAL use was not without side effects. BAL ointment itself was a minor skin irritant. More significant side effects were associated with BAL injections. Patients experienced increased blood pressure, nausea, vomiting, burning sensations in the throat, eye tearing and inflammation, salivation, and a runny nose. But these symptoms were temporary and far less serious than the original conditions.

BAL also came to play a major role in the career of a renowned British neurologist, Derek Denny-Brown. In 1939 Harvard University hired the thirty-eight-year-old Denny-Brown to direct its neurological unit at Boston City Hospital. Unfortunately, Denny-Brown could not assume the position immediately because he was an officer in the Royal Medical Corps and was needed in the war effort. However, in 1941, after a personal appeal to Winston Churchill by the same James Conant who helped develop lewisite, now president of Harvard and in London on behalf of the United States government (see chapter 8), Denny-Brown was released from military service and allowed to assume the position at Harvard.

Once settled in Boston, Denny-Brown initiated a very active research program and in the early 1950s began treating patients with an obscure and relatively rare neurological disease, Wilson's disease. These patients exhibit a variety of strange and uncontrollable movements, including a bizarre flapping of the arms called "wing beating." Although the cause of this condition was unknown, there was mounting evidence that patients with Wilson's disease had abnormally high amounts of copper in their bodies. Could this excess copper be causing the strange movements? Denny-Brown and his colleague, Huntington Porter, reasoned that if BAL could remove other metals from the human body (a process called chelating) it might also remove copper. Would such removal result in an amelioration of symptoms? It was worth investigating, since the prognosis for Wilson's disease patients was premature death.

Denny-Brown and Porter conducted a long-term study of the effects of BAL in five patients severely incapacitated with Wilson's disease. The effects were definitive and dramatic; the patients greatly improved, and the improvement was accompanied by the excretion of copper in their urine. Denny-Brown showed films of these patients at the 1951 meeting of the American Neurological Association. The audience was stunned by the success. One of the neurologists present said Denny-Brown's BAL therapy represented a milestone in neurological treatment—for the first time, an adult movement disorders disease had been "cured," not just palliated. The accomplishment was announced in the popular press. BAL was a hero. Denny-Brown's discovery also had a more general but profoundly great influence on the further development of the discipline of neurology: now cures for other adult conditions were considered possible.

Although BAL was effective in treating Wilson's disease, it was not a perfect cure. The injections had to be given often and were painful. And,

The New England
Journal of Medicine

Copyright, 1951, by the Massachusetts Medical Society

Volume 245   DECEMBER 13, 1951   Number 24

THE EFFECT OF BAL (2,3-DIMERCAPTOPROPANOL) ON HEPATOLENTICULAR DEGENERATION (WILSON'S DISEASE)*

D. Denny-Brown, M.D.,[†] and Huntington Porter, M.D.[‡]

BOSTON

HEPATOLENTICULAR degeneration is an uncommon but not rare disease that is generally regarded as incurable. In our experience one or two cases may be found in the outpatient department of any large general hospital, often mistakenly labeled as multiple sclerosis or Parkinsonism. The more chronic type of the disease, earlier known as "pseudosclerosis" because of the prominence of an intention tremor as a symptom, is grouped with the "progressive lenticular degeneration" of Wilson, under the general heading of "hepatolenticular degeneration."[1,2] This disease is of considerable interest, for it is one of the few chronic degenerative diseases of the nervous system in which an asso-

and nervous system. Studies of the metallic content of those tissues were at first inconclusive. Vogt[11] and others strongly advocated the theory of silver intoxication, but it now appears likely that abnormal findings in relation to this metal were due to the prevalent use of silver salvarsan in treatment of nervous diseases in that period.[12] Gerlach and Rohrschneider[13] in 1923 failed to find silver in the eye by spectroscopic tests but found traces of copper in the cornea. A marked increase in copper content of both brain and liver was shown by Haurowitz[14] and by Glazebrook.[15] Cumings,[16] in the first controlled study, has com-

20. First page of article by Derek Denny-Brown and Huntington Porter about the use of BAL to treat Wilson's disease, and portrait of Denny-Brown.

Courtesy Sid Gilman.

with time, the beneficial effects became less evident. In 1956 a better chelating agent for copper, penicillamine, was developed, and even better agents have been discovered since.

BAL was the premier chelating agent for poisoning from many types of metal, including arsenic, gold, mercury, and lead, during the middle to late parts of the twentieth century. It was deemed one of the five leading medical discoveries of World War II. Amazingly, BAL is still manufactured in both the United States and Britain. It is a recommended treatment for high levels of blood lead in children, and it would also be available should lewisite be used in warfare or by terrorists. A trip to the pharmacy of my local hospital found a supply of injectable BAL, albeit an outdated one! Akorn Incorporation, which manufactures BAL in the United States, sold over four thousand three-milliliter ampoules in 2003.

Strangely, a recent report by the army indicated that exposure to lewisite should be treated with 10 percent sodium carbonate and then flushed with soap and water before transferring the patient to a medical facility. The army has either forgotten about BAL or considered the sodium carbonate therapy to be more effective, which is highly unlikely.

Despite BAL's success at reversing the toxic effects of lewisite, the original hypothesis explaining its efficacy may not have been completely correct. Stocken and his colleagues had hypothesized that BAL acted by restoring activity of the cellular enzyme pyruvate dehydrogenase. Recently a German report suggested that lewisite acts on additional enzymes besides pyruvate dehydrogenase, reinforcing the concept discussed earlier in the chapter that the precise cause of lewisite's toxicity is still a mystery. Also interesting is that the article described the authors as being able to obtain lewisite from the German Ministry of Defense. Presumably, the ministry produces small quantities of lewisite for experimental and training purposes.

Lewisite and BAL were both stockpiled during the Second World War. Fortunately and surprisingly, neither proved to be necessary.

8 World War II: The Gas War That Never Happened

During the World War II years the War Department was charged with the role of producing lewisite; but a civilian agency, the National Defense Research Committee (NDRC), was formed in June 1940 to develop and improve military weapons, including poison gases. This agency was responsible for the great improvements in radar made by American engineers during the war and for the development of the atomic bomb. The NDRC's Division B (Bombs, Fuels, Gases, and Chemical Problems) investigated issues pertaining to chemical weapons, and one of its major emphases (CWS project 3) was to improve ways of synthesizing organic arsenic compounds. Who was initially in charge of Division B? None other than James B. Conant, who had directed Willoughby's lewisite factory during the First World War. Further, in 1942, the NDRC was reorganized into twenty-three divisions, with Conant appointed overall chairman.

After his demobilization following World War I, Conant had returned to Harvard, where he became an assistant professor of chemistry on September 1, 1919. Conant's chemical brilliance flourished there; he rapidly achieved an international reputation in organic chemistry and won every major chemistry award short of the Nobel Prize. By 1927 he had completed his academic progression from assistant professor to associate professor to professor. During this ascent to chemical fame, Conant visited the chemistry departments of the major European universities. In 1925 his travels led to the Kaiser-Wilhelm Institut für Physikalische Chemie in Dahlem, a Berlin suburb, at which he paid his respects to Fritz Haber, who had fathered chemical warfare during the First World War. A very cordial meeting thus occurred between two individuals who had each sought, just eight years earlier, more effective chemical ways to enable his country to massacre the other's young men by the millions. Did lewisite arise in their conversation? Haber's scientific group had investigated lewisite for potential use in World War I but had concluded that its toxic effects were less than those of mustard. Maybe Haber shared this information with Conant, although it is more likely that neither felt at liberty to discuss their efforts during the war.

Conant continued his academic progression, becoming chairman of Harvard's Department of Chemistry in 1930. In 1933, six months after Franklin D. Roosevelt was elected President of the United States, a search committee at Harvard recommended to the Board of Overseers that Conant be approved as the twenty-third president of the university. Conant worked diligently as Harvard's president, but as the situation in Europe deteriorated, his attention became more focused on the role that science would inevitably play in the war he knew was coming. His name reached the White House as one who would not hesitate to speak out against isolationism. Thus was Conant recruited to join the newly formed NDRC.

As chairman of the NDRC Conant led a scientific mission to England, traveling through U-boat infested waters to London, which was under daily aerial bombardment. Among his many meetings in London, two are particularly relevant to the story of lewisite. In one meeting he met with British chemists working on lewisite, presumably at the British chemical warfare establishment at Porton Down, and learned of a new manufacturing technique using mercury chloride as a catalyst, instead of aluminum chloride. It was at the other, with Winston Churchill, that he made his unusual, somewhat selfish request that benefited Harvard, the institution to which he was still loyal; he asked Churchill to release Denny-Brown from his military obligation. His request was honored and helped propel Denny-Brown into international prominence, based partly on his use of British Anti-Lewisite (BAL) to treat patients with Wilson's disease.

Upon returning from England, Conant's role as NDRC chairman required that he begin investigating nuclear research because of the belief among military and civilian scientists that this line of inquiry, which became known as the Manhattan Project, could produce a massively powerful bomb. The urgency of the Manhattan Project was heightened when it was learned that Germany, too, was working on such a weapon. Accordingly, this project consumed Conant's attention for the rest of the war. He made frequent trips to laboratories and universities in the United States to recruit nuclear scientists, and he set policy as to which scientific paths to the bomb's development would be followed. In essence, he had to determine which nuclear "horse" to "bet" the government's research money on. J. Robert Oppenheimer, the scientific head of the project, was pleased to find in Conant a government bureaucrat who understood the science involved in developing this weapon.

How much of Conant's skillful management of the Manhattan Project, which required him to control the complex and sometimes strident relationships between the military overseers and the civilian scientists, can be directly traced to his World War I experience? He never spoke or wrote about this publicly. But the situations are analogous, and it seems safe to speculate that his intimate knowledge of the unique psychology of both groups contributed to the success of the later project. Furthermore, it is a remarkable coincidence that the same individual chemist supervised the two most secret American military projects of both major twentieth-century wars.

Once the atomic bombs "Fat Man" and "Little Boy" were built and ready to be used against Japan, Conant had to decide whether to endorse their use. Seeing no credible alternative, he supported their use; he only regretted that the bombs had not been finished sooner. This was consistent with Conant's worldview; he saw the world as imperfect, which required making unpleasant compromises to achieve results. This attitude had its germination in his World War I efforts with chemical weapons, during which he concluded that because all war was immoral, no one weapon could be more immoral than another.

Conant, however, opposed the use of poison gas during the Second World War; he did not, by this time, consider it an effective battlefield agent. (It is not clear when he changed his mind, or if he also quietly held this opinion during the First World War.) The public distaste for poison gas contributed to Conant's negative feelings about its use, and he confessed to a friend his great relief that lewisite had not been named conantite, or something similar, although he probably had more to do with actually raising lewisite to the status of a war gas than did Lewis.

After World War II ended, Conant continued serving as Harvard's president until 1953, when he was appointed ambassador to Germany. He resigned his diplomatic post in 1957 and then began a well-publicized study evaluating American high school, and later teacher, education. Conant suffered a series of debilitating strokes in 1977 and died in Hanover, Massachusetts, on February 11, 1978, at the age of eighty-five. His autobiography was aptly titled *My Several Lives*.

As described in chapter 6, the CWS barely survived the inter-war years, receiving minimal funding during this period. Some chemical warfare research was nevertheless conducted in preparation for the future war or wars many suspected were coming. Accordingly, in 1925, the CWS constructed a small plant at Edgewood Arsenal to manufacture lewisite. The decision to construct a small plant rather than a large one was apparently based on a report that there were difficulties associated with the large-scale production of lewisite that had yet to be overcome (pertaining to the Willoughby plant, this concern is ambiguous—does it mean that the Willoughby plant was not really successful, or does it mean that ten tons per day of lewisite was not considered "large-scale?"). The report also included specific recommendations for methods of lewisite production, including the most effective temperatures and pressures.

A 1926 document summarizing the operation of the EA plant stated that 1,805 pounds of lewisite with an average purity of 92 to 93 percent had been made. It was estimated that the cost of lewisite produced at this plant was $0.60 per pound, and the document expressed doubt that a larger plant could produce the substance substantially cheaper. Interestingly, a different CWS document (from 1925) reported that an investigation into the hydrolysis of lewisite had been suspended because of a lack of personnel (presumably reflecting a lack of funding). However, a 1923 CWS report on lewisite described the difficulty of developing vapor concentrations that would be sufficiently toxic for battlefield use, a concern that was prescient in light of a mid–World War II evaluation of lewisite that is discussed later.

Similarly, a classified publication of the CWS, *A Handbook of Chemical Warfare Agents*, that was available in 1936 (its date of publication is uncertain) stated, "This agent [lewisite] is useful in cold frozen countries and in hot very dry countries; i.e., where hydrolysis is of little importance."[1] The report also mentioned that lewisite munitions were designated by two green bands, and that lewisite could be sprayed from an airplane or used in airplane bombs and artillery shells.

Apparently, both this evaluation and the 1923 report that questioned the battlefield effectiveness of lewisite were disregarded. As World War II approached, lewisite was held in high regard by the CWS, which developed plans to manufacture it in large quantities and further test its effectiveness. Lewisite's reduced flammability compared to mustard was probably a major factor that favored its further development at this time despite the earlier negative evaluations.

By 1940, lewisite and mustard were considered the World War I gases that had the greatest potential for use in the anticipated conflict. In 1941 the budget of the CWS was bolstered by a thirty-fold increase, rising from $2 million in 1940 to more than $60 million in 1941. This money was used for offensive and defensive research and production.

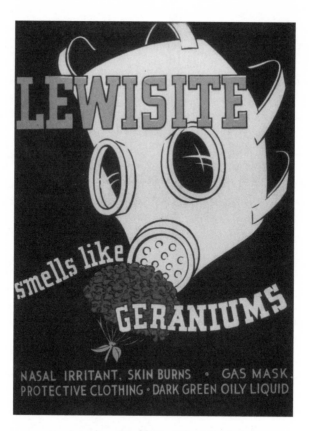

21. American World War II lewisite poster.
Courtesy National Museum of Health and Medicine,
Washington, D.C.

The promise of lewisite propelled the CWS to include it as one of five chemical warfare agents packaged in a civil defense preparatory kit (the other four were mustard, phosgene, chloropicrin, and tear gas). The "Sniff Kit" was to be used to acquaint civil defense authorities with the characteristics of each gas; each one was made of wood and contained small labeled bottles of each sample agent. The kit was approved for sale for $5 and was manufactured and sold by the Northam Warren Corporation of Stamford, Connecticut.

To the surprise of the belligerents, the initial battles of World War II ensued without the use of poison gas. On October 28, 1939, Lewis wrote a long essay for the *Riverside (California) Press* addressing the "delay" in the

22. "Sniff Kit" containing sample chemical agents, including lewisite, that was used by Civil Defense workers during World War II. Courtesy Florida State Archives, Tallahassee.

use of gas in the current conflict in Europe. He suggested that gas had not yet been used for three reasons: (1) the opprobrium associated with gas warfare; (2) the lack of chemical industrialization in some of the countries involved; and, (3) the poor fit of gas weapons with the then current military campaign. He fully expected, however, that gas would eventually be used in the conflict. In this essay Lewis made the perceptive point that as a weapon in the present conflict (as opposed to World War I) gas had lost two of its most effective attributes: surprise, and use against defenseless troops.

Lewis's speculation proved untrue. Poison gas was never used by the major powers against each other during World War II. Why? There has been much conjecture about this question, with hypotheses ranging from Hitler's disagreeable experience being gassed with mustard during World War I, to the fear of each belligerent that the other had better agents, to an unwillingness to be the first to use gas, to a belief by the belligerents that gas had not proved decisive in the First World War. A recent analysis found that Germany's dependence on tanks and speed, plus its lack of preparedness for defense against a chemical attack, explain why German chemical attacks were not used when such attacks could have been devastatingly effective (e.g., battle of Dunkirk, D-Day).

Although poison gas was not used by the major powers against each other, each expected it to be. Lewisite's prospective role received a boost in the United States when Conant brought home from England the new manufacturing process that used mercury chloride. The use of this compound both simplified lewisite's manufacture and alleviated the need for aluminum (for the aluminum chloride catalyst), which was required for the manufacture of other war-related equipment. The mercury chloride process also produced a greater percentage of L_1 than the aluminum chloride process. The CWS built a pilot lewisite plant based on the new mercury process at EA in 1941. Once completed, the plant produced a small quantity of lewisite at an enormous cost in energy. One engineer recalled that the power consumption could have made a substantial contribution to reversing the flow of water at Niagara Falls!

In 1942, larger and presumably more efficient lewisite plants were constructed at the Pine Bluff Arsenal and Huntsville Arsenal (HA, now called Redstone Arsenal), and a still larger plant was finished in 1943 at the Rocky Mountain Arsenal (RMA) outside Denver. In total, these plants produced about twenty thousand tons of lewisite, some of which was loaded into munitions that were stored as far away as Australia. Producing this much lewisite between the time the first plant went on line in 1941 and the time all were closed in 1943 was a notable achievement considering that the use of mercury chloride for a catalyst had not been tried in the United States prior to 1941. In fact, an engineer in 1959 described the new process as one of the easiest and most economical in the metal-organic field, regretting that no other use had ever been found for the compound. The engineer also stated that the Chemical Corps (as CWS was renamed in 1946) still had stocks of lewisite available, which it would sell to any interested purchaser. Apparently there were no al-Qaeda terrorist groups interested in chemical weapons in 1959!

Although the engineer praised the mercury chloride process, an RMA report from 1945 described many problems associated with the production of lewisite at this site. This plant operated from April through November 1943, and produced 4,553.5 tons, which means it never reached its production capacity of 50 tons per day, or 1,500 tons per month. The report detailed continuous problems with corrosion and with pipes plugging and breaking, which resulted in the release of lewisite vapors. Inadvertent production of sludge, which had to be removed from the reactors, was also a continuous source of difficulty, and much higher quantities of mercury chloride were needed than had been predicted. The report stated that in the Control Laboratory, "fumes were so heavy . . . that it was difficult for chemists to work except when wearing a gas mask."[2] On one occasion approximately 3,500 gallons of crude lewisite spilled on the floor, which presented a difficult and dangerous cleanup task. The room in which the finished lewisite was stored had no flooring; the earth absorbed spills and leaks, which became a continuous source of lewisite fumes.

There was so much lewisite in the plant's air that some of the personnel apparently developed a tolerance to it. New personnel would frequently find themselves forced to leave the building or don gas masks, whereas personnel who had worked at the plant for a longer period could function without any apparent discomfort, although many of the workers did suffer from conjunctivitis (pinkeye).

The RMA report also described one accident in which a plant mechanic who was working without any special precautions inadvertently loosened a pipe fitting and released crude lewisite onto his face. In addition to serious burns, he lost the use of one eye. Overall the manufacture of mustard and lewisite produced hundreds and "probably thousands" of unintentional injuries during World War II. Fortunately, the availability of BAL reduced the severity of some of these injuries. "The introduction of BAL compound saved numerous skin burns from liquid L [lewisite]. This compound, when applied within two minutes after spilling liquid on the skin, prevented the development of vesicant action."[3]

In contrast to the RMA, a shift foreman I interviewed paints an entirely different picture at the HA. Ellis T. Baggs was an eighty-one-year-old retired electrical engineer in 2004; as a nineteen-year-old in 1942 he was employed at the HA lewisite plant. Prior to beginning his employment he had to enroll in a six-week chemistry course at the University of Alabama. He began at the arsenal's mustard plant but was then transferred to the lewisite plant. Baggs stated that virtually everyone working at the plant was an "amateur," and that they all learned how to operate the plant from a book. Baggs surprisingly said that he did not perceive his work as especially dangerous; he recalled very few accidents or spills, all of which were minor. Two to three dozen workers, many of whom were women, operated the plant during each of the three daily shifts, according to Baggs. He reflected that he found the work to be fun, and that he "could go back there right now and take over again." Finally, Baggs indicated that during his employment at HA he was not allowed to discuss his work with anyone.

23. Lewisite reactor and distillation building at Rocky Mountain Arsenal.
Photographs by Clayton B. Fraser courtesy National Parks Service.

He was never told the disposition of the final product, although he did not believe that any of it was loaded into artillery shells there.

Some of the lewisite produced at the arsenals was used for testing purposes. For example, in field tests at EA, lewisite liquid was sprayed from airplanes, after which ground concentrations were determined from measurements made on paper panels, buildings, and goats. In one experiment, an airplane sprayed 610 pounds of lewisite from an altitude of 75 feet over an area of 76,250 square yards. Subsequently, lewisite vapor on the ground was found to be significantly toxic for only ten minutes after the spraying. The rapid decline in lewisite's vapor concentration and toxicity was attributed to hydrolysis, degradation by alkaline soil, and explosive detonation. The CWS thickened and increased the droplet size of lewisite in an attempt to increase its effectiveness when sprayed from the air. However, the droplets tended to harden, rendering them less effective. A comparison of thickened and unthickened lewisite sprayed on the goats from low flying planes found that the thickened lewisite caused less severe injury than the unthickened form.

A CWS summary document discussing the overall effectiveness of lewisite bombs and shells stated that, although immediately after an explosion vaporized lewisite may reach very high concentrations, the spatial range is very small, no larger than that of an explosive shell of similar size. Similarly, the vapor sprayed from an airplane was found to be very transient, odorous, and not sufficiently concentrated on the ground to produce casualties. The results of eleven such tests at EA indicated that lewisite would be effective only as a direct liquid contaminant (i.e., not as a vapor).

Although there is no available record of the United States military conducting formal field tests of lewisite toxicity on humans (soldiers) in addition to the tests on goats, a contemporaneous report detailing a test on "observers" appeared in 1943 in the prestigious *Journal of the American Medical Association*. The test occurred in mid-January on a 25°F day during which there was considerable wind. A group of volunteers stood in an open field fifty to eighty feet downwind from a hundred-milliliter vial of 5 percent lewisite dissolved in chloroform. Of the 33 men in the group, 19 developed cutaneous lesions, 2 developed eye lesions, and 10 showed eye tearing after the lewisite was vaporized by a small explosion. The report's author, Harvard ophthalmologist David Cogan, described in detail the eye lesions, both of which resolved after treatment. Dr. Cogan further noted the differences in effects between lewisite and mustard. Most importantly, when the subjects were exposed to lewisite, their eyes reacted immediately with tearing and blinking, which lessened the severity of lewisite-induced injury. But when eyes were exposed to mustard, there was no such protective response; symptoms developed only after several hours, and were more severe than after lewisite exposure. Publication of this study was approved by the Committee on the Treatment of Gas Casualties, which presumably was affiliated to the United States government (War Department) in some manner.

Another open-air lewisite test involving humans occurred on December 18, 1940. Thirty-five intelligence officers were exposed to it so that they could recognize lewisite in a combat situation. In this test, the officers stood twenty paces away from a small pit, with their backs turned towards it. Following a small explosion in the pit, the men were instructed to turn around and face it. Initially they sensed nothing unusual, but soon they experienced a burning sensation and smelled the odor of geraniums, which permeated their clothing.

In total, the field tests on lewisite concentrations and toxicities conducted by the War Department indicated that lewisite was a less effective war gas than mustard. The experiments suggested that unless a soldier was defenseless or unconscious, the immediate pain, eye irritation, and geranium odor allowed ample opportunity for evacuation before significant injury occurred. The tests similarly suggested that the hydrolysis of lewisite quickly degraded the potency of its vapor, rendering it ineffective.

In contrast to the field tests, the CWS conducted formal laboratory tests of lewisite toxicity on humans, as well as human laboratory and field tests of mustard toxicity. The laboratory tests were of two types: tests similar to those conducted at the American University Experimental Station in 1918, in which drops of liquid agents were applied to the skin of volunteers to determine the toxicity of the agents and to develop treatments; and tests in chambers in which the subjects wore varying types of protective clothing to assess the effectiveness of the clothing for retarding the penetration of the vapor. These tests, which involved at least four thousand soldiers, were conducted at EA, Maryland; the Naval Training Center, Maryland; Camp Sibert, Alabama; the Naval Research Laboratory, Virginia; the Great Lakes Naval Training Center, Illinois; Camp Lejeune, North Carolina; and San Jose Island, Canal Zone. Most of the lewisite tests involved application of the vesicant to two to three forearm sites, one of which had protective ointment (BAL) applied before or after application. The amount of lewisite applied ranged from 1.4 to 7 milligrams (0.0003 to 0.0015 teaspoon).

Why did the CWS, in essence, repeat the skin drop tests of lewisite done during World War I? In considering a similar situation at England's Porton Down facility, at which the lewisite tests of World War I were repeated during World War II, Rob Evans in his book *Gassed,* both asks and answers this question. During the Second World War dosages could be much more accurately determined than during the earlier war. Furthermore, the World War I experiments were done in an atmosphere of urgency, and there were suspicions that record keeping was not very accurate.

For the chamber tests, revealingly called "man-break" tests, the men would enter the chamber and remain there for periods ranging from one to four hours. The chambers were often hot (90°F) and humid (65 percent relative humidity) because the investigators were particularly interested in how well protective clothing performed under hot and humid conditions such as might occur using the gas against Japanese troops on tropical Pacific islands. Following chamber exposure, the men remained in their suits for four to twenty-four hours and were then examined for skin burns, the presence of which would indicate that the vapor had penetrated the protective clothing. The men were required to repeat the activity either every day or every other day until blisters developed. The anatomical location of the blisters were noted; some individuals showed very severe burns of their scrotal and buttock areas.

The results of the lewisite laboratory tests on humans were consistent with the field tests leading the CWS to conclude that lewisite would not be effective under battlefield conditions. Accordingly, on November 8, 1943, an order was issued to suspend lewisite production. The order stated that production of lewisite and procurement of raw materials should be halted on or about November 15, 1943, and that current stocks of lewisite would be maintained as a supplement to mustard to "confuse and harass the enemy."[4] In a January 17, 1944, letter to Colonel W. A. Copthorne, General Alden H. Waitt, Assistant Chief of the CWS at the time, commented on the new view of lewisite, "I fully realize this information conflicts seriously with our previous thoughts on L." This admission by Waitt reveals how completely the CWS had changed its opinion on the effectiveness of lewisite during the course of World War II.

I submitted a request under the Freedom of Information Act in April 2002 to the United States Army Soldier Biological and Chemical Command for information on lewisite. Because this request involved a weapon of mass destruction, it was forwarded to the Deputy Chiefs of Staff Office in the Pentagon. The request was finally filled in June 2003 with partial documents, most of which were heavily "redacted" (parts blackened). Among the material the army sent me were the first three pages of chapter 7 ("Arsenicals") of an eighteen-chapter, four-hundred-page 1946 document by the NDRC summarizing its work during the war. The accompanying letter explained that I did not receive the entire chapter because it "contains a technical discussion of a variety of means to increase the yield of different lewisite catalysts and of the ultimate product, lewisite."[5] However, later in 2002 I discovered a more complete reference to this summary document and simply requested a copy of chapter 7 from Indiana University's Ruth Lilly Medical Library. The librarian there had no trouble filling the request via interlibrary services. The library of the National Research Council of Canada had a copy of the "declassified" document and sent the chapter for ten dollars! So much for the American government's attempt to contain sixty-year-old information.

The conclusions of the summary document were:

> The use of liquid L for gross contamination of personnel seems feasible only when the agent is dispersed as low altitude airplane spray, and the effects produced on contaminated personnel are so inferior to those produced by mustard as to create strong prejudice against the use of L.
>
> Since the powerful antiarsenical agent, BAL, available to Britain and the United States in World War II, will be available to all in the future, there seems to be little likelihood that there will ever be any incentive for the use of L as a chemical warfare agent.[6]

Most of America's allies also pursued lewisite production during World War II. Britain's association with lewisite began during World War I when it initiated plans to build a lewisite plant at a naval station near London. After that war ended, the British Chemical Warfare Experimental Station at Porton Down conducted a modest amount of research and field trials with lewisite, and as described in chapter 6, two of their scientists described publicly how to manufacture it. Later, about 1938, British chemists developed the mercury chloride process, and a plant was built that was capable of manufacturing 14.9 tons per week. Subsequently the British switched to a process based on copper chloride, which was less expensive than mercury chloride but which also produced less product. By early World War II (1942), the British had produced only 156 tons of lewisite, which was mainly used for field testing at Porton Down, although some was put into munitions. The British produced only this limited amount before concluding, based on human testing and similar results to those of the CWS in the United States, that lewisite was less effective than mustard, and that BAL significantly reduced its potential as an effective agent (because they believed the Germans too had discovered BAL).

Because the British authorities were sure that gas would be used in World War II, they thoroughly prepared their civilians for gas attacks, distributing thirty-eight million gas masks by the time the war began. To enable their civil defense workers to identify which gases the enemy might be using, the British distributed a box similar to the United States "Sniff Kit" that contained vials of the agents most likely to be used, including lewisite and mustard. Today, immediately upon entering the restored underground Cabinet War Rooms in London (from which Churchill directed the war effort), one encounters a chemical warfare exhibit in the first panel on the left, in which a vial of lewisite from one of these kits is displayed. Had gas been used against London, the city's civil defense workers were to identify the agent and then paint the tops of city pillar (mail) boxes green if lewisite, and yellow if mustard.

The British military, like that of the United States, conducted experiments to evaluate the toxicity of lewisite on humans. These tests were conducted in Britain and, in conjunction with their Commonwealth allies, in Australia, India, and Canada. Three books have been published that describe the testing done in three of these countries: the previously mentioned *Gassed*, by Rob Evans (2000), described the tests done in England; *Keen as Mustard*, by Bridget Goodwin (1998), described the Australian tests (Goodwin also produced a documentary film on this topic with the same title); and *Deadly Allies*, by John Bryden (1989), described the Canadian tests (Bryden later became a member of the Canadian Parliament).

The exact number of soldiers tested by the British at their Porton Down facility is unknown, but Evans estimates it to be about thirty thousand over the past eighty years. As discussed in chapter 11, many of the volunteers in the United States now claim health problems caused by their exposure to chemical agents. The British government has typically refuted these claims.

One participant, a twenty-year-old British soldier named Sydney Pepper, did not find the tests to be at all unpleasant. Pepper volunteered in January 1940 to be tested, reasoning that it would be better to know what to expect from the enemy than not to know. In the course of two days, drops of both lewisite and mustard were applied to his forearms and the blisters were then treated with an experimental ointment (presumably

BAL). He said the blisters hurt a bit, similar to a burn. Pepper spent a week at Porton reading, playing music, and relaxing in the canteen while the doctors recorded the healing of the blisters. Pepper considered it to be a pleasant but dull break, and the blisters all healed completely.

The British conducted one highly unusual experiment: they impregnated underwear with zinc oxide to determine if it protected underlying skin from lewisite drops placed on outer garments. The impregnated undergarments did provide some degree of protection. For example, when untreated fabrics were worn, twenty minutes of exposure resulted in blister formation, but when impregnated fabric was worn, the underlying skin was protected for up to two hours. The British expanded their tests to include impregnated flannel shirts, long cotton underpants, and "cellular" drawers. This experiment resulted in a detailed report on how undergarments, whether new or "soiled," could be washed under field or base conditions in a zinc oxide solution to obtain the protective effect.

The CWS of both Britain and the United States wished to know how mustard and lewisite would perform under tropical conditions. To determine this, the British exploited the stoic Australian character and exposed their Commonwealth brothers to mustard and lewisite, in some cases, without protective clothing. Goodwin's book and documentary on the Australian poison gas experiments portray the British as unfeeling overseers who solicited volunteers by misrepresenting the tests as "experiments in the tropics." The British also asserted that the Australians had an "imperial responsibility" to volunteer. And the Australians responded with enthusiasm; in British slang they were "keen as mustard." These keen volunteers suffered terrible pain and developed huge blisters, especially in sensitive areas such as the scrotum, which are depicted in the documentary. There was even a contest to see which man sustained the worst burns. The Goodwin book does not provide much detail about the results of the lewisite tests but does state that lewisite drops, like drops of mustard, were very effective under tropical conditions, requiring only approximately 25 percent of the temperate climate dosage to produce a comparably sized lesion.

Military reports from the Queensland, Australia, testing site provide additional details about liquid lewisite's effectiveness under the tropical conditions. Amazingly, and in great contrast to the United States, the National Archives of Australia provides these reports freely over the internet. They clearly reveal the efficacy of liquid lewisite for raising blisters in the tropics, and the protective value of BAL, which was found to be far more efficacious than other ointments.

Both the United States and Britain continued to subject human volunteers to lewisite's effects even after concluding that it would not be an effective battlefield agent. For example, in April 1945 and, curiously, at the request of the American CWS representatives in India, the British tested lewisite there. The tests included both chamber and outdoor tests using exercised (sweating) and non-exercised soldiers. The study found that "lewisite vapor [as opposed to lewisite liquid] is relatively ineffective in causing casualties in a warm, humid climate"[7] and that the effects of lewisite were more severe on resting than on exercising men. It was thought that the presence of sweat might explain the latter finding.

Most of the chemical warfare tests in Canada were conducted at Suffield, a military research station near Medicine Hat, Alberta. Again "volunteer" soldiers were subjected to mustard and lewisite exposure, with some of the lewisite being delivered by spray from airplanes. At the time, the British expected a German invasion, and such tests were conducted to determine if an invasion could be repulsed by chemical agent spraying (Churchill was prepared to douse German troops with chemical weapons the moment they landed on English beaches). Accordingly, one of the final reports produced by the scientists at Suffield was "The Casualty Producing Power of Thickened Lewisite Sprayed From Aircraft on Troops, June 30, 1944." This document concluded that mustard sprayed from airplanes was more effective than lewisite. The number of goats, cattle, horses, and mice killed at Suffield in the poison gas tests was in the thousands.

The Soviet Union also manufactured and tested lewisite during World War II, reportedly producing 22,700 tons between 1939 and 1945. Lewisite was tested in its *sharashkas*, as described in chapter 6.

The final major United States ally of World War II, France, has also been reported to have produced lewisite during World War II, although I have been unable to locate any primary evidence or details.

The British development of BAL during the Second World War was specifically triggered because of Allied fears that lewisite would be used by Germany. However, there has been some doubt as to whether Germany did manufacture lewisite during World War II. One military source stated specifically that although German chemists were familiar with lewisite, they preferred to rely on other arsenicals, for which they sequestered all of the available arsenic on the world market before the war began. Accordingly, a report listing German chemical weapons stockpiles captured by the Allies at the end of war does not include lewisite. Similarly, there is a 1993 report by the German Maritime and Hydrographic Agency in Hamburg, "Chemical Munitions in the Southern and Western Baltic Seas," that does not list lewisite in a table titled "Important chemical warfare agents produced in the Third Reich between 1935 and 1945."

To the contrary, a 1998 report available from Aberdeen Proving Ground (APG; formerly EA), "Old Chemical Weapons Reference Guide," lists lewisite as a German chemical warfare agent, but it does not describe it being loaded into munitions. However, the report does list artillery shells, aerial bombs, mortars, land mines, and rockets being filled with a 50/50 mustard/lewisite mixture called "*winterlost*." This name is quite revealing because "*lost*" (also called "*summerlost*") was the German code name for mustard. Thus, *winterlost* was winter mustard gas. Lewisite lowers the freezing temperature of mustard (mustard normally freezes at 57°F whereas lewisite freezes at 0°F resulting in a mixture that freezes at 14.4°F) allowing its use in cold climates, e.g., in the Soviet Union during the winter. Furthermore, the mixture had some of the "best" attributes of both compounds, including the immediate effects and systemic toxicity of lewisite and the greater persistence of mustard. Such mustard/lewisite mixtures were also manufactured by the Allies and, as described later, by Japan for the same reasons. Thus, part of the ambiguity surrounding Germany's World War II production of lewisite is due to Germany's focus on *winterlost,* rather than on lewisite as a stand-alone battlefield agent.

In addition to the APG report, one German military book in the 1968 edition supports the view that Germany produced lewisite during World War II, although this claim is absent in the 1976 edition. Furthermore, a 1978 article in *Der Hautarzt* (*The Dermatologist*) describes one case of Bowen's disease (skin cancer) in a former German infantryman who was exposed to lewisite approximately forty years previously near the Belgian town of Bastogne. The seventy-eight-year-old patient had been inadvertently exposed to lewisite in 1940 after he opened yellow barrels stored in a train tunnel that were labeled "lewisite." The oily substance soaked his trousers and socks, and later that evening he had intense itching and burning of the affected areas. Blisters appeared the next day and cancer developed almost forty years later.

In the United States, the press speculated that Germany was producing lewisite for battlefield use. For example, a May 14, 1940, *New York Times* article claimed that a new "paralyzing" gas was used by German forces in

Belgium. The article concluded that the agent was lewisite because, among other attributes, it was poisonous and smelled like geraniums.

Why did Germany not load pure lewisite into munitions? Probably because, as described previously, German scientists had evaluated it during the First World War and concluded that it would not be an effective battlefield agent for the same reasons that persuaded the Allies, albeit some twenty-five years later. This German evaluation was in the public record and available to the Allies. Büscher mentioned it in his 1931 book on the effects of mustard and lewisite on human skin, and, as described in chapter 5, Ulrich Mueller indicated in his 1932 book, *Die Chemische Waffe* (Chemical weapons), that lewisite would have been a great disappointment had it been used by the Allies during World War I because it hydrolyzes so readily. In addition, in *Chemical Warfare,* which was published in the United States in 1941, Curt Wachtel described Germany's evaluation of lewisite. Wachtel had personally evaluated lewisite while working in Germany under Haber during World War I, concluding that it is a poor agent for battlefield use. Surprisingly, by 1941 Wachtel had emigrated to the United States and, according to the book's foreword, had written it to be "helpful to the military of his adopted country."[8] Unfortunately, I have found no indication that the CWS paid any attention to this book, apparently because German authors were not trusted. It would be interesting to know whether Wachtel tried to assist the CWS in any other way, and whether any such efforts were rebuffed (I did not find any letters from him in the CWS archives). However, Wachtel did lament in a 1941 *Newsweek* interview that scientists like himself are typically condemned for their work on poison gases: "Nobody likes us. Nobody likes gas."[9]

Although Germany did not rely heavily on lewisite as a primary battlefield agent, their scientists tested it on human guinea pigs in concentration camps. On January 12, 1948, Major D. C. Evans filed a report for the British Ministry of Supply, "German CW [chemical warfare] Experiments on Human Beings." These chemical warfare experiments were conducted by three physiologists, Drs. Picker, Wimmer, and Hirt, from Strasbourg University, working directly under Holocaust architect Heinrich Himmler on inmates at the adjacent Natzweiler concentration camp. Evans reported that he found records of human experiments with mustard and lewisite as well as other toxic agents. He also found a German document revealing that on October 13, 1939, 23 inmates at the Sachsenhausen concentration camp were "vaccinated" with lewisite and subsequently treated with an experimental ointment. Additionally, 150 inmates at the Neuengamme concentration camp were forced to drink water contaminated with lewisite and other agents (it is unclear whether the water was contaminated with a single agent or a combination of compounds). It may be that this experiment was conducted because the German military feared that the Allies would contaminate German water supplies with chemical agents. However, this was never an Allied plan and would not seem very credible considering that the lewisite would be severely degraded by hydrolysis and dilution.

During its tenure as Germany's ally during World War II, Italy produced lewisite at a rate of five tons per day. Italian forces were experienced in the use of poison gas from their conquest of Ethiopia, an operation in which, as described previously, they reportedly used mustard and lewisite.

Of the three major Axis Powers, the most extensive information on the production of lewisite for military use exists for Japan. Ōkunojima is one of a dozen small islands that divide Japan's mainland, Honshu, from the large island of Shikoku. Today visitors to the state-run summer resort on this island often comment on the many white rabbits residing there. The visitors are unaware that the rabbits are descended from an initial group released in 1962 to commemorate the victims of the poison gases produced by a secret plant on the island that operated prior to and during World War II. Lewisite was one of the products manufactured at the plant.

The leaders of the Japanese Imperial Army had carefully observed the use of gas during World War I and had become concerned that Russia might use poison gas against their troops in Siberia. Consequently, after the war Japan began an active research program in chemical weapons, with some help from a German scientist. By 1928 the Japanese chemical warfare agency had completed experiments on the production of mustard and lewisite. The agency began looking for a site to manufacture these agents, as well as others, in massive quantities. They chose the island of Ōkunojima because it was relatively isolated. To ensure the operation's secrecy, the island was subsequently deleted from civilian maps of Japan. The plant complex was dedicated on May 19, 1929. Mustard and tear gas were the first agents to be produced there, but by 1935 other gases, including lewisite, were being manufactured in quantity. In 1937 the plant was making 2 tons of lewisite per day, although by the end of the war it had produced only 1,381 tons of lewisite.

The legacy of the Ōkunojima plant is threefold: the use of the chemicals on Chinese civilians and soldiers and on prisoners of war during World

24. World War II chemical weapons plant on Ōkunojima, Japan.
Courtesy Takata Makoto, arch-Hiroshima website,
http://www.arch.hiroshima.net.

War II; the effects on the men and women who labored at the plant; and the leftover munitions that were buried in China.

In 1931 Japan invaded Manchuria and then, in 1937, invaded the remainder of China (although the Chinese government never completely surrendered). During Japan's invasion of these regions, chemical and biological weapons (including lewisite) were used secretly. Against untrained and poorly equipped Chinese troops and civilians, the weapons were very effective. In my search of CWS documents at the National Archives and Records Administration, I located a letter about the Japanese use of lewisite in China. The letter, dated July 12, 1938, referred to a report (which I could not locate) by a Dr. H. Talbot, who had been stationed in Nanchang, China. The report described the symptoms of several people who were victims of Japanese gas attacks. Dr. Talbot indicated that the symptoms were consistent with exposure to lewisite and stated that he was strongly of the opinion that "the Japanese have been conducting a fairly small field test with the crude lewisite using the Chinese for test animals."[10] Similarly, between September 7 and 11, 1940, the Japanese conducted experiments on five Chinese prisoners who, like the prisoners in the German concentration camps, were forced to drink lewisite or mustard.

In 1937 the Japanese army occupying Manchuria (the Kwantung army) created the Kwantung Army Technical Section in the small city of Qiqihar in Heilongjiang Province. A subdivision of the Technical Section became the Chemical Weapons Research Squad, or Unit 516. This unit was organized in a manner similar to the better-known biological warfare division, Unit 731. At its peak, Unit 516 was composed of three thousand soldiers; some of its buildings persist today as crumbling shells, and the local population still considers an area of the unit's former base where chemical weapons were stored to be hazardous. Unit 516's mandate was to test chemical weapons on prisoners and, when a prospective battlefield agent showed potential in these tests, to conduct field tests on Chinese communities.

The Japanese army is estimated to have conducted 889–2,900 chemical warfare attacks in China, usually as a last resort when they were experiencing heavy losses. Reports indicate that entire Chinese battalions were killed by gas. Altogether, it is estimated that Japanese chemical warfare killed 10,500 people and injured 80,000–94,000. An article in *Time* magazine dated May 25, 1942, stated that lewisite "is now a favorite of the Japs."[11] However, after the war, Japanese officers testified that lewisite was manufactured solely to serve as an additive to mustard, allowing mustard to be effective at cold temperatures. Nevertheless, Japan had artillery shells that were filled with lewisite alone, as well as ones with lewisite and mustard. The Japanese names for lewisite and mustard were *ruisaito* and *masutādo,* respectively.

The use of mustard gas and lewisite by the Japanese army against the defenders of the Chinese city of Hengyang was described to the American public in a *New York Times* article dated July 7, 1944. The article referred to a military report by Captain Ralph Thompson, a United States Army chemical warfare intelligence officer, who had investigated a specific allegation by the Chinese that the Japanese were using poison gas. Captain Thompson stated that he observed gas victims who had burns and blisters on their legs, between their ankles, and on their thighs—all places with exposed skin due to the wearing of summer uniforms. The captain hypothesized that the Japanese were firing seventy-five-millimeter shells containing a mustard/lewisite mixture. He surmised that the mustard was causing one-half-inch-high blisters filled with a yellow fluid, whereas the lewisite was causing smaller, bluish blisters.

President Roosevelt was aware of the Japanese use of poison gas in China, and in 1942 he sent a warning to the government of Japan:

> Authoritative reports are reaching this Government of the use by Japanese armed forces in various localities of China of poisonous or noxious gases. I desire to make it unmistakably clear that, if Japan persists

> in this inhuman form of warfare against China, or against any other of
> the United Nations, such actions will be regarded by this Government
> as though taken against the United States, and retaliation in kind and
> in full measure will be meted out. We shall be prepared to enforce com-
> plete retribution. Upon Japan will rest the responsibility.

Japan apparently responded with the message that if the United States uses gas, "Uncle Sam's boys will be given a smell of their own Du Pont gas which the Japanese captured at Guam."[12]

Between 1937 and 1944 the Japanese poison gas plant operated twenty-four hours per day, seven days a week, employing 5,000–6,000 people, including women and school children. This plant produced over 7.5 million weapons, with 1,200 tons of chemical agents manufactured annually during 1940–43. Women played an important role; they primarily put the finishing touches on the gas-filled artillery shells. Supposedly, these shells had been wiped clean by the male workers, but lewisite and mustard residues persisted. The women handled the shells with only cloth gloves, which were easily penetrated by the vesicants. The women then transferred the agents to their genitals after using the toilet, causing terribly painful blisters to appear in this area of their bodies. This effect was amplified because the factory was so permeated with poison gas vapors that the toilet paper was contaminated. Thus, women may have been affected more than the men at the plant; but after the war both sexes began suffering and dying from lung cancer, cancer of the larynx, stomach cancer, chronic bronchitis, and other ailments. Some of the workers referred to the plant as "the Island of Great Hardships." In 1988 a Toxic Gas Museum was established on the island.

World War II ended with sighs of relief that lewisite and other poison gases had played virtually no part in it. But now the Cold War was to begin, and lewisite is especially effective at "cold" temperatures.

9 Lewisite Production, Use, and Sea Dumping after World War II

When World War II began, both sides regarded lewisite as a powerful potential weapon. When the war ended without poison gas having played a major role, most countries regarded it as antiquated. Nevertheless, the antipathy between the East and West would not let it die.

The United States

The CWS was demobilized at the end of World War II. To preserve it from total elimination, Major General Porter (director of the CWS 1941–45) made a vigorous defense of the organization, reminiscent of that made by General Fries during the 1920s. Like his predecessor in the years between the wars, Porter too was helped by an organization, the Chemical Corps Association, which was composed of officers, enlisted men and civilians who served in the CWS during World War II. The group published *The Chemical Warfare Service in World War II: A Record of Accomplishments* in 1948 to publicize the contributions of the Service to the nation during the war.

As in the 1920s, the campaign to preserve the military's chemical warfare division was successful, and the Chemical Corps was invigorated during the Korean conflict (1950–53). The overwhelming number of troops possessed by North Korea's ally, the People's Republic of China, led some to advocate for the United States to use chemical weapons in this conflict. One officer stated:

> The use of mustard, lewisite and phosgene in the vast quantities which we are capable of making and distributing offers the only sure way of holding Korea at the present time. We are not playing marbles. We are fighting for our lives. Let's use the best means we have to overwhelm the enemy scientifically and intelligently.[1]

However, senior military officers rejected all suggestions to use chemical weapons during the Korean conflict.

After that conflict ended, the Cold War continued to supply the Chemical Corps with a justification for survival as it prepared for chemical battles against the Soviet Union. Once again the Corps evaluated the effectiveness of its chemical agents. Lewisite was reviewed on October 3, 1955, by the Chemical Corps Technical Committee, which at that time acted to "obsolete" lewisite from American stockpiles based on World War II data indicating that lewisite would not be effective under typical battlefield conditions. Subsequently, in 1957, the committee authorized that the remaining three thousand tons of the United States lewisite stockpile be dumped into the sea. The Chemical Corps' directive ordering lewisite's dumping stated that "burial in deep water" was the only feasible means of elimination because efforts to sell lewisite to private parties had failed. The directive also estimated that the sea dumping would cost $500,000 and ordered that, for safety reasons, the lewisite should be transported only during cold weather (less vaporization if there was a spill).

Most of the approximately twenty-thousand-ton World War II lewisite stockpile had been dumped into the sea prior to the committee's order. For example, the June 28, 1946, *New York Times* described the dumping of an estimated ten thousand tons of lewisite 165 miles off the Charleston, South Carolina, coast in waters approximately one mile deep. The lewisite containers—bulky fifty-five-gallon steel barrels—were shipped to the Small Boat Wet Storage Basin in Charleston by trains from Huntsville Arsenal in Alabama, Pine Bluff Arsenal in Arkansas, and Edgewood Arsenal in Maryland, where they were transferred to three barges, each of which had a special mechanism that dropped the barrels over the sides. In 1948 more bulk lewisite was shipped to Charleston; the *SS Joshua Alexander* transported approximately 3,150 tons from there and dumped it at sea. This latter operation was referred to as Operation Geranium, because of lewisite's odor.

In the spring of 1958, lewisite was dumped off the West Coast of the United States. In this case, a liberty ship, the *SS William C. Ralston,* was loaded with 6,832 tons of mustard bombs and 448 tons of "cylinders" containing lewisite, and scuttled 129 miles west of the Golden Gate Bridge in waters over two miles deep. A military spokesmen said the dumping presented no danger to humans or fish and that, although this was the first such operation on the West Coast, similar operations had been performed previously in the Atlantic Ocean. The military also dumped 948 containers of chemical agents (each containing 150 gallons; 997 tons of lewisite) in waters twelve miles northeast of Attu Island (Alaska) after World War II.

During World War II the United States had stockpiled lewisite outside the United States, presumably in case it was needed quickly in either the European or Pacific theaters. After the war these reserves were apparently dumped into the nearest ocean. Thus, in November 1945 approximately 925 tons of lewisite, which presumably had been stored in India, were dumped in the Bay of Bengal in the Indian Ocean, and between October 2 and December 20, 1945, the Allies dumped ninety-three containers (of unknown size) containing lewisite twenty-five miles off of Cape Moreton, Australia. Although the exact amount of lewisite dumped there is unknown, a 1943 inventory showed that the United States had 195 tons of bulk lewisite stored in Australia in 1943, and an unknown number of lewisite munitions. Lastly, in April 1946, the army sea dumped an unspecified number of lewisite bombs previously stored at a United States base in Auera, Italy, at an unspecified location in the Atlantic Ocean.

In addition to dumping these major amounts of lewisite at sea, smaller amounts of it were frequently jettisoned in the same way until 1968. For example, two to three tons of lewisite were dumped off Port Henry, Virginia, from the United States Army vessel *Pvt. Carl Sheridan* on June 16, 1960. But indiscriminate dumping of chemical weapons into the seas was halted abruptly in 1972 by the passage of Public Law 92-532, the Marine Protection, Research and Sanctuaries Act, which specifically prohibited the sea dumping of United States chemical weapons. Also in 1972, the United States signed the Convention of Marine Pollution by Dumping of Wastes and Other Matter, which also specifically prohibited the dumping of materials "produced for biological or chemical warfare."[2]

Passage of the law and the signing of the convention was preceded by the suspension of plans by the Department of Defense to dispose of approximately twenty-seven thousand tons of chemical weapons by ocean dumping in accordance with a program known as Operation Chase ("Cut Holes and Sink 'Em"). The suspension was in response to public concerns over the transportation of these agents and the impact on marine life at the dump site.

Although there was no movement of large amounts of lewisite in the United States after 1968, small samples of it were still shipped to military bases within Chemical Agent Identification Sets. These sets were distributed to troops to facilitate the detection of chemical agents and their decontamination during combat. The inclusion of lewisite in these sets implied that the United States military continued to believe it was an agent that could be used against American troops. Approximately fourteen hundred pounds of lewisite from these kits have been destroyed.

The Soviet Union

After World War II, the Soviet Union continued to manufacture large quantities of lewisite and other First World War–era chemical agents, as well as newer agents such as tabun, because Joseph Stalin saw chemical weapons as a cheap alternative to tactical nuclear weapons. Stalin's commitment to a chemical weapons philosophy and his material investment in it continued even after the Soviet Union successfully detonated an atomic bomb in August 1949. Indeed, during the 1950s, Soviet military doctrine was that chemical and biological weapons were part of its usable arsenal in any war. At the time, chemical munitions constituted up to one-third of Soviet artillery shells. This investment kept the United States Chemical Corps alive: Its director said in 1953, "Today, thanks to Joe Stalin, we are back in business."[3]

The use of lewisite was an integral part of the Soviet chemical warfare strategy. Thus, Soviet munitions utilizing lewisite (and lewisite/mustard mixtures) included artillery shells, airplane bombs, and special canisters that were designed to be attached to spraying units on airplanes. A United States Chemical Corps scientist told me recently that the Soviets also mixed lewisite with nerve agents; this produced a particularly insidious poison because the victim immediately begins scratching the affected area, forcing the deadly nerve agent into his body.

The importance of chemical weapons to the Soviet Union became especially apparent to the United States after the 1973 Arab-Israeli War when it was learned from captured equipment that the Soviet Union had supplied the Arabs with equipment designed to work in a chemical warfare environment. And this equipment included a detector for lewisite.

Did the Soviet Union ever use its chemical weapons in a military conflict? Possibly. In 1982 Deputy Assistant Secretary of State Walter J. Stoessel, Jr., testified (based on information obtained from defectors) that the ongoing Soviet invasion of Afghanistan involved the use of poison gas, including lewisite, which by then had allegedly killed 3,042 people. However, the use of chemical weapons by the Soviet Union in that conflict has never been substantiated.

As the Soviet Union made new chemical weapons, it also disposed of some of its older stockpiles, mainly by dumping the material into the Arctic Ocean (White, Kara, and Barents Seas). Perhaps as much as 40,000 tons of mustard and lewisite were dumped into the White Sea, and as much as 75,000 tons were dumped into the Kara and Barents Seas during the 1940s and 1950s. These dumping sites are labeled "Hazardous Dump Site" on Russian shipping charts, and of the 115,000 tons, 20,000 are believed to be lewisite.

In April 1987 Soviet Premier Mikhail Gorbachev announced that the Soviet Union would halt production of chemical weapons. Two years later the Soviet Union and the United States signed the Wyoming Memorandum of Understanding, agreeing to the exchange of confidential data pertaining to the two countries' chemical weapons inventories. They also pledged to begin to destroy their respective stockpiles of chemical weapons. This memorandum also allowed for a small number of "challenge inspections" to verify the provisions of the multinational Chemical Weapons Convention (CWC), which banned the production of chemical weapons.

Iraq

On September 22, 1980, Iraq invaded its neighbor, Iran. The Iraqi army, trained by Soviet advisors, was prepared for offensive and defensive chemical warfare. When, instead of the expected quick victory, the war stalemated, and waves of Iranian soldiers began attacking Iraqi forces, the Iraqis attacked with chemical weapons. The first reported use of chemical weapons occurred in November 1980, with Iraq continuing to use chemical agents during the next few years. This resulted in a November 1983 Iranian complaint to the United Nations (UN) that Iraq was using such weapons, including "compounds containing arsenic." The agents were delivered by aerial bombs, artillery shells, and rockets and were used against civilians as well as military forces. Roughly 5 percent of Iranian casualties during the war were attributed to chemical weapons. The war ended in 1988 when the belligerents accepted a UN sponsored cease-fire plan.

A UN investigative team confirmed Iraq's use of chemical weapons, reporting that the principal chemical agents used by Iraq were mustard and the nerve agent tabun. However, in accordance with the strategy of their Soviet mentors, lewisite was apparently also used, either alone or in combination with mustard. Lewisite, although probably ineffective as an agent in most climates, would be at least as effective as mustard in the hot and dry climate of the Middle East.

The primary evidence for Iraq's use of lewisite is the condition of Iranian soldiers who were victims of gas and were treated in Europe. Eight victims of a chemical attack arrived in London on March 22, 1985, for treatment at the Hospital of St. John and St. Elizabeth. One of the victims, Amin Ali Saidy, presented with burns on his forehead, cheek, arm, armpit, chest, legs, hip region, and groin. He reported that he felt burning on his face immediately after an explosion, that within fifteen minutes his whole body was burning, and that he was blinded by the gas for a week. All of these symptoms were considered consistent with lewisite poisoning.

On January 16, 1991, a United States–led coalition of military forces initiated Operation Desert Storm to liberate Kuwait from its recent conquest by Iraq. President George H. W. Bush ordered the cessation of military operations on February 28. Although there were no chemical battles during this short war, some of the coalition forces suffered a mysterious malady, which came to be known as Gulf War Syndrome. This syndrome has been attributed to inadvertent or deliberate low-level release of chemical and/or biological agents. In *Gassed in the Gulf,* Patrick Eddington, a former Central Intelligence Agency analyst, compiled all of the evidence in support of a chemical/biological agent etiology for the condition, which is characterized by very vague symptoms such as headache, fatigue, neurological degeneration, and gastrointestinal distress. Eddington detailed the detection of lewisite by one chemical unit on February 24 and 25. He also reported that one Iraqi prisoner of war from the 30th Infantry Division stated that Iraq possessed lewisite-filled munitions. A United States soldier, Corporal Santos, developed blisters after cleaning bunkers and touching prisoner of war clothing. When he placed his arm near a chemical agent detection unit, it registered "lewisite." However, the United States military considers any chemical detection of lewisite during the Gulf War to have been erroneous, and a RAND Corporation study in 2000 concluded that there was no indication of sufficient exposure to lewisite during the Gulf War to produce chronic health problems.

On Monday, April 7, 2003, during Operation Iraqi Freedom, Major Michael Hamlet of the United States 101st Airborne Division reported finding fourteen barrels of chemical agents, which he believed to contain the nerve agents tabun and sarin, as well as lewisite. Later, his report was determined to be erroneous. Chemical weapon stockpiles have not been found in Iraq since the overthrow of the Hussein regime. However, Major Hamlet's initial report, which was released to the national media, suggested that the United States forces fully expected to find lewisite among Iraq's arsenal.

Libya

Since the 1970s and until very recently Libya, under the control of Colonel Muammar Qadhafi, had sought to amass weapons of mass destruction, particularly chemical and biological agents, and showed a willingness to use them; in 1987, Libya used mustard gas against Chadian troops. Qadhafi's decision to pursue and use chemical weapons probably reflected an attempt to bolster Libya's relatively ineffective conventional military capacities and might also have been a response to Israel's nuclear capabilities. Libya is believed to have had three major chemical weapons production facilities, Pharma 150 at Rabta, Pharma 200 at Sebha and an underground facility at Tarhunah. One of these, the Pharma 200 plant, reportedly produced both lewisite and sarin nerve gas.

In an unexpected announcement on December 20, 2003, Colonel Qadhafi pledged to abandon Libya's pursuit of WMD, including chemical weapons, and to dismantle its WMD programs. This reversal occurred after months of secret diplomacy and visits by American and British weapons experts to Libyan weapons manufacturing sites, where they found "significant quantities of chemical agents."[4] Apparently Colonel Qadhafi believed that abandoning the program would lead to the end of economic sanctions against his country and the return of American oil company investments.

The Former Yugoslavia

Beginning in 1989 the Yugoslavian army had a working relationship with Iraqi military specialists that presumably involved chemical weapons technology. President Slobodan Milosevic is believed to have considered using chemical weapons when North Atlantic Treaty Organization troops entered the conflict associated with the dissolution of Yugoslavia. Total Yugoslavian production of lewisite is estimated to have been about thirty tons.

Japan

When World War II ended, the factory on Ōkunojima was destroyed, and the remaining 3,000 tons of chemical agents on the island were dumped into the ocean under the supervision of U.S. occupation forces. Of these, 827 tons were lewisite, which were sea dumped under "Operation Lewisite." Additionally, near the end of World War II the Japanese Imperial Army may have dumped chemical weapons, presumably including lewisite, into the sea at unmarked disposal sites.

England

England produced only about 156 tons of lewisite during World War II, all of which was manufactured at the Chemical Defense Research Establishment, Sutton Oaks, St. Helens, Lancaster. It was destroyed after the war.

Yemen and Egypt

During the years 1963–67 a civil war occurred in Yemen between the Republican forces of Brigadier Abdullah Al-Sallal, who had staged a coup d'état against the Imam in September 1962, and Royalist forces. Whereas the Republicans under Al-Sallal occupied the main towns of Yemen, the Royalists occupied most of the mountain ranges in the north and center of the country and the rocky plateaus and deserts to the east. President Gamal Abdel Nasser of Egypt initially sent three thousand troops into Yemen on the Republican side, expecting quick pacification of the Royalist forces. However, this did not occur, and eventually Nasser ordered approximately sixty thousand troops into the conflict. The war became protracted, costly, and inconclusive for Egypt, even though Egypt almost certainly used poison gas—specifically, bombs containing blister agents—within months of the outbreak of hostilities. Two retired British officers who were advising the Royalist leadership examined some of the evidence for gas use; one of them, Colonel David de C. Smiley, reported after having sniffed one of the bomb craters, "there was a pronounced smell of geranium, and suddenly I felt queer and almost fainted. There seemed little doubt that these were gas bombs."[5] Because the Egyptians had probably received their gas from Soviet sources, it seems likely that they were using lewisite or mustard/lewisite bombs. Accordingly, Professor Lauppi of the Institute of Forensic Medicine at the University of Berne in Switzerland studied the medical records of the victims and concluded that the agent most likely used was mustard, lewisite, or adamsite (another arsenic-based agent that was developed during World War I). The

Egyptians withdrew their forces when these tactics failed to dislodge the Royalists.

Sudan

The alleged association between Sudan and chemical weapons first achieved international notoriety in 1998 when President Clinton ordered a cruise missile attack on a pharmaceutical plant in Khartoum (its capital) that was suspected of manufacturing chemical weapons. Clinton believed at the time that the factory was owned by Osama bin Laden. No credible evidence that the plant was in fact making such weapons has ever been found, and the plant was later found to be owned by a Saudi Arabian businessman.

Less well known are the allegations that the Sudanese government has been using chemical weapons against rebel forces within the country. The National Islamic Front, which has controlled the government of Sudan since 1989, has been accused of using chemical weapons against rebels in remote regions of the country, including the Nuba Mountains and southern Blue Nile regions. Individuals from these regions reported to investigators from Christian Solidarity Worldwide in 1999 that bombs were dropped over their regions that produced sore eyes, skin irritation, acute nausea, vomiting, and bleeding, all of which are consistent with lewisite exposure. In addition, British television reported in 1998 that Sudan may have received chemical weapons from Iraq, and Baroness Cox, in a speech delivered to the British House of Lords on October 13, 1999, accused Sudan of having used chemical weapons. Similar accusations have also appeared in British newspapers.

The Sudanese government has denied the use of any chemical weapons. Sudanese Foreign Minister Dr. Mustafa Osman Ismail stated on August 5, 1999, that the Sudanese government does not possess chemical weapons. To back its claim, the Sudanese government noted that the UN had failed to find any evidence of chemical weapons usage in the country.

China

When China ratified the CWC, it declared two chemical weapons facilities. There is little doubt that China's large petrochemical facilities could have produced mustard and lewisite in large quantities, presumably during the 1950s. There are no good data, however, verifying that China ever actually produced lewisite.

North Korea

Not surprisingly, North Korea's military doctrine was heavily influenced by Soviet doctrine, which envisioned the use of chemical warfare as an integral part of any offensive operation. There is no indication that the end of the Cold War has altered this view. In fact, as recently as 2002, the commander of United States forces in Korea issued a report stating that North Korea was self-sufficient in production of First World War–era chemical agents, including lewisite. Similarly, in 1997, Ch'oe Ju Hwal, a former member of the North Korean armed forces, testified before the United States Congress that North Korea maintains a chemical arsenal that includes "luzit" (lewisite).

North Korea is believed to have produced lewisite at a number of factories, including the April 25 Vinalon Factory, Factory No. 297, February 8 Vinalon Factory, Manp'o Chemical Factory, Namhumg Youth Chemical Plant, Sunch'on Calcium Cyanamide Fertilizer Factory, and Sunch'on Vinalon Complex. Estimates of how much lewisite North Korea has stockpiled are not available, although it is believed that the country may possess a total of 2,500–5,000 tons of chemical weapons.

The information in this chapter suggests that worldwide, most of the lewisite that was produced after 1918 has been disposed of by ocean dumping. Lesser amounts have been deposited in burial pits, and thousands of tons still languish in stockpiles of rusting munitions and steel containers, resulting in hazardous conditions for the surrounding communities. Furthermore, chemical weapons from World War I are still regularly unearthed on the battlefields of that war.

10 Lewisite Stockpiles and Terrestrial Residues

How much lewisite has been produced since 1903? Unfortunately, relatively accurate information is available only for a few countries. The United States produced 20,150 tons. The Soviet Union produced at least 22,700 tons and probably much more, with one source reporting that over 47,000 tons was dumped at one burial site alone. Japan produced approximately 1,400 tons, and together the other countries (e.g., England, Iraq, North Korea, Italy, etc.) perhaps another 2,000 tons. Thus, at a minimum, slightly over 45,000 tons were produced, and perhaps that much by the Soviet Union alone. But only a very tiny amount of it was actually used in combat. So—where is the rest?

Most of the world's lewisite was dumped into the ocean, but a substantial portion was not. Some that was not sea dumped has been destroyed (chemically neutralized), whereas the remainder exists in stockpiled containers, stockpiled munitions and, unfortunately, in designated and undesignated burial pits. Within these pits are the toxic degradation products (see chapter 11 and appendix 3) that result when lewisite contacts the surrounding moisture and combines with the compounds that exist in the soil. Furthermore, the development of lewisite resulted in arsenic-tainted experimental apparatus and substantial amounts of arsenic-tainted waste products (tars). These materials had to be deposited someplace.

In 1993 the nations of the world recognized the huge problems posed by the production and disposal of chemical weapons by implementing the Chemical Weapons Convention (CWC), an international treaty. The major goal of the CWC is the destruction of all existing chemical weapons and the destruction of all facilities used to produce them, or their conversion to peaceful purposes. The Convention provides the administrative structure by which the Organization for the Prohibition of Chemical Weapons (OPCW), which was formed in 1997, can monitor the destruction of existing stockpiles of chemical weapons and the factories that produced them. Each country that is a member of the OPCW pledges:

1. Never to use chemical weapons.
2. Never to develop, produce, acquire, or keep chemical weapons, or transfer chemical weapons to any other entity, anywhere in the world.
3. Never to assist or encourage, in any way, anything that is prohibited by the Convention.

As of September 2004, 164 countries have become members of the Convention. Both the United States and Russian Federation are members and, accordingly, technically obligated to destroy all weapons and eliminate all production facilities by April 29, 2007, although it is likely that the Convention will grant a five-year extension beyond this date. Only two other signatory countries besides the United States and Russia have admitted to currently possessing stockpiles of chemical weapons: India and one country that prefers to remain anonymous.

The OPCW is particularly concerned about the use of chemical weapons by terrorists, and lewisite has been listed in its Category 1, which includes the most threatening chemical agents. Category 1 agents also include mustard, sarin, tabun, and VX. As of December 31, 2000, the OPCW reported the worldwide stockpile of lewisite as 7,433 tons, and 380 tons of lewisite/mustard mixtures, the vast majority of which are in the Russian Federation. But it is important to understand that the OPCW estimate is based on self-declaration and assumes honesty, which means that this estimate is likely to be far too low. In fact, some estimates suggest that Russia alone has more than 8,000 tons of lewisite, not to mention stockpiles of other agents.

Between November 11 and 20, 2000, the OPCW conducted a chemical weapons training exercise for weapons inspectors and associated health and safety personnel at Vyskov in the Czech Republic. The purpose of the exercise, which was deemed successful, was to familiarize participants with the requirements of working in a chemical environment. It included training in the detection and decontamination of four chemical agents: sarin, VX, mustard, and lewisite. The presence of lewisite on this list is indicative of the OPCW's belief that it is a weapon that would appeal to terrorists and be accessible to them.

What follows is a discussion of lewisite stockpiles and terrestrial residues by country or region.

The United States

The Tooele Chemical Agent Disposal Facility is the only remaining depot for lewisite in the United States. It is located at the United States Army's Deseret Chemical Depot, twenty-two miles south of Tooele, Utah. This site was at one time part of the Tooele Army Depot. As of the beginning of 2004 the facility held fifteen tons of lewisite that was awaiting destruction using a process developed by Canadian chemical engineer and former dean of the College of Engineering at the University of Calgary Robert Ritter. Ritter described the process, known as Swiftsure, as involving three steps, resulting in a compound " . . . sorta like salt, but you wouldn't want to put it on your eggs."[1]

The Tooele facility was specifically built to destroy chemical weapons under the CWC, which the United States signed in 1993. Although the United States is obligated to destroy all of its lewisite by 2007, it is unlikely that this task will be completed before 2012 because of technical difficulties that required Dr. Ritter to visit Tooele in 2003 to review the Swiftsure procedures. Dr. Ritter told me on March 15, 2004, that, although the lewisite destruction facility had been built years ago, it had not been utilized by 2003 and, accordingly, the chemists at Tooele wanted a refresher course before they initiated the process.

The sites in the United States that are definitively or presumptively contaminated from the production and testing of lewisite are: AU and the adjoining Spring Valley neighborhood in Washington, D.C.; CUA, also in Washington, D.C.; Willoughby, Ohio; Rocky Mountain Arsenal (RMA) near Denver, Colorado; Pine Bluff Arsenal (PBA) in Central Arkansas (about thirty-five miles southeast of Little Rock); Huntsville Arsenal (HA) in northern Alabama (about a hundred miles north of Birmingham); Dugway Proving Ground (DPG) in Utah; Attu Island, Alaska; and a housing subdivision in Columbia, South Carolina.

As mentioned in chapter 4, lewisite was developed and tested (on humans and animals) at the American University Experiment Station. Probably also at the AUES lewisite was poured into bombs that were exploded to determine their range and effectiveness. As quoted below, the United States Army Corps of Engineers expressed doubt that lewisite was loaded into bombs, but there is evidence to the contrary. Of the bombs that were tested, some failed to explode (duds), which were then typically disposed of by burying on site. Thus, when World War I ended, the AUES contained

REACTOR

25. Lewisite destruction facility at Deseret Chemical Depot, Utah.
Photograph by Geri Lawrence courtesy U.S. Army.

areas of soil contaminated with lewisite (arsenic) from the exploded bombs and perhaps areas where lewisite-containing duds were buried. Further, there should have been lewisite-contaminated equipment and waste products associated with its production, and it is reasonable to assume that some or all of that was buried on the grounds. But how much contamination is there, where are the specific areas that are contaminated, and what, specifically, is the nature and degree of the contamination at each? Unfortunately, no one knows. And because an inventory completed when the war ended has been lost, estimates of the amount of lewisite buried are difficult to make. This situation accentuates the anxiety and uncertainty felt by some AU personnel and well-to-do residents of the neighborhood adjoining AU known as Spring Valley.

Spring Valley, a 690-acre community in Northwest Washington, D.C., has been home to many government officials, including three presidents: George H. W. Bush, Richard Nixon and Lyndon Johnson. It contains fifteen hundred homes, mainly brick colonials, and commercial shops. Sibley Memorial Hospital and twenty-seven embassies are also located there. During World War I, soldiers referred to some of the Spring Valley area as "Death Valley" and "Arsenic Valley" because of all the animals killed and the experiments conducted there on arsenic-based poison gases, of which lewisite was one. When residential construction began in 1927, the area was prudently renamed "Spring Valley."

Once World War I ended, the army began to transfer personnel and equipment from the AUES to Edgewood Arsenal (EA) in Maryland. However, not everything was transferred, especially materials that had been buried in pits. In a March 11, 1920, agreement between the army and AU, the army pledged to restore the property to its original 1917 condition. However, in a later Memorandum of Agreement (June 21, 1920), AU released the army from this obligation in exchange for transfer of title of certain buildings erected by the army on campus. In a real sense, then, AU willfully granted permission to the army to depart without removing the buried materials on its campus.

After the army departed from AU, the university began selling some of the land the army had used. This land, which became the Spring Valley neighborhood, was developed primarily by the W. C. & A. N. Miller Company. By 1928 the company had platted three hundred acres of land in Spring Valley, and it began developing homes for the affluent there. According to anecdotal stories, the first post-war residents of the newly developed houses found their back yards pitted with shell holes and bomb dugouts, the remains of the army's occupation of the campus.

Despite such stories from the initial residents, in time the World War I operation at the AUES was largely forgotten. However, in 1986, when AU initiated plans to construct a new athletic facility, university officials discovered a 1921 newspaper article referring to buried munitions from the World War I military station that occupied its campus. Nevertheless, after consultations with the army, AU proceeded with its plans and the facility was built without incident.

In 1990, AU again sold land adjacent to it for residential development, this time to a company called Glenbrook-Brandt, which began construction of two homes (4825 and 4835 Glenbrook Road). During the excavation associated with the development of these properties, some of Brandt's workers experienced skin burning and eye pain severe enough to warrant a visit to the emergency room. According to a District of Columbia Department of Health memo, one of the workers had black spots on his skin, which was considered consistent with exposure to a vesicant agent such as lewisite. Brandt's workers also unearthed antique laboratory equipment, broken jars, and a fifty-five gallon drum. Brandt notified AU, which hired an environmental consulting firm to investigate. The firm attributed the workers' symptoms to the presence of an herbicide in the soil. Later, a Washington, D.C., Health Department scientist said this attribution was ludicrous.

At another section of Spring Valley approximately one mile from the Glenbrook Road properties (at 52nd Court), while digging a utility trench for new houses on January 5, 1993, construction workers unearthed rusted bombs. The army was notified, and within a few hours helicopters brought gas-mask equipped bomb-removal experts from nearby Aberdeen Proving Ground (part of which used to be known as EA) in Maryland. The residents of the area became very concerned, and army officers held a town meeting that evening at a nearby church. The officers told the residents that the bombs were from World War I and assured them that the situation at this Formerly Used Defense Site would be cleansed of all bomb-related residues. An Army Corps of Engineers operation, part of "Operation Safe Removal Formerly Used Defense Site" was initiated.

The Corps' efforts continued through the remainder of that year and into 1994. In total, 141 munitions were recovered, including 43 shells suspected of containing poison gas, as well as glassware and other lab equipment. Some of the recovered materials (presumably liquids) tested positive for L2, L3, and chlorovinylarsonous acid (CVAA, a lewisite degradation product; see appendix 3). As part of this investigation, the army tested soil on the Brandt properties and concluded that no hazardous materials were present on the lot at 4825 Glenbrook, which was purchased in 1994 by Thomas and Kathi Loughlin. In 1995 the Army Corps of Engineers issued a Record of Decision indicating that all poison gas related materials had been removed and that Spring Valley was safe; that is, "no further action" was required. This Record also stated:

> The primary contaminants of concern at the OSR FUDS are the mustard agents and lewisite. . . . Lewisite, a compound similar to mustard but arsenic based, was developed at AUES; however, it was not believed to have been loaded in ordnance. Lewisite also breaks down in the presence of moisture resulting in chlorovinylarsenious [chlorovinyl-

arsonous] acid (CVAA). While samples were analyzed for lewisite and CVAA, arsenic is the most persistent and readily analyzed indicator for lewisite and CVAA.[2]

Although the Army Corps of Engineers was satisfied that residues from the World War I AUES work no longer posed a health risk for Spring Valley's residents, an environmental lawyer and scientist working for the District of Columbia, Richard Albright, was not. His lack of confidence in the Corps' "Record of Decision" was initially based on the vastness of the World War I operation at AUES. The Corps' investigation did not seem to Albright to be commensurate with the amount of munitions testing that was done there in 1917 and 1918. Albright was also concerned because this was the first time the army had conducted an ordnance and chemical warfare removal operation in a residential area. Albright believed, as did an Environmental Protection Agency investigator, that there was an immediate threat to the health and safety of the people of Spring Valley and, in a report he wrote for the District of Columbia, referred to the AUES as the "worst defense site in the country."[3]

The Washington Post also found flaws in the Corps' work:

1. The Corps initially failed to test soil at the correct depth at the Sedgwick Street site. More recent tests found arsenic levels at four homes to be twenty times higher than EPA allowable levels.
2. The metal detector used by the Corps was designed to find burial pits, but not single munitions. Thus, such munitions may not have registered with the device.
3. The Corps' findings that arsenic levels at AU were not significantly elevated compared to other areas in Spring Valley may not be meaningful because all of Spring Valley could be contaminated from the open-air testing done there during WWI.

A further development occurred in June 1996, when workers planting a tree on the grounds of AU President Ladner's property at 4835 Glenbrook (adjacent to the Loughlin property) were overcome by fumes that caused severe eye burning. The workers subsequently found broken bottles and glassware containing liquids. An environmental firm confirmed the presence of high levels of arsenic (twenty-eight times above the allowable EPA level) in the soil at the property.

In January 1998 the Corps responded to the calls to reopen its investigation with a report rejecting the notion of any continuing problem. It all

26. Excavation site located on 52nd Court NW in Spring Valley, Washington, D.C., January 1993.
Courtesy U.S. Army, Research Development and Engineering Command.

**27. The pit called "Hades" at the AUES, ca. 1918. The bottles contain mustard to
be deposited in the pit.**
Courtesy Addie Ruth Maurer Olson.

might have ended there, except that the Corps agreed in this report that it
had searched in the wrong place for one of the possible burial pits and
would examine what their historians now believed to be the more likely
location.

Early in 1999 the Corps began excavating the new site: the South Korean
Ambassador's residence at 4801 Glenbrook Road. Here they discovered extremely high levels of arsenic, up to a thousand parts per million (ppm).
With this excavation, the Corps believed they may have found a pit in
which carboys (large liquid containers) of chemical agents were reported
to have been buried, and which was referred to in some historic documents
as Hades. Their excavation unearthed 250 shells and 175 bottles, but no carboys or their remnants, and thus this pit was determined not to be Hades.
A subsequent excavation next door, at the Loughlin property, identified
380 shells, several 50-gallon drums and 40 bottles, most containing mustard or lewisite. However, this pit was still not considered to be the one
referred to as Hades. The Corps' final analysis for the properties concluded
that there was "an unacceptable hazard from arsenic on the property."[4]
These findings eventually led the Corps in January 2000 to agree to reopen
and expand the investigation.

A plan was implemented to conduct arsenic sampling on sixty-one private residences and the southern portion of AU. The land surrounding the AU childcare center showed arsenic levels that averaged 60 ppm, with a high of 498 ppm. One sample with a reading of 400 ppm originated in an area of the center where the children had planted a vegetable garden, from which they had harvested and eaten the vegetables. The Loughlin house on Glenbrook Road showed an average of 241 ppm, with some areas greater than 600 ppm. EPA guidelines call for soil removal when levels are higher than 43 ppm.

The elevated arsenic levels at the AU childcare center understandably alarmed parents and university officials alike. In 2001 the university relocated the childcare center. The Corps agreed to remove and replace the soil from the property (to a depth of two feet), and to test the children and selected AU personnel for systemic arsenic levels. This was accomplished by taking two-inch hair samples (arsenic is deposited in hair roots as they grow) from twenty-eight children and four adults. None exhibited elevated arsenic levels. The report on the children, which was prepared by the Agency for Toxic Substances and Disease Registration of the United States Department of Health and Human Services, suggested that a layer of mulch and grass overlying the playground soil may have minimized the children's exposure to the arsenic.

Thirty-two other Spring Valley residents also were tested for arsenic poisoning by the same agency. Again, the results did not indicate systemic exposure to high levels of arsenic. Thus United States government tests suggested that neither the children who attended the childcare center nor Spring Valley residents had been harmed by the high levels of arsenic in the soil. Similarly, an analysis of cancer data by the District of Columbia government did not find that Spring Valley had a higher than expected rate of cancer. However, a more recent analysis suggests that cancer rates may be higher than normal in this area, and Richard Albright wondered whether the tests done on the children from the childcare center included hair samples that represented the period when the children would have been playing in the soil and thereby exposed to arsenic.

In 2001 the Army Corps again expanded its efforts and agreed to test every property in Spring Valley for arsenic. Any property that had a sample that exceeded 13 ppm would have additional samples taken. At the date of this writing (October 2004) 1,484 of 1,602 residential and business properties have been tested, with 139 found to have arsenic levels higher than 20 ppm, the level at which the Corps agreed to remove and replace the upper two feet of soil from the properties. This has been accomplished for 27 of the 139 properties.

As of July 2003 a total of 655 shells and 220 bottles of chemicals had been excavated in Spring Valley. But according to Richard Albright there may be as many as 4,300 shells buried on the site. The Army Corps has spent about $91 million since 1993; it estimates that the project will not be completed until 2008, and that a total of $34 million more will be required to complete it. As recently as September 3, 2003, the Corps announced that a newly found sealed vial containing a small amount of lewisite (about a tablespoon) had been excavated. Although not a large amount, the findings heightened residents' fears because the material was found in a "low-priority" area.

The empirical data thus far compiled suggest that the residents of Spring Valley have not been harmed by the arsenic compounds that contaminate their neighborhood. However, not all are convinced that these tests have revealed the true effects of their exposure, especially chronic low-level exposure. The Loughlins are one family that remains unconvinced. While growing up in Spring Valley the Loughlin children, like all children, played in their yards. Unlike all children, however, they developed skin rashes that their pediatrician could not explain. Finally, after many tests and having learned of Spring Valley's history, their pediatrician suggested the Loughlins move out of their house, which they did permanently in 1999. In addition to the rashes experienced by the Loughlin children, Kathi Loughlin developed a brain tumor in 1997, from which she has recovered. The Loughlins believe the rashes and the brain tumor were caused by the chemicals in the soil, most probably the elevated levels of arsenic.

The Loughlins want accountability. They, their nanny, and a neighbor filed a civil action suit against the army for dumping mustard gas, cyanide, phosgene, arsenic, and lewisite, when World War I ended in 1918, on the land that became their properties. Unfortunately for them, in 2003, United States District Judge Ellen Segal Huvelle ruled that the residents could not hold the Federal Government responsible for this action and any associated decrease in the value of their homes. The judge indicated in her ruling that the Federal Government is immune from such suits because the decisions made by the army at the time cannot be challenged unless the officers violated a clear directive, and there is no evidence that the burial of chemical weapons violated army policy. To the contrary—such burials were common. The judge, however, citing the document by which AU relieved the army of its responsibility to remediate the area after World War I, left open the possibility for residents to sue AU and various Spring Valley developers.

Interestingly, in 2001, before the Loughlins' lawsuit, AU filed an $86.6 million damage claim against the army. In the suit AU alleged that the discovery of the army's World War I chemical warfare material forced the university to take significant measures to ensure the safety and health of AU personnel and children attending the childcare center. Further, AU alleged that the Corps' conduct resulted in financial losses associated with disruption of normal operations, temporary relocations, construction delays, potential loss of donors, and harm to the university's academic reputation. However, the ruling by Judge Huvelle also applied to AU's suit. Currently AU is appealing the ruling.

Forty-six-year-old Zachary Wilnowski (an alias), another Spring Valley resident who believes his strange illnesses were caused by living in his contaminated neighborhood, has been very active in trying to secure what he considers to be justice for the community. Zachary was one of eight children who grew up in an area adjacent to Spring Valley that also may have been used by the army for chemical weapons testing. I met Zachary in March of 2002 when he guided me on a tour of Spring Valley. At the time the Corps was sampling the soil at some of the homes in the area, and it was quite eerie when Zachary pointed out World War I concrete bunkers situated in the front yards of some $1-million-plus Spring Valley homes.

Many of Zachary's siblings had unusual ailments while growing up, and he himself suffered from frequent gastrointestinal problems. Upon reaching adulthood, Zachary became a landscape architect and regularly worked on Spring Valley properties. Beginning in 2001 he started experiencing headaches, memory loss, numbness, and muscle twitching throughout his body, which forced him to stop working. He and his doctors thought his symptoms might be due to lewisite residues in the soil, and, when the symptoms became so severe that he sought treatment at the Johns Hopkins University Medical Center Emergency Room, he was actually offered BAL. He declined BAL treatment, however, because the physician indicated it might cause more symptoms than it could cure. None of the medical treatments offered by the many physicians he consulted provided any relief for his symptoms. Zachary is just now (early 2004) beginning to return to work.

Is it possible that the Loughlins and Zachary are correct in attributing their symptoms to chronic low-level arsenic poisoning in Spring Valley? Chapter 11 discusses the known health effects of such exposure.

Very recently the Army Corps of Engineers began testing a new technique to remove arsenic residue from Spring Valley soil: planting ferns. These feathery plants have been demonstrated to possess a sponge-like ability to absorb arsenic. One hundred thirty thousand dollars have been allocated to test the effectiveness of two fern species, *Pteris multifida* and *Pteris cretica* in Spring Valley. If successful, planting and later removing the plants might alleviate some of the need for soil removal in this neighborhood.

AU is not the only Washington area suspected of having been contaminated with residues from lewisite. In 1993 the Army Corps of Engineers began an investigation of the grounds of CUA to determine whether chemical weapon residues, especially those of lewisite, were buried somewhere on the campus. Corps personnel interviewed long-time (since 1959) CUA chemistry professor Leopold May, who was at the time seventy years old (I also met and interviewed Dr. May during my 2003 visit to Washington). Professor May recalled that a former CUA chemistry professor, the late Henry Ward (who was talking to Nieuwland when Nieuwland died), had been concerned during the 1960s that a new construction site overlay an area where some barrels of World War I–related toxic materials had been buried. But no such barrels were found, and the Corps concluded in 1995 that there was no evidence that hazardous materials from the World War I CWS research unit had been buried on campus property. Nevertheless, in 2001, as work continued in Spring Valley, District of Columbia health officials requested that the Corps review its 1995 findings. Thus far, the Corps has not done so.

In 1993 the Army Corps initiated an Archives Search Report for the grounds surrounding the plant in Willoughby, Ohio, at which lewisite had been manufactured during World War I. The Corps surveyed the site using ground-penetrating radar, but failed to locate any buried equipment. But this method was not capable of locating any pit where lewisite residues were simply poured into the ground. Because during the World War I era "an open pit disposal of wastes was commonplace, we [the Army Corps] find the probability of CWM [chemical weapons materials] contamination to be high."[5] Indeed, as previously described, some buried glassware containing lewisite had been found during construction at the site in 1957. Furthermore, the process used to manufacture lewisite included steps in which hazardous tars were formed that were disposed of in some manner.

A representative of a recent corporate owner of the Willoughby site, Eagle Picher, was quoted in the *Willoughby News-Herald* in 2002 as stating that this "scare" has cropped up before and, despite repeated probings, no gas has been found. However, Eagle Picher would not release details on these "probing" studies to the *News-Herald's* reporter, Jeffery Frischkorn. Frischkorn authored two articles for the paper describing the World War I activity at the site and the planned additional radar scans and possible soil-sampling tests that were scheduled to be done by the Corps in 2003. However, presumably because of budgetary constraints, neither scans nor soil tests were conducted in that year. Furthermore, Kevin Jasper, project manager for the Corps' Louisville, Kentucky, office, indicated to me late in that year that further work at the plant site is unlikely unless there is new definitive evidence that lewisite or its precursors had been buried at the site. Mr. Frank DeMilta, who currently owns the scrap metal yard that is located on the Willoughby property, did not respond to a letter requesting an interview, or his written opinion, about the possibility that his property might be contaminated with arsenic.

The production of lewisite during the Second World War also produced hazardous byproducts, which is a source of concern. In 1986 the United States Department of Justice completed a report on the environmental impact of chemical warfare agent production at the RMA during World War II, and calculated (according to worst-case scenarios) that the manufacture of lewisite produced the following "waste" products: 11,700 pounds of antimony hydroxide, 6,221 pounds of calcium arsenide, 331,000 pounds of calcium arsenite, 1,500,000 pounds of arsenic trichloride, 172,000 pounds of mercuric chloride, and 129,000 pounds of arsenic trioxide. Whatever the precise amounts of these wastes, the chemicals were usually treated in some manner and deposited in two basins on the property. The contents of one of these basins have since been further treated, excavated, and placed in a designated hazardous landfill as part of the army's remediation of the site. The other basin is still being used for deposition of low-level hazardous wastes and will eventually be capped with a soil cover.

During the 1950s there was some concern that contamination from the RMA was causing crop damage and polluting wells to the north. To alleviate these concerns, residents in the affected areas were provided with municipal water. In any event, although most of RMA was designated by Congress to become a natural wildlife refuge, the areas where waste is stored will remain inaccessible to the public and under army jurisdiction indefinitely, with a program for soil remediation scheduled for completion by 2011.

During World War II, lewisite was also produced at PBA and HA. At

PBA, undetermined amounts of residues of lewisite and mercury were deposited in a four-acre lagoon located in the north-central part of the arsenal, where they formed a white sludge up to seven feet deep. As part of the remediation process, this lagoon was capped with three feet of topsoil, and the Arkansas Department of Environmental Quality is committed to a long-term program to monitor the lagoon. At HA (now called Redstone Arsenal) the lewisite residues were placed in three lagoons that have since been capped. These lagoons are surrounded by barbed wire and not accessible without special permission.

Attu Island is the westernmost island in the Aleutian chain of Alaskan islands. This island was captured in 1942 by the Japanese during World War II, but was retaken by the United States Army in 1943. Subsequently the army stored chemical munitions on the island, including 997 tons of lewisite. After the war most of the lewisite (all but ten containers totaling about eleven tons) was dumped at sea. The remaining ten containers were transferred to the Cape Yakak Radio Station located on Adak Island, which is another island in the Aleutian chain. The final disposition of these ten containers is unknown, although they may have been buried.

During World War II the army used an area of Columbia, South Carolina, for aerial bombing practice. The site was known as the Pontiac Precision Bombing Range. According to army records, only practice bombs were tested at the range. It was strange, then, that in early June 2001 a construction worker excavating a trench at the site, which is now a residential housing development (The Summit), experienced a burning sensation on his skin followed by the appearance of a rash and blisters. The EPA was consulted and soil samples were tested for lewisite and mustard; one of them tested positive for lewisite.

A few months after the worker's incident, a resident of the community, Elijah Robinson, was digging in the patio of his new home when he suddenly felt as if "his body had just been hurled into a fire." Subsequently his face and neck swelled, and blisters appeared. Robinson and his wife also began to smell the odor of geraniums in their house. "It was so sweet, it would nauseate you," said his wife, Darlene, who then consulted with Washington, D.C., scientist Richard Albright.[6] He suggested that Elijah and Darlene, who also had developed blisters, were suffering from symptoms consistent with lewisite exposure. University of Texas medical toxicologist Chip Carson also expressed the opinion that the Robinsons had symptoms consistent with lewisite exposure.

Following the EPA's positive findings and the suspected exposures to lewisite at The Summit, the army sampled the soil and also found low levels of lewisite in two of eighteen cases (although a different laboratory analyzing the samples could not confirm lewisite residues). The army then explored the subsurface soil and obtained additional samples, which were also tested; although some arsenic residues were identified, lewisite residues were not. Nevertheless, Albright suspects that chemical weapons were indeed tested during World War II at bombing ranges such as Pontiac, which were not specifically designated for chemical weapons testing. The Robinsons are currently living in an apartment. Darlene said in a recent interview, "We were attacked by an unseen enemy, and everything we had was taken from us."[7] Other residents also complain of rashes, but at this time no remediative action is planned for the site because there is no known historical data suggesting that chemical weapons were tested there.

The possibility that lewisite residues might be found in Utah would never have been revealed except for the efforts of a gadfly, David W. Hall, a Ph.D. chemist the army surely regrets ever having hired. He was assigned to the DPG in Utah, an army base that comprises almost eight hundred thousand acres in the middle of the Great Salt Lake Desert. The DPG is responsible for testing military equipment used to protect against chemical and biological agents.

Hall received a doctorate in organic chemistry in 1963 from the California Institute of Technology. He subsequently worked as a research chemist for Marathon Oil Company, a professor of chemistry at the Colorado School of Mines, a research chemist at Loctite Corporation, an engineer/chemist at IBM, and as a high school science teacher before being hired by the United States Army as a civilian chemist in 1986.

While employed at DPG, Hall continually raised safety issues, including improper storage of incompatible, ignitable, and explosive waste chemicals, illegal dumping of toxic chemicals into DPG laboratory drains, defects in gas masks, and defects in devices for identifying the contents of recovered chemical munitions. In addition, Hall raised issues about how lewisite was used at two DPG facilities. The first, the Carr Facility, is a site contaminated with lewisite and mustard after the agents were deliberately released to test the efficacy of protective equipment on soldiers. The second site, Simpson Butte, is where lewisite waste had historically been dumped.

Hall's issue with the Carr Facility was that the army had made no attempt to decontaminate the area. And, although the army had decontaminated the Simpson Butte site, Hall demonstrated that a degradation product (chlorovinylarsonous acid, CVAO) was still present. Furthermore, Hall was concerned because lab workers receiving samples of CVAO from the site were not informed that if it is mixed with an acid, lewisite is re-formed. Hall was also concerned that lewisite breakdown products from these sites could migrate to other areas via contaminated rainwater and groundwater.

Hall's army superiors were not pleased when he raised these issues. Eventually their lack of corrective action forced Hall to forward his concerns for the environment and DPG workers to the state of Utah. In other words, Hall became a "whistle-blower." Accordingly, Hall's supervisors at DPG penalized him by reassignment, unjustly lowering his performance evaluations, writing negative comments in his personnel record, requiring that he undergo several psychiatric exams, making false allegations of misconduct, suspending his security clearance, verbally referring to him as a traitor, and directly threatening him with job termination. This hostility severely affected his health, necessitating his retirement on June 12, 1997.

Following his "forced" retirement Hall filed a legal complaint against the army alleging that he had been subject to retaliatory treatment for his public exposure of the army's failure to properly dispose of chemical (including lewisite) wastes and the army's inaccurate evaluation of chemical protective equipment. The complaint was initially reviewed by the Occupations Safety and Health Administration, followed by a fifty-seven day hearing held before Department of Labor Administrative Law judge David W. Di Nardi. Judge Di Nardi's ruling on August 8, 2002, was a stinging rebuke to the army; he found Hall to be a "dedicated, conscientious and highly-motivated public citizen who has manifested these qualities throughout his many years as a public servant, no matter the task assigned."[8] He concluded that Hall, after his internal complaints did not result in any change in procedures, was justified in bringing his concerns to the state of Utah, and that the army had retaliated against him. Judge Di Nardi awarded Hall $1.5 million in compensatory and punitive damages, plus $400,000 in attorney fees. The army is currently appealing the verdict, and Hall is living on Social Security and a small pension in Salt Lake City.

The Soviet Union

In contrast to all of the other World War II combatants, as described previously, the Soviet Union continued to manufacture lewisite and other antiquated chemical agents after the war. Currently lewisite is the second largest component of Russian chemical weapons stockpiles (the nerve agents sarin, soman, and VX are the largest).

During World War II, the Soviet Union produced lewisite at several of its chemical warfare facilities, including Chapayevsk (Kuybyshev region). At Chapayevsk, lewisite was produced in shop no. 7, which had the capacity to produce forty-four hundred tons per year. The arsenic trichloride required for lewisite production was also manufactured at this plant. When batches of lewisite were completed at Chapayevsk, they were put into artillery shells in the "women's shops," nos. 52–55, by pouring the liquid from kettles; safer technology was not introduced until the 1950s. The initial primitive technology used at the plant resulted in the death of many of the Chapayevsk workers, endangered the health of nearby residents, and polluted nearby waterways. An article in *Izvestia* in 1992 stated that "During the war young men unfit for the front line and girls arrived by the trainload—and just as quickly became ill and died."[9] Air from the shops was exhausted directly to the city air. Although there were facilities for treating the waste water, these facilities were often broken, resulting in the waste water spilling directly into the Chapayevka River, and from there to the Volga River. Eventually this chemical warfare plant was converted into one making fertilizer.

The conversion of the Chapayevsk chemical weapons plant necessitated disposing of the chemical agents stored there. The plant's supervisors ordered the burial of the agents in the nearby village of Pokrovka, whose residents recall the ground releasing heat in the 1980s. A recent analysis of soil near shop no. 7 showed arsenic levels 7,000–8,500 times higher than permissible. The highly toxic product associated with lewisite degradation, CVAO, was found in residential areas downwind of the factory, and in 1995 premature births and cases of hydrocephalus were shown to be seven times higher than in neighboring regions.

Similarly hazardous conditions exist at a former mustard/lewisite plant site at Dzerzhinsk (Nizhny Novgorod region), where large amounts of toxic wastes were buried on site, dumped into the Oka River, or burned in the open air. The soil around the plant remains contaminated with arsenic compounds.

Near the small rural community of Leonidovka (Penza Region) and nearby Lake Mokhovoe, during the 1950s, some of the lewisite, mustard, and phosgene that had been stored aboard about 620 railway cars was incinerated or simply poured into streams. Henceforth the lake became known as Lake Mertvoe ("the dead lake"). A recent analysis of underground water in the area showed that the concentration of arsenic near the ground surface was twenty thousand times higher than the permissible maximum.

At other Soviet chemical warfare depots, lewisite was often incinerated in the open air, allowing the arsenic to waft away with the smoke and eventually to settle on the surrounding ground. At a plant in Volgograd, lewisite waste was stored in the open air or deposited in a massive toxic lake. In the spring of 1965 this lake overflowed into the Volga River, producing an infamous event known to the locals as the "white sea" accident—the river turned white from the bellies of all the upturned dead fish.

Unfortunately, little data exist on the amounts of lewisite deposited at these Russian sites, although one report indicated that a huge amount, over forty-seven thousand tons, was buried in the ground at Kambarka alone, a site where lewisite is also stockpiled.

One man who has investigated a Soviet lewisite dump site is Vladimir Pankratov. Although once in the Soviet military, he now labors to reveal its transgressions. Pankratov has found aerial bombs containing lewisite/mustard mixtures slightly below the surface in an unmarked pine forest outside of Leonidovka. He also has found in nearby streams, which supply the reservoir for the city of Penza (population 530,000), arsenic levels that are ten times higher than normal. In the forest itself, arsenic levels are fifteen thousand times above allowable limits. These high levels are believed to result from the dumping of lewisite-filled railroad cars at this location.

Finally, a lewisite-contaminated site is thought to exist in the southeastern Kuzminki district of Moscow, an area of leafy birch trees that some Muscovites refer to as "infectionland." Barrels of lewisite and other agents are believed to be buried somewhere in these woods, although the exact burial location is unknown even to the military, which abandoned the site in 1961. The barrels, some of which date to the First World War, are likely located near the shores of two swampy pools in which residents swim and sunbathe, and adjacent to where they pick wild berries and mushrooms during the summer. There are no warning signs at this site, only the debris of poolside parties. In 2000 Moscow's mayor asked the military to clean up the site, which it has not done, officially stating instead that there is no risk to swimmers.

Russia signed the CWC in 1993 and ratified it in 1997, renouncing the development of chemical weapons, their manufacture, their stockpiling, and their future use. It pledged to destroy its stockpile, which contains the largest lewisite reserve of any country, by 2007. Unfortunately, because of financial constraints including limited Western aid, this deadline will not be met. The cost to completely destroy all of Russia's chemical arsenal is estimated to be $6–10 billion—and this may be an optimistic estimate. Further, the money thus far available from both domestic and Western sources is well short of this amount. Initially Russia hoped that its lewisite reserves would provide a source of revenue for the country's chemical weapons destruction program. Because lewisite is 36 percent arsenic, Russian scientists believed that the arsenic could be sold for inclusion in electrical semiconductors. At the time (mid- to late 1990s) this proposal seemed viable, because semiconductor-grade arsenic was selling for $450–900 per pound. However, later analysis indicated that there was not a market for the large amount of arsenic that could be produced and that the cost to extract the arsenic from the lewisite was too high to make this proposition economically viable.

Russia has declared its chemical weapons reserve to include approximately 8,280 tons of lewisite, which is stored at Kambarka, Kizner, and Gorny. The Kambarka site was constructed in the early 1940s about two miles from the town of the same name (population 17,100), which is located in the Urdmurtia region, about 650 miles east of Moscow. Approximately 7,053 tons of lewisite are stored here, which represents about 16 percent of Russia's total chemical arsenal and probably also represents the largest quantity of lewisite stored anywhere in the world. The agent is stored in five stone-walled, wooden-roofed buildings that each contain sixteen 13,209-gallon steel tanks, filled to various levels with lewisite. Destruction of the lewisite here is scheduled to begin in 2005.

The storage site at Gorny was founded in 1943 as People's Commissariat of Defense Warehouse No. 276. Gorny is in the Saratov region (about 500 miles southeast of Moscow) and is a repository for stocks of lewisite/mustard mixtures that were transferred from Chapayevsk. As of early 2003 there were 248 tons of lewisite and 231 tons of a lewisite/mustard mixture stored here. Eighty-two hundred people live within six miles of the site. All of the agents are stored in bulk railroad tank cars. Destruction of the agents here began in December 2002, with the workers operating the neutralization plant conspicuously wearing chemical protective "moon-suits."

Originally the Gorny neutralization plant was supposed to have two lines operating simultaneously—one for lewisite and the lewisite/mustard combination, and one for mustard alone. However, technical problems forced the Russian scientists to concentrate on neutralizing the 680 tons of mustard first, a process that was finished in November 2003. In May 2003 the lewisite line began test runs, and as of August 2004 eighty-four tons of lewisite had been destroyed. The final product of the lewisite neutralization process is called hydrolysate. Current plans are to store it on site, and Russian scientists continue to assess whether it would be economically feasible to extract arsenic for sale from the hydrolysate.

The Kizner storage site is located in the Urdmurtia region about 550 miles east of Moscow. It lacks an automatic alarm system for chemical vapor detection and is a repository for rocket and nonrocket artillery ammunition filled with a variety of chemical weapons, about 804 tons of which contain lewisite.

Because of the environmental dangers associated with lewisite and its degradation products, European countries and the European Union are assisting Russia with the destruction of lewisite at Kambarka and Gorny. In 1992 Germany committed $60 million to construct a plant at Gorny to destroy the lewisite and mustard stored there, with an additional $6 million contributed by the European Union. At the ceremonial opening of the plant in 2002, German Ambassador Hans-Joachim Daerr said this was the first "small step" in the destruction of Russia's stockpile of chemical weapons.

In 1996 Netherlands Minister of Defense Joris Voorhoeve formally announced that the Netherlands would provide $16 million to Russia, primarily for the destruction of the lewisite stored at Kambarka. At the same time Sweden pledged approximately $125,000 to analyze the risks associated with the storage and destruction of lewisite and $350,000 for implementing measures that will reduce accidents at the site. More recently, Germany pledged $300 million for the construction of a disposal plant at Kambarka, at which Russia will provide infrastructure in the form of housing, roads, and utilities.

Local residents at Gorny and Kambarka have raised concerns about the ultimate disposition of the lewisite neutralization products; they fear that once Russia meets its CWC destruction goals it will delay determination of the final disposition of the hydrolysate for decades.

China and Japan

Qiqihar is an industrial city in northeastern China (Heilongjiang Province). A popular teenage hangout there is the Nen River bridge, at which youths gather and walk along the water's edge to collect freshwater clams, apparently unaware that dislodging these clams could be fatal to them due to the presence of lewisite and mustard. The Japanese Imperial Army occupied the city during the Second World War and on August 12, 1945, as the war was ending, dumped barrels of lewisite and mustard into the Nen River. This action was part of the Japanese army's effort to eliminate all evidence of its chemical weapons program in China. Former Japanese soldier Takahashi Masaji supervised the dumping of the chemicals into the river, following orders that he should "throw them [the barrels] from the bridge."[10]

Mudanjiang City, with a population of more than a million, is also located in Heilongjiang Province. It is a city best known for its nearby summer tourist attractions, Mirror Lake and the Underground Forest. In 1982 four barrels (more than 880 pounds) of a lewisite/mustard mixture were found there and destroyed. Then in 1995, 104 artillery shells filled with a mustard/lewisite mixture were found by a Japanese team searching for chemical weapons in this area.

Heilongjiang Province is not the only one in which the Japanese abandoned their chemical weapons and agents; many were abandoned in Jilin Province, which is also in northeastern China. In 1951 Chinese officials in Dunhua, a city in the province, located and collected some of the weapons buried by the Japanese and decided to rebury them in a cave on the west side of Haerba Mountain. Since then officials have found tons of additional chemical agents and weapons in Jilin Province that are rusting and leaking their poisons into the soil. Similarly, in the town of Weijin in the Meihekou region of Jilin Province, seventy-four tons of the mixture were "solidified with lime."

In total there are believed to be five hundred thousand munitions in Jilin Province which, because of their volatility, must be individually excavated. Furthermore, because of the abandoned chemical weapons, farming and herding are considered two of the most dangerous occupations in Jilin Province. One official in Dunhua stated that an accidental explosion would kill everything, even grass, within a 125-mile radius.

During 1937–45 Japan produced an estimated seven million chemical munitions, of which four million are currently unaccounted for. The Chinese government estimates that about two million chemical weapons, totaling almost a hundred tons in weight, were abandoned by Japan in the northeastern provinces of Heilongjiang, Liaoning and Jilin. The Japanese government, however, has conceded only that about seven hundred thousand weapons remain there, most of which were filled with a mustard/

28. Abandoned Japanese chemical weapons from World War II found in China. Courtesy Professor Tsuneishi Keiichi, Kanagawa University.

lewisite mixture. Based on a 1999 estimate from previously unearthed weapons, 18 percent still contain explosives and 53 percent still contain chemical agents.

The Chinese and Japanese governments have agreed on a plan to remediate these weapon sites, ideally by 2007, at an estimated cost of $1.6 billion, to be paid by the government of Japan. In 1999 funds for initiating this project were allocated to a newly established Japanese government department, the Office for Abandoned Chemical Weapons. In 2002 a Japanese team led by the director of the department, Iwatani Shigeo, uncovered 193 chemical shells in Heilongjiang Province and remediated 1.8 tons of contaminated soil, some of which presumably contained arsenic residues from lewisite. It is estimated that the abandoned Japanese weapons have accidentally injured or killed a total of two thousand Chinese since World War II.

Most recently, in Qiqihar on August 4, 2003, one worker was killed when a sixty-year-old Japanese bomb, probably containing a mixture of mustard and lewisite, was accidentally exposed at a construction site. The Japanese government granted about $900,000 in "sympathy money" to the relatives of the man killed. In referring to this incident, Chinese Defense Minister

Cao Gangchuan said, "The chemical weapons left by the invading Japanese armies still remain a threat to the safety of the Chinese people and China's environment."[11]

In April 2003 Chinese and Japanese negotiators agreed that a plant to destroy the chemical weapons would be built in the vicinity of Haerbaling (Jilin Province). In the meantime, unearthed weapons are stored in warehouses.

Apparently, the Japanese army also disposed of some lewisite within its own country during World War II. In 2003 the Japanese government approved a financial aid program to compensate residents of the town of Kamisu, whose drinking water has extremely high arsenic levels attributed to the burial of lewisite munitions in the area.

Canada

When World War II ended, Canada had approximately 2.75 tons of lewisite within its boundaries, mainly at the Defence Research Establishment, Suffield, Experimental Proving Ground Range. It is probably that all of this was United States–made lewisite given to Canada for research, although I have found documentation (dated October 27, 1941) authorizing the transfer of only 1.2 tons. Project Swiftsure, mentioned above, was initiated in 1991 to dispose of Canadian mustard gas, lewisite, nerve agents, and contaminated scrap by incineration or chemical neutralization. The lewisite was chemically neutralized and the byproducts stabilized in concrete for disposal in a marked landfill on-site.

England

During World War II, because the British military never believed that lewisite would be very effective, England only produced 156 tons of lewisite. After the war, most of the lewisite was sent to the War Department Factory at Randle for destruction. By 1968 all of it had been destroyed except for a small quantity that was transferred to Porton Down for defensive research.

Although during World War II the British CWS was never very enthusiastic about using lewisite, some small amount was put into munitions. This became an issue in a court case in 2002 in which Angela Cannings was accused of smothering two of her children. Cannings's attorneys insisted that the children died of "cot death" (Sudden Infant Death Syndrome) associated with exposure to poisonous toxins in the environment from the CWS Porton Down base, less than two hundred yards from her home. Group Captain Ian McPhee testified at the trial that although 1,088 munitions had been found on land around Porton Down in a clearance operation, there was no indication of soil or water contamination. Nevertheless, he further testified that three of the bombs contained lewisite and mustard gas and that the Porton records were incomplete. The jury did not accept Mrs. Cannings's defense, and she was convicted of killing her children. She served twenty months of a life sentence and then was released when her conviction was overturned by an Appeals Court that ruled that her children had probably died of cot death, although not due to lewisite poisoning. A story about Mrs. Cannings's initial conviction and appeal (among other mothers who had similarly been accused of murdering their children in England) was broadcast on the CBS news show *60 Minutes II*, on April 21, 2004.

France, Iraq, Italy, Libya, North Korea, Poland, Yugoslavia

As mentioned in previous chapters, some or all of these countries at one time produced (or are still producing) lewisite. How this material was or is stored, or if destroyed, when, is not currently known.

Many people, possibly hundreds of thousands, live in the vicinity of the lewisite burial and stockpile sites in the United States, Russia, and China. They may well be exposed to low doses of lewisite degradation products including arsenic on a daily basis. Some, but not all, of the possible health consequences are known.

11 Human and Environmental Toxicology

Many people live in close proximity to lewisite deposits in the United States, Russia, and China. Are these individuals at increased risk for contracting life-threatening illnesses? Similarly, do the great quantities of lewisite that have been dumped in bodies of water around the world constitute a hazard for animal (especially marine) and/or human life?

The answers to these two questions are, in turn, based on two additional questions: What are lewisite's degradation products, and how toxic are these products? Unfortunately, the answers to these two questions are dependent on many factors, making absolute determinations of risk impossible.

The degradation of lewisite both on land and in water has been inadequately investigated, and the studies that have been performed have produced confusing and contradictory conclusions. Still, some facts are known, perhaps the most important of which is that lewisite breakdown products contain arsenic. As discussed previously, in the presence of moisture lewisite rapidly undergoes hydrolysis. This reaction results in the formation of chlorovinylarsonous acid and hydrochloric acid; it proceeds very quickly and is reversible. In the presence of additional quantities of water, the hydrolysis reaction will continue resulting in chlorovinylarsonous oxide (CVAO; see appendix 3).

CVAO is a white powdery substance that is poorly soluble in water. Thus, if an area in which lewisite was deposited was at first very moist and then dries, the resulting lewisite degradation product will most likely be a very stable dry white powder that is easily carried by the wind and that can be ingested by a children putting dirt in their mouths. Further chemical degradation, especially in soils that are high in pH (alkaline soils), may occur, resulting in inorganic arsenic compounds. In seawater, lewisite degradation produces both organic and inorganic arsenic compounds.

In addition to concerns about lewisite's breakdown products, whenever lewisite is manufactured, substantial quantities of arsenic-tainted waste products are also produced, especially associated with the catalyst (typically aluminum or mercury chloride; see appendix 2 for more details).

The toxicity of arsenic compounds varies. Thus, to determine the precise health risks of a lewisite-contaminated area, it is essential that the specific degradation compounds be known. Unfortunately, because of inadequacies in chemical analysis or financial considerations, this is rarely the situation. Nevertheless, it is possible to describe some general symptoms associated with arsenic toxicity.

Ingestion of a large quantity of arsenic results in a metallic taste in the mouth and excessive salivation within about thirty minutes. Subsequent symptoms include vomiting, perspiring, a garlic-like breath odor, and diarrhea. Finally, seizures occur, and death follows from generalized organ failure due to low blood pressure. This occurs because of decreased blood volume when excessive amounts of blood plasma escape from arteries and veins. Similar symptoms of acute intoxication are caused by arsenic entering the body by other routes (surface contact or inhalation), although higher levels of exposure are required to produce symptoms equal to those produced by arsenic ingestion.

It is possible for people living near lewisite-contaminated sites or storage facilities to suffer from the symptoms described above—but that would require direct exposure to lots of lewisite residues. It is more likely that people living near lewisite-contaminated areas would be exposed to relatively chronic, low dose levels of arsenic, through either inhalation (e.g., of dust containing arsenic), skin contact, or ingestion of drinking water. The deleterious health effects caused by chronic arsenic exposure are sometimes referred to as arsenicosis and often do not become evident until after a few years of exposure (e.g., two to five years).

Unfortunately, arsenicosis is endemic in many parts of the world where water supplies are contaminated by arsenic. The most disturbing example is Bangladesh, where thirty-seventy million people currently consume arsenic-contaminated water; the World Health Organization has described this as the largest mass poisoning in history. But other countries face this problem too, including Argentina, Chile, China, Hungary, India, Mexico, Nepal, Pakistan, Thailand, Taiwan, and Vietnam. There are even some localities in the United States where drinking water is contaminated with arsenic.

The most common early signs of chronic arsenic poisoning are muscle weakness and aching, increased skin pigmentation, hardening of the skin, and edema (swelling). Other signs are garlic odor of the breath and perspiration, excessive salivation and sweating, generalized itching, sore throat, nasal discharge, lacrimation (tearing of the eyes), numbness, burning or tingling of the extremities, dermatitis (skin inflammation), formation of white skin patches, and hair loss. Chronic exposure may also lead to diabetes and may cause cancer, especially of the skin, bladder, and lung.

Are there any definitive examples that lewisite has caused arsenic-related illnesses? During World War II, a few thousand Allied soldiers were directly exposed to lewisite and mustard. In 1991 the CBS television network news magazine *60 Minutes* broadcast a story on the World War II soldiers who had participated in these mustard/lewisite experiments. Mike Wallace, the *60 Minutes* correspondent, interviewed one of them, Nathan Schnurman. Schnurman's saga also was described in a 1993 article in the *Bulletin of Atomic Scientists* and in a video program for the Center for Defense Information.

Schnurman was a seventeen-year-old seaman in training at Bainbridge Naval Station, when he volunteered for "tests of summer clothing" at Edgewood Arsenal. However, when he arrived at EA he was given a gas mask, a protective suit, and rubber boots. The corpsman told Schnurman he would be participating in an experiment involving a combination of mustard and lewisite but would experience no more than a mild to severe sunburn. Schnurman was not concerned, because he did not believe the government would do anything to harm him; he dutifully entered the gas chamber six times, with his mask failing during the sixth test. He called for help but was not allowed to leave the chamber for a few additional minutes, by which time he had vomited into his mask and fainted. "I was carried from the chamber and left for dead by the side of the road. I tried to get up to remove my mask to get a breath of air because I'd thrown up into it." When Schnurman did regain consciousness he related, "My nose was burning, my eyes were burning, my throat was burning."[1] The next day Schnurman was sent home for ten days. During this time his nasal membranes sloughed off and he became ill with pneumonia.

Schnurman appeared to recover from this experience and illness, but in 1948 he became ill and sought medical attention, which included a blood test. His physician, upon seeing the results of the test, told him he had been "poisoned." Schnurman's physical condition deteriorated for the next thirty years (he has been hospitalized approximately two dozen times), and only when he became completely disabled did he finally tell his wife how he had been "poisoned" during the war. By this time his legs were numb, and he had lung, kidney, heart, and eye diseases. In the *60 Minutes* interview,

Wallace asked Schnurman why he waited so long to tell his wife about this experience. Schnurman responded that he had been sworn to secrecy by the Navy about the mustard/lewisite tests.

Recently one of Schnurman's physicians insisted that he seek his medical records from the Department of Defense. Schnurman told his physician that he had previously done so and received a letter from the Navy insisting that there were no records indicating that he had participated in any mustard/lewisite experiments at EA. Furthermore, the *Bulletin* article stated that all of Schnurmann's fourteen attempts to receive compensation from the Veterans Administration had been rejected. During one of these attempts, a clerk commented to another within earshot of Schnurman, "That man thinks he was in World War I."[2]

Schnurman, however, was eventually able to obtain his service records, which showed a gap of two weeks during his training at Bainbridge; that is, the two weeks during which he was at EA and at home. Nevertheless, Schnurman was unsuccessful in the legal suit he filed to obtain compensation for his injuries from the government.

In the *60 Minutes* broadcast Wallace also questioned Anthony J. Principi, deputy secretary of the United States Department of Veterans Affairs, asking why the country had not offered assistance to those servicemen who participated in these tests. Principi responded, "You're absolutely right. They should be praised."[3]

A few days before this *60 Minutes* interview was to be broadcast, the United States Department of Veterans Affairs announced that it was relaxing the rules for the victims of these experiments so that they could receive compensation. Schnurman was given a full disability pension.

Publicity stemming from the Schnurman interviews helped convince the United States Department of Veterans Affairs to sponsor a study of the effects of mustard and lewisite exposure on the World War II volunteers. In the same year as the interview, 1991, the Committee to Survey the Health Effects of Mustard Gas and Lewisite, Division of Health Promotion and Disease Prevention, Institute of Medicine was constituted. The committee was composed of experts in the fields of toxicology, epidemiology, occupational and environmental medicine, ophthalmology, dermatology, oncology, chemistry, and psychology. The committee's specific assignment was to survey the strengths of the association between exposure to these agents (mustard and lewisite) and the development of specific diseases, identify the gaps in the literature, and recommend how these gaps could be filled. To accomplish its goal, the committee met four times, examined nearly 2,000 scientific reports, received input from 13 civilian and military experts and over 250 affected veterans. The committee's endeavors resulted in a 1993 report that was published as a book, *Veterans at Risk: The Health Effects of Mustard Gas and Lewisite.*

The committee castigated the military for the way it recruited and treated the "volunteer-soldiers" who had participated in the experiments. Committee members heard testimony revealing that those who had participated in the chamber tests were commonly told that they would be "testing summer clothing" in exchange for some extra leave time prior to being sent overseas. As Schnurman had said earlier, the soldiers were unaware that they had volunteered for gas chamber experiments until they arrived at the test location and even then were not told what to expect. The committee's report used the terms "lies and half-truths" with reference to how the men were recruited and treated. Some men testified that they were threatened with court-martial if they did not reenter the test chamber. Others testified that they witnessed subjects collapsing within the chamber, never to be seen again. The witnesses assumed that these subjects had died. The volunteers recalled that they had been told that they would be sentenced to prison if they revealed their participation in these tests. Accordingly, most did not inform their wives, parents, family doctors, or anyone else about their poison gas exposure. The committee also noted that the safety records of the bases (arsenals) at which chemical weapons were produced during World War II were the worst in the military during the peak years of production.

Whereas the committee was probably correct in criticizing the manner in which the soldiers were recruited and the World War II tests conducted, it is important to remember that this happened during a time of war in which the future of the country was at stake. At such times the priorities of one's values can be distorted. For example, Harold Stranks, a chemist who was involved in the testing of chemical agents on British "volunteers" at Porton Down, said, "To a large extent, ethics did not occur to you. One finds it very difficult in the present climate to explain what it was like to live through a war." Then, Stranks indicated, it was as if nothing was beyond acceptance, especially if a superior officer ordered it to be done, "You did not think twice if it was thought necessary."[4]

Because of the lack of adequate quantitative data on the amount of chemical agents used in the experiments and the absence of meaningful studies, the committee found it very difficult to accurately assess the long-term consequences to the "volunteers" of having been directly exposed to lewisite and mustard. To overcome the lack of data on the amount, frequency, and duration of agent exposure that individual soldiers had been subjected to, the committee tried to obtain details on the testing regimens. Unfortunately, it then found that "an atmosphere of lingering secrecy still existed in the Department of Defense pertaining to some of the testing programs."[5] The committee was also appalled that no long-term health care monitoring of any kind was provided for any of the soldiers despite knowledge that lewisite and mustard exposure could have long-term effects. Even immediately after the experiments, some of the blistered men were simply released without any instruction as to how to care for their lesions. In addition to hearing from the soldiers who were tested with the agents, the committee also received testimony from CWS soldiers who were assigned the task of handling mustard and/or lewisite.

Much of the committee's concern centered on whether, in the long-term, acute exposure to lewisite could increase the risk of cancer. Indeed, many of the veterans who testified before the committee reported that they had cancers, the most common of which were skin cancers, followed by lung or laryngeal cancers, bladder cancer, and prostate cancer, a distribution of disease that is similar to that which occurs among people who ingest arsenic in their drinking water. The committee concluded that because lewisite induces chromosomal aberrations in one type of cellular assay, and because arsenicals in general have been shown to cause chromosomal breakdown and to enhance the chromosomal damage caused by known carcinogenic compounds, lewisite exposure could increase the risk of cancer. However, the committee specifically stated that the evidence is insufficient to establish a causal relationship between lewisite exposure and carcinogenesis. Significantly, the use of arsenic-based drugs to treat syphilis during the 1930s and 1940s was not associated with an increased rate of cancer in the patients.

The soldiers who were exposed to mustard gas and lewisite suffered a number of nonmalignant ailments, the most frequent being pulmonary and respiratory diseases including asthma, chronic bronchitis, emphysema, laryngitis, sinusitis, and bouts of pneumonia and respiratory infections. Cardiovascular problems, including heart attack, stroke, and hypertension also occurred. Additionally, there were reports of gastrointestinal diseases and stomach ulcers, and some veterans reported neurological problems such as multiple sclerosis, abnormal sensory loss, and chronic pain. Some of the men reported sexual problems associated with scarring of their genital region from the tests. It is important to note that the committee was unable to properly compare these reported conditions with a nonexposed population because of the uncontrolled manner in which the data were collected.

Although the committee concluded that mustard gas caused respiratory cancers, leukemia, corneal ulcerative disease, chronic respiratory diseases, skin cancers, skin pigmentation and depigmentation, chronic skin ulceration, scar formation, bone marrow depression, and immune system dysfunction, it could not demonstrate that lewisite caused health problems other than respiratory diseases. However, the committee also noted that any corneal scarring caused by lewisite would persist after recovery. There simply were not enough data to determine whether or not exposure to lewisite caused long-term adverse effects on the skin, or if there was any reproductive toxicity or effects on gastrointestinal, hematological, or neurological systems. The committee recommended that the human subjects involved in these tests be, if possible, identified and notified of the potential health risks associated with their exposure. Although this was not done, the United States Department of Veterans Affairs website does list the conditions whereby veterans exposed to these agents may be eligible for compensation.

In a related investigation, 363 of the "volunteers" were interviewed in 1996 to assess whether they suffered from post-traumatic stress disorder as a result of their participation in the mustard and lewisite tests during World War II. Thirty-two percent were found to have full post-traumatic stress disorder, and 10 percent had partial disorder. These percentages are higher than that of combat victims.

Although not definitive, *Veterans at Risk* and the more recent study strongly suggest that some of the men exposed to lewisite as part of America's military testing during World War II did suffer long-term detrimental health effects. As described previously, similar lewisite and mustard tests were done in England, Canada, Australia, and India with presumably similar long-term health effects. In light of these possible detrimental health effects to the approximately thirty-seven hundred Canadian volunteers, the Canadian government is paying each $24,000. I have found no indication that any of the other countries have provided such blanket compensation.

In 1996 Oak Ridge National Laboratory (ORNL), at the request of the United States Army, studied lewisite's biological properties and proposed that the highest daily dosage of lewisite that humans could endure without detrimental effects was 0.0001 mg/kg body weight.

The ORNL's finding was primarily based on a 1989 study by Sasser and colleagues in which lewisite was intubated into the forestomach of rats. The ORNL determination was based on the maximum dosage administered to the rats over varying periods (three to thirteen weeks) divided by what is known as "uncertainty factors," which are used to extrapolate animal data to humans. The Environmental Risk Assessment Program, which represents a multiagency group (Environmental Protection Agency, departments of Defense and Energy), accepted the ORNL recommendation based on both the rat study and its belief (erroneous, see above) that lewisite in the environment primarily degrades to inorganic arsenic. The army provisionally accepted the results of the ORNL study pending further evaluation by the National Research Council.

The NRC evaluated the ORNL's finding in 2000 and concluded that it is flawed. Instead of basing its estimate for the minimum allowable daily lewisite exposure on the rat study, the NRC used a 1987 study by Hackett and colleagues in which rabbits were administered lewisite by stomach intubation at six to nineteen days of gestation. The NRC expressed the belief that the results of this study indicated that rabbits might be more susceptible to lewisite toxicity than rats and also that lewisite has a toxic effect exceeding that of inorganic arsenic. The NRC concluded that the minimum acceptable daily dosage for lewisite is 0.00001 mg/kg, or one order of magnitude lower than that reached by ORNL. The NRC also indicated that the available animal studies on lewisite toxicity are less than ideal and called for additional studies.

Undoubtedly, chronic arsenic exposure and acute exposure to lewisite can have long-term deleterious effects on health. Is there any evidence that the people who now reside in areas known to be high in arsenic resulting from lewisite dumping have suffered such effects?

Charlie Bermpohl is a sixtyish reporter for a suburban Washington, D.C., newspaper, the *Northwest Current*. With a raincoat and cigar Charlie would be the perfect image of a stereotyped 1930s reporter. Tall, thin, craggy-faced, and ornery, Charlie may claim persistence as his most redeeming characteristic. He wants to learn and describe the complete Spring Valley situation, primarily how much arsenic and other agents were dumped into the ground and whether this dumping has harmed the community's residents. In addition to his dogged questioning of the Corps and his search for relevant military documents, Charlie has conducted an unscientific health survey of some of the residents of Spring Valley. In his survey he found sixty-one houses in which there are or were 171 diseases, including

55 cancers, 33 blood diseases and at least 9 diseases of the thyroid. As an example of the illnesses, in one household he found that the occupant's husband had died of esophageal cancer; her older daughter has irritable bowel disease; her youngest daughter has Grave's disease; a tenant suffered from multiple sclerosis; and her dog died of a blood disease. Charlie readily admits that his data prove nothing. Because of human genetic variability and differences in activities, it is exceedingly difficult to prove a link between environmental toxins and human illnesses. Charlie's data are intriguing and raise suspicions, and they suggest that a comprehensive scientific health survey of Spring Valley is warranted. Other than Charlie's data, there are only the anecdotal reports, such as those presented in chapter 10, by individual residents who believe they have been harmed by their neighborhood. Further, some Spring Valley residents may be reluctant to come forward with any unusual illnesses in their family because they are afraid that such publicity may decrease their property values.

Unfortunately, except for the report of increasing frequency in premature births and hydrocephalus near the lewisite factory at Chapayevsk, there have not been any investigations on the effects of the massive Russian lewisite-related deposits on the health of the residents near the contaminated areas. Similarly, other than acute injuries from exposure to the agents, there are no records detailing any detrimental health effects that Chinese citizens might have experienced from the lewisite the Japanese abandoned in China.

There have been some studies on the health of the workers at the Japanese poison gas factory at Ōkunojima. Unfortunately, because these workers were involved in the production of many agents, it is impossible to distinguish between the effects of lewisite and those of other agents, alone or in combination. In one survey, conducted twenty-five years after the plant closed, when workers were asked about respiratory problems, they reported higher than expected levels of bronchitis and chronic coughs. A different study found that of 488 workers surveyed, 115 exhibited spotty skin pigmentation, and another 22 had developed either skin cancer or Bowen's disease, a precancerous skin condition. Although the authors of the study did not specifically relate Bowen's disease to lewisite exposure, there is the report of the World War II German soldier who developed the same disease after he was accidentally exposed to lewisite (presented in chapter 8). Yet another report found it likely that some of the Ōkunojima workers had higher than expected rates of lung cancer.

What about the health effects of dumping lewisite into the ocean? The

United States stopped ocean dumping chemical weapons partly from concern that the practice could harm the ocean environment and marine life, although there was no evidence that this had occurred. Furthermore, because the United States confined its dumping predominantly to the deep waters of the Atlantic and Pacific (a frigid environment with few lifeforms), the likelihood of lewisite degradation products (i.e., arsenic) entering the food chain or causing severe harm to much marine life via skin absorption seems quite remote. Unfortunately, this is not the case for the ocean dumping of lewisite by the Soviet Union.

As described in chapter 9, the Soviet Union dumped at least twenty thousand tons of lewisite and probably much more in the Arctic Ocean, of which 50 percent comprises continental shelf, a relatively shallow extension of the land mass from nearby continents (tens of meters deep compared to the thousands of meters deep in open ocean). Further, the continental shelf is important for marine life because it is here that sediments from the erosion of land surfaces are washed into the sea by rivers and waves, nourishing microscopic plants and animals. Larger animals, such as fish, feed on these microscopic organisms, and some large Arctic mammals (e.g., polar bears) feed on these fish. The continental shelf contains the highest concentration of plant and animal life in the ocean. Unfortunately, all of the Russian lewisite dump sites in the Arctic are located in the vicinity of the continental shelf. Thus, given the sensitive ecology of this region, it is reasonable that concerns have been raised about the Soviet Union's sea dumping of chemical warfare agents.

In 1997, a 110-page color-illustrated book, *Ocean Dumping of Chemical Munitions: Environmental Effects in Arctic Seas*, was published by an unusual organization named MEDEA. Both the publication and the group were products of the CIA, formed only as a result of prodding by former United States Vice President Al Gore. Prior to his becoming vice president, as a senator from Tennessee, Gore was very interested in national security issues and the environment. He became aware that the Arctic Ocean, because of its strategic importance, had been intensely studied during the Cold War by both the Soviet Union and the United States. Both countries had viewed this region as a potential staging area for World War III, which would probably have involved Soviet Typhoon class submarines rising through the Arctic ice to fire ballistic missiles at United States targets (the ice provides very good cover and impedes detection). Thus, both sides wanted to know as much about the ice and ocean topography of this region as possible.

In May 1990 Gore sent a letter to the CIA asking if it possessed environmental data on the Arctic Ocean. The CIA staff person assigned to respond to the letter was Linda Zall. She determined that, yes, the CIA had volumes of data on the Arctic Ocean, and she began to understand that these data might be useful apart from their military value. After learning that such data existed, Gore asked then CIA Director Robert Gates to allow scientists selected by Zall to peruse the CIA's Arctic data and extract information that would be scientifically useful, but not endanger national security. Gates agreed to grant these scientists security clearances, and thus was MEDEA born. Zall named the group MEDEA after the character in Greek mythology who did not let anything—even her children—stand in her way.

The MEDEA group stated that contamination by the arsenic compounds formed when lewisite breaks down in seawater represented one of the main threats to marine life in the Arctic Ocean. The book also stated that since arsenic can bio-accumulate in the food chain, human health is put at risk when humans eat fish that have themselves eaten contaminated food. Moreover, the likely effect of significant arsenic in sediments would be to reduce biomass and species diversity permanently. Finally, the MEDEA group expressed some concern that there were risks to humans involved in offshore activities such as fishing and oil/gas drilling.

Lewisite dumping both on land and at sea has not been innocuous. The precise risk to human and animal health is difficult, if not impossible, to assess accurately, and there have been few attempts anywhere to do so. People living in lewisite-(arsenic-) contaminated areas will continue to wonder which of their health problems, if any, can be attributed to their government's dismantling of its chemical weapons production programs, and the neutralization and disposal of its chemical agents and their residues.

The United States is currently involved in a "war on terrorism." The final chapter discusses lewisite's role in this war.

12 Lewisite, Terrorism, and the Future

On March 19, 2002, Andrew H. Card, Jr., President George W. Bush's chief of staff, issued a "memorandum for the heads of executive departments and agencies" titled "Action to Safeguard Information Regarding Weapons of Mass Destruction and Other Sensitive Documents Related to Homeland Security." This memo came in response to the September 11, 2001, terrorist attack on the World Trade Center. It stated that government departments or agencies have an obligation to safeguard records that provide information about WMD (i.e., chemical, biological, radiological, and nuclear weapons), *regardless of age.* Card requested that the director of the Information Security Oversight Office and the codirectors of the Justice Department's Office of Information and Privacy prepare specific guidelines for implementing the policy. The guidelines issued allowed for any information, regardless of age, to, in essence, become "classified."

Implementation of Card's memo has resulted in many government documents pertaining to lewisite and other World War I weapons no longer being available for historical research. Locked in a vault at Fort Leonard Wood, Missouri, are approximately fifteen thousand reports pertaining to the work of the CWS work during the First World War. Approximately eighty-two of these documents relate directly or indirectly to lewisite. Four of the more interesting titles are: "Report on Lewisite (Skin Irritant)," "Penetration of Lewisite and Mustard," "Surveillance Tests on Shell Filled with Lewisite," and "Kerosene Treatment of Lewisite." I requested copies of these as well as the seventy-eight other lewisite documents in a Freedom of Information request. The army agreed to copy only seven of them for me, at a cost of $260. I declined the offer as none of the seven appeared (based on their titles) to contain information that I didn't already have.

The stated reason for the army's denial of my request to obtain most of the other seventy-five lewisite documents was the "White House Memo on WMD 19 March 2002," i.e., Card's memo. Other investigators—Richard Albright of the District of Columbia Department of Health, the Environmental Protection Agency official involved with the Spring Valley remediation, and even the historian for the army's own Corps of Engineers, who is also working on the Spring Valley project—have had similar frustrating experiences while attempting to gain access to the World War I materials at the Fort.

Although the intention of Card's memo was certainly good, it will not impede the ability of terrorists to manufacture lewisite if they choose to. Lewisite production information is easily obtainable through public sources, as revealed by this book. A further example of the futility of the government's application of Mr. Card's memo is my quest to obtain a copy of a 1977 two-volume book, *Lehrbuch der Militärchemie* (*Textbook of Military Chemistry*) by Siegfried Franke, which was published in East Germany. Although few libraries own this book, the Technical Library of the United States Army Natick Research and Development Laboratories does possess one. I requested this copy through Interlibrary Loan and received both German-language volumes from the Technical Library. However, after requesting this book, I learned that the CWS had had the book translated into English, and that the English version was available from the Department of Commerce's National Technical Information Service. Unfortunately, when I tried to order the English version, the representative told me that this document had been withdrawn after September 11, presumably as a result of Mr. Card's memo. Apparently, someone in the government believes that terrorists cannot read German!

Any dedicated terrorist group that has within its midst bachelor's level chemists could easily obtain and understand from scientific journal articles all the necessary information to produce lewisite. Lewis himself made this point in 1937 when he was asked to travel to the Soviet Union to help design a lewisite factory there. As described in chapter 6, he declined the invitation but said in a letter that any competent chemical engineer using public sources could design such a plant. Thus, I do not believe that national security has been enhanced by the government's refusal to allow access to relevant documents about lewisite. Rather, all that has been accomplished is the positioning of impediments to pure historical research and to those trying to determine the full extent of the Spring Valley contamination. If anything, the restraints on access have greatly impaired the "security" (used broadly) of the residents of Spring Valley who are still trying to understand the environmental risks associated with living in their neighborhood.

Is it reasonable to believe that some terrorist group would at some time use lewisite? Chemical weapons are the easiest to use of the nuclear, biological, and chemical group of weapons. And, if the purpose of such use would be to create fear, panic, and revulsion, then lewisite, with its ability to cause immediate pain, blisters, and blindness, might be more effective than more deadly agents. Eric Croddy, in his 2002 book *Chemical and Biological Warfare,* states that if a modern military is seeking a low-cost, effective chemical agent that can be mass-produced easily, then mustard and lewisite are the logical choices. Presumably the same could be said for a terrorist group. Croddy continues that although mustard and lewisite would not cause large numbers of deaths, they would put enormous stress on the medical and logistical systems of the attacked country.

Is it realistic that a group of terrorists could synthesize lewisite? Laboratory quantities could certainly be produced. Production of larger quantities would take more effort, but would also seem reasonable with chemical engineering expertise. Further, as Croddy emphasizes, the basic ingredients are inexpensive and readily available. A terrorist group would be subjecting itself to some risk of injury in the process of making lewisite, but simple precautions could probably result in a reasonably safe procedure. There is also the possibility that terrorists could hire experts to produce chemical weapons for them, perhaps from the pool of under- or unemployed chemical weapons specialists living in the former Soviet Union, Iraq, or some other country.

It is also feasible, and perhaps more likely, that a terrorist group could obtain lewisite from a rogue nation. Iraq, under Saddam Hussein, might have been a primary source. However, that is clearly no longer the case. North Korea is another possibility. And lewisite might also be obtained from Sudan, if the country does indeed possess chemical agents. As of March 28, 2004, former United Nations weapons inspector Hans Blix estimated that thirty-five to forty countries still have chemical weapons stockpiles, although he did not speculate on how many of these countries possess lewisite. Terrorists could also steal lewisite from old stockpiles, most likely in the former Soviet Union. Or it is even possible that they could find a cache of old World War II Japanese weapons in China.

The possibility exists that a terrorist group has already obtained chemical weapons from Sudan. Former United States National Security Advisor Sandy Berger told a press conference in February 1999 that "we know bin Laden was seeking chemical weapons," and "we know that he had worked with the Sudanese government to acquire chemical weapons."[1] There have also been reports of contacts between bin Laden and Iraqi personnel who were responsible for chemical weapons.

It does not seem unreasonable that a dedicated group of terrorists would be able to obtain lewisite one way or another. Could they then get it into the United States? Smuggling large quantities of lewisite would seem difficult, but possible, for a group with sufficient funds. Obviously, the larger the amount the more difficult the task becomes; but it might only take a few gallons of lewisite to accomplish some missions. On the other hand, lewisite could perhaps be made surreptitiously in the United States in the first place.

Delivery would probably be the most difficult aspect, for a terrorist group, of using lewisite. Certainly it could be detonated from an explosive shell in an enclosed location, for example, a subway car. Lewisite vapors could also probably be effectively delivered via a building's heating and/or air conditioning systems. Even simply spreading it on the ground in a public area such as a park could create serious injury and panic.

The question of lewisite use by terrorists must always be considered relative to whether such groups would ever choose to use chemical weapons rather than explosives. Explosives are more easily handled and the pertinent expertise is more readily available than for chemical weapons. Nevertheless, some experts have predicted that to increase the terror value of their attacks, fringe groups will eventually switch to chemical and biological weapons, arguing that the effects of poisonous gas use must be measured not merely in statistical terms (e.g., number of injuries and deaths, costs of medical care, etc.) but also by the indirect psychological effects resulting from the changes in behavior associated with the fear of exposure.

With a few limited exceptions, terrorist groups have not yet used poisonous weapons. But, considering the risk, it does not seem imprudent for United States communities to continue to prepare for a terrorist attack based on lewisite. Such preparation involves developing and practicing procedures to be used in a lewisite attack. One such exercise was conducted on June 26, 2002, in Lemon Grove, California, a part of San Diego County. A "terrorist" entered Palm Middle School's auditorium and exploded three bombs containing mock lewisite. Two students pretended to be "fatally" burned and twenty-three pretended to be injured. Nearly two hundred county safety and medical personnel were involved in the exercise, which was directed by Steve Wood. When I asked Mr. Wood why he chose lewisite for the exercise, he said that whereas many communities choose more toxic agents, such as sarin or VX, he chose lewisite because it has the potential to cause more serious injuries with fewer deaths than those agents, thereby requiring much higher "staffing."

Another lewisite training exercise was staged on February 20, 2002, in St. Petersburg, Florida. The scenario for this exercise was that an international volleyball tournament was under way at the Bayfront Center when an explosion occurred releasing lewisite. The exercise involved 200 emergency personnel and 120 "victims." I was able to obtain a videotape of the exercise in which the victims were shown removing their outer clothing and undergoing water decontamination procedures. None, however, of the mock victims were acting as if they were in great pain, and none were showing any signs of eye pain, which would be the first and most immediate consequence of exposure to lewisite. Apparently the victims needed some acting lessons! Similar full-scale lewisite exercises have been conducted in twelve other major United States cities since February 2002, including Tacoma, Washington; Lincoln, Nebraska; and Lexington, Kentucky.

The necessity for lewisite preparedness in American cities is at such a level that it is now possible to buy fake lewisite for the training exercises. The material, sold by Servamer Corporation of Henderson, Nevada, is called TAGGER. TAGGER is available for all the major chemical warfare agents, with each mock agent duplicating the viscosity of the real one. TAGGER is designed to be sprayed on "victims," who are then decontaminated. Because TAGGER fluoresces under ultraviolet light, emergency workers can perform a post-contamination evaluation of the effectiveness of their decontamination regimens.

In addition to the preparations for lewisite attacks, some new treatments for lewisite injuries have been developed. As recently as 2002 an article in the journal *Burns* described an improved procedure, lasablation, for treating lewisite burns using a laser. Similarly, an article in the *Journal of Chromatography* in that same year described a novel sensitive technique for the detection of chlorovinylarsonous acid in humans. This technique could be used to measure CVAA exposure levels following lewisite's use in warfare, in a terrorist attack or by chemical workers involved in its cleanup.

Approximately a hundred years ago lewisite was inadvertently born in a chemistry laboratory at Catholic University of America. Father Nieuwland could never have predicted that his innocent experiments would result in the development of a compound considered a weapon of mass destruction a century later. Remarkably, there is no evidence that lewisite would actually be effective as a weapon of mass destruction, at least on the battlefield, and even its use as a weapon of terror is uncertain. On the other hand, fear of lewisite use resulted in British Anti-Lewisite, which has had a beneficial effect on the health of many individuals.

Will lewisite still be able to produce eleven thousand "Google" hits (or the equivalent) a hundred years from now? Or, will lewisite finally fade out of the current lexicon and terrorism awareness into the realm of ancient weapons, such as the crossbow? The United States military considers lewisite an outdated and ineffective weapon. Nevertheless, when I tried to obtain the lewisite.com domain name on the internet, I was not surprised to find that the United States Army already "owned" the name. If you type "lewisite.com" into your browser's address bar, it is automatically forwarded to the army's Center for Health Promotion and Preventive Medicine. Searching for lewisite on that page yields twenty-eight hits.

Clearly lewisite is still of active concern to the United States military. Accordingly, I suggest that its amazing resilience over the past century gives some reason to expect that "lewisite" may still appear one hundred years from now in a *New York Times* crossword puzzle, as it did in a Sunday edition in 2003 (8 down; "poison gas").

Appendix 1
Lewisite's Chemical and Physical Properties

Chemical Formula	$C_2H_2AsCl_3$
Chemical Abstracts Registry #	541-25-3
Synonyms	Dichloro-(2-chlorovinyl) arsine
	Arsine, (2-chlorovinyl) dichloro-
	Chlorovinylarsine dichloride
	2-Chlorovinyldichloroarsine
	2-Chlorovinylarsonous dichloride
	Beta-Chlorovinyldichloroarsine
American Code Names	L
	M-1
	G-34
	Methyl
Type of Chemical Agent	Arsenical (vesicant)
Appearance	Oily, colorless liquid (pure)
	Amber to dark brown liquid (impure)
Odor	Geraniums
Freezing/Melting Point	−18.2 to 0.1°C (depending on purity)
Boiling Point	190°C @ 760 mm Hg
Molecular Weight	207.32
Solubility	Negligible in water
	Soluble in ordinary organic solvents
Vapor Pressure	0.22 mm Hg @ 20°C
Specific Gravity (Liquid Density)	1.89 @ 20°C ($H_2O = 1$)
Vapor Density	7.1 (air = 1.0)
Flash Point	Does not flash
Volatility	2,500 mg/m^3 @ 20°C
Stability	Stable in steel or glass below 50°C

Source: ATSDR website, "Medical Management Guidelines"; CDC website, "Emergency Response Card"; SBCCOM website, "MSDS on Lewisite"; Pechura and Rall, *Veterans at Risk* (when there was a difference in values the MSDS by SBCCOM was used).

Appendix 2
Lewisite Production

The chemical process that was used to produce lewisite during World War II is detailed in a Department of Justice document pertaining to the waste product remediation done at Rocky Mountain Arsenal. Production was based on a process using mercury chloride as a catalyst, whereas earlier production (e.g., World War I) had used aluminum chloride. At all the arsenals, the production processes included synthesizing the two primary compounds involved in the production of lewisite: arsenic trichloride and acetylene.

ARSENIC TRICHLORIDE
1. Reactions to Make Disulfur Dichloride
Chlorine (Cl_2) was produced in two ways: some made by re-vaporizing liquid chlorine that was purchased as a raw material; most, however, was made by electrolyzing aqueous brine (NaCl; salt) solutions:

$$2\ NaCl + 2\ H_2O \rightarrow H_2 + \textbf{Cl}_2 + 2\ NaOH$$

Disulfur dichloride (S_2Cl_2) was then made by reacting sulfur and chlorine.

$$S_8 + 4\ Cl_2 \rightarrow 4\ \textbf{S}_2\textbf{Cl}_2$$

2. Reaction to Make Arsenic Trichloride
The disulfur dichloride (S_2Cl_2) produced in #1 was reacted with purchased arsenic trioxide (As_2O_3) to give arsenic trichloride ($AsCl_3$).

$$16\ As_2O_3 + 48\ S_2Cl_2 \rightarrow 32\ \textbf{AsCl}_3 + 9\ S_8 + 24\ SO_2$$

Not detailed here is the manufacture of an intermediate product, thionyl chloride ($SOCl_2$), which improved the efficiency of the production of disulfur dichloride.

ACETYLENE
3. Reaction to Make Acetylene
Calcium carbide (CaC_2) was reacted with water to produce acetylene (C_2H_2).

$$CaC_2 + 2\ H_2O \rightarrow \textbf{C}_2\textbf{H}_2 + Ca(OH)_2$$

LEWISITE

4. Reaction to Make Lewisite

The arsenic trichloride ($AsCl_3$) made in #2 was reacted with the acetylene (C_2H_2) made in #3 with a catalyst (aqueous hydrochloric acid solution of mercury chloride) to produce lewisite ($C_2H_2AsCl_3$; can also be represented as $ClCH=CHAsCl_2$).

$$AsCl_3 + C_2H_2 \xrightarrow{\text{catalyst}} \mathbf{C_2H_2AsCl_3}$$

Source: USDOJ, "Assessment of CERCLA."

Appendix 3
Lewisite Degradation

The primary issue pertaining to lewisite degradation is its reaction upon contact with water (soil environments, except in arid regions, can be expected to have relative humidities in excess of 90 percent). Lewisite hydrolysis (reaction with water) is critical not only for understanding lewisite degradation, but also whether lewisite would have been effective on the battlefield.

The complexity associated with lewisite hydrolysis begins with the differences found with each type of lewisite. L1 and L2 will hydrolyze, but L3 will not because there is no "free" chlorine atom that can be replaced by water. Thus, L3 can remain indefinitely in the environment as L3. Pertaining to L1 and L2, if either compound is exposed to a limited amount of water (for example, soil moisture, water vapor in the air, or sweat on human skin) the hydrolysis reaction is:

$$ClCH=CHAsCl_2 + 2\ H_2O \leftrightarrow ClCH=CHAs(OH)_2 + 2\ HCl.$$

In words, this process is: lewisite (L1 in this case) reacted with water yields an arsenic-containing compound called chlorovinylarsonous acid (CVAA) and hydrochloric acid (HCl). This reaction proceeds very quickly and is reversible, depending on how much water and HCl are present.

In contrast to the limited water situation described above, if water is abundant (for example, pouring lewisite into a river, lake, or ocean, or after it has spent some time in the soil) the reaction will proceed further:

$$ClCH=CHAs(OH)_2 \leftrightarrow ClCH=CHAsO + H_2O.$$

This reaction indicates that CVAA will decompose to form a compound called lewisite oxide (chlorovinylarsonous oxide; CVAO) and water. This reaction will occur because CVAO is a far more chemically stable compound than CVAA.

CVAO can exist in either monomeric or polymeric forms. In the case of L2, only the monomeric form will result. CVAA and the monomer form of CVAO can only exist in solution, whereas the polymer is virtually insoluble in water. Depending on a variety of conditions including relative volumes of water and lewisite, CVAO may remain a monomer and be dissolved in water or may precipitate out of solution as a white powder polymer. Regardless, as the solution dries, all of the CVAO will be converted to the white powder polymer. The conversion of lewisite to CVAO is not reversible unless there is excess acid present.[1]

The ultimate meaning of these reactions in terms of lewisite residues is that if lewisite is deposited in the soil, assuming sufficient moisture is present, it will be converted to CVAO, which is a white powder. CVAO may undergo further degradation if the soil is strongly alkaline, including the formation of inorganic arsenic compounds.[2]

---

1. Munro et al., "Sources, fate and toxicology"; Pechura and Rall, *Veterans at Risk.*
2. Goldman and Dacre, "Lewisite"; Munro et al., "Sources, fate and toxicology."

Notes

Abbreviations

AU	American University
AUES	American University Experimental Station
BAL	British Anti-Lewisite
CUA	Catholic University of America
CWC	Chemical Weapons Convention
CWS	Chemical Warfare Service
DPG	Dugway Proving Ground
EA	Edgewood Arsenal
EPA	Environmental Protection Agency
HA	Huntsville Arsenal
NDRC	National Defense Research Committee
NRC	National Research Council
OPCW	Organization for the Prohibition of Chemical Weapons
ORNL	Oak Ridge National Laboratory
PBA	Pine Bluff Arsenal
RMA	Rocky Mountain Arsenal
WMD	Weapon of Mass Destruction

1. 1878: Two Stars are Born

Direct Citations

1. Nieuwland, "Some Reactions," 123–24.
2. Lewis, "Why I became a chemist," 100.
3. Lewis, "Certain Organic Compounds," 2.
4. Lewis, "How the American chemists," 5.
5. "Hundreds attend tablet unveiling," *Gridley Herald*.
6. "Prof. Lewis honored," *Alumni News*.
7. "Four alumni chemists," *Washington Alumnus*, 10.
8. Lewis, "Why I became a chemist," 105.

Sources

Nieuwland's Role in Invention of Duprene: Inventor Hall of Fame website, "Inventor Profile."

Biography of Nieuwland: "Dr. J. A. Nieuwland," *New York Times;* Froning, "Father Nieuwland"; Hartnett, "Father Nieuwland"; Hope, *Notre Dame;* "Julius A.

Nieuwland obituary," *Catholic World;* "Julius A. Nieuwland obituary," *Commonweal;* Lyon, "Father Nieuwland"; Lyon, "Julius Arthur Nieuwland obituary"; May, "Early days of chemistry"; Notre Dame Athletics website, "Notre Dame Football Memories"; Notre Dame website, "Congregation of the Holy Cross"; Rutherford, "Julius A. Nieuwland."

Acetylene: Miller, *Acetylene;* Nieuwland, "Some Reactions."

Nieuwland's Experiments with Acetylene: Froning, "Father Nieuwland"; Nieuwland, "Some Reactions"; "Notre Dame dean," *South Bend Tribune;* Rutherford, "Julius A. Nieuwland."

Lewisite Characteristics: CDC website, "Emergency Response Card"; SBCCOM website, "MSDS on Lewisite."

Nieuwland's Reflections on His Role in Developing Lewisite: "Priest on poison," *Time.*

Biography of Lewis: Biographical record, Winford Lee Lewis (from Northwestern University Archives); "Capture Him with Tear Gas!" *Cleveland Plain Dealer; Evanston News Index,* Jan. 8, 1918; *Evanston News Index,* Jan. 18, 1918; "Four alumni chemists," *Washington Alumnus;* Lee Harwood (daughter of W. Lee Lewis), e-mail message to author, Apr. 20, 2003; Lee Harwood, e-mail message to author, Mar. 22, 2004; Wilson Harwood (husband of Lee Harwood), e-mail message to author, Apr. 23, 2003; Hurd, "Development of chemical research"; Hurd, "The scientific contribution"; "Kraybill heads research," *Chicago Tribune;* Lewis, "Certain Organic Compounds"; Myrtilla Lewis (wife of W. Lee Lewis), notes about job offers for W. Lee Lewis, Dec. 29, 1918 (from Phil Reiss); Lewis, "Some features"; W. Lee Lewis, telegram to Mrs. W. Lee Lewis, Oct. 9, 1917 (from Phil Reiss); Lewis, "Why I became a chemist"; "Lewis-Hughes grenade," *Cleveland Plain Dealer;* E. J. Ragsdale, letter to W. Lee Lewis, Dec. 22, 1917 (from Phil Reiss); Resume, Winford Lee Lewis (from Northwestern University Archives); "Tear gas bomb," *Evanston News Index;* "W. Lee Lewis, the new chairman," *Chemical Bulletin;* "Winford Lee Lewis," in *National Cyclopaedia;* "Winford Lee Lewis obituary," Unidentified newspaper.

1920s and 1930s Reports on Lewis's Role in Lewisite Development: "America had deadliest poison," *Philadelphia Press;* "America reveals deadliest poison," *Shreveport Times;* "American gas," *Columbus Tribune;* "Another new gas?" *Chemical Bulletin;* "Armistice saved German people," *New York Herald;* "Chicagoan finds deadliest drug," Unidentified newspaper; "Controversy over poison gas," *Washington Post;* "Deadliest gas," *Nashville Tennessean;* "Deadliest gas was never used," *Terre Haute Star;* "Deadliest poison known," *Barber County Index;* "Deadly American gas," *Washington Post;* "Deadly drug ready," *Minneapolis Tribune;* "Famed inventor former Gridleyan," *Gridley Herald;* "Former Oroville man," Unidentified newspaper; "Former University student," *Seattle Post Intelligencer;* "Had deadliest gas," *New York Times;* "Interior Exposition," *Washington Post;* "Is Chicago teacher," Unidentified newspaper; "Lewis invents deadliest gas," *Northwestern Alumni;* "Lewisite," *Topeka Capital;* " 'Lewisite,' deadliest of poisons," *Cincinnati Tribune;* " 'Lewisite' deadliest poison known," *St. Louis Republic;* " 'Lewisite,' deadliest poison yet discovered," *Commerce and Finance;* "'Lewisite' is revealed," *New York Times;* "'Lewisite' would have annihilated," *Little Rock Gazette;* "Man who found deadliest poison," Unidentified newspaper; "Methyl, deadliest of gases," *Philadelphia Ledger;* "New invention," *Central Christian Advocate;* "New poison gas," *Chicago Tribune;* "Poison that can wipe," *Mid-Cumberland and North Westmorland Herald;* "Poison that may kill," Unidentified newspaper from London; Stockbridge, "War inventions"; "Terrible U.S. war poison," *Detroit News;* "Truce saves million lives," *San Francisco Examiner;* "U.S. had awful preparation," *Punxsutawney Spirit;* "W. Lee Lewis inventor," *Evanston News Index;* "Yankee gas," *Salt Lake City Herald.*

Lewis Honored for Lewisite Development: "Hundreds attend tablet unveiling," *Gridley Herald;* Milt and Kathy McClung (Family History Center, Gridley, California), e-mail message to author, Apr. 15, 2002; "Prof. Lewis honored," *Alumni News.*

Lewis's Character and Interests: Eisenschiml, "W. Lee Lewis obituary"; Lee Harwood (daughter of W. Lee Lewis), e-mail message to author, Mar. 22, 2004; Lee Harwood, e-mail message to author, Apr. 20, 2003; Lee Harwood, e-mail message to author, May 26, 2003; Lewis, "Why I became a chemist."

2. The Poisonous Yellow Cloud and the American Response

Direct Citations

1. Hessel, Hessel, and Martin, *Chemistry in Warfare*, 82.
2. Dixon, "Catholic University of America," 151.
3. Thomas J. Shahan, letter to "Students, Alumni and Parents of Catholic University," Apr. 26, 1917 (from USACE, "Defense Environmental Restoration Program: Catholic University," appendix A).
4. Jones, "Role of Chemists," 120.

Sources

History of Chemical Weapons Use in World War I: Bancroft, *Bancroft's History;* BOC Gases website, "MSDS on Phosgene"; Cook, *No Place to Run;* Croddy, *Chemical and Biological Warfare;* Emedicine website, Noltkamper and Burgher; Evans, *Gassed;* Haber, *Poisonous Cloud;* Heller, *Chemical Warfare;* Hershberg, *James B. Conant;* Hessel, Hessel, and Martin, *Chemistry in Warfare;* Jones, "Role of Chemists"; Pechura and Rall, *Veterans at Risk;* Smart, "History of chemical and biological warfare"; Spiers, *Chemical Weaponry;* Warthin and Weller, *Medical Aspects.*

Beginnings of the United States Chemical Warfare Program: Heller, *Chemical Warfare;* Jones, "Role of Chemists."

CUA and its Role in the Early Chemical Weapons Program: Dixon, "Catholic University of America"; Gillis, *Roman Catholicism in America;* Thomas J. Shahan, letter to "Students, Alumni and Parents of Catholic University," Apr. 26, 1917 (from USACE, "Defense Environmental Restoration Program: Catholic University"); USACE, "Defense Environmental Restoration Program: Catholic University"; Walch, *Catholicism in America.*

AU and its Role in the Early Chemical Weapons Program: Albright, "American University Experimental Station"; Bancroft, *Bancroft's History;* Burrell, "Contributions"; Gordon, Sude, and Overbeck, "Chemical testing"; Hershberg, *James B. Conant;* Jones, "Role of Chemists"; USACE, "Brief History"; USACE, "Remedial Investigation Report."

Birth of the CWS: Jones, "Role of Chemists."

William Sibert: Arlington National Cemetery website, "William Luther Sibert"; Clark, *William L. Sibert.*

3. The Hunt for a New King

Direct Citations

1. Burrell, "Contributions," 100.
2. Lewis, "Report for the Week," (from USACE, "Defense Environmental Restoration Program: Catholic University," appendix A).
3. Julius A. Nieuwland, letter to Amos A. Fries, Nov. 14, 1922 (from University of Notre Dame Archives).
4. "Notre Dame dean," *South Bend Tribune.*
5. "Dr. J. A. Nieuwland," *New York Times.*
6. Wood, "The chemistry," 331–32.
7. W. Lee Lewis, letter to Amos A. Fries, Jan. 15, 1929 (from National Archives and Records Administration).
8. W. Lee Lewis, letter to Amos A. Fries, Dec. 11, 1929 (from National Archives and Records Administration).
9. Lewis and Perkins, "Beta-chlorovinyl chloroarsines," 290.
10. Meyer, *Der Gaskampf,* 426.

Sources

Development of Lewisite at CUA and Early Testing: "Chemical Warfare Agents"; Green and Price, "Chlorovinylchloroarsines"; Jones, "Offense Chemical Research Section"; Jones, "Role of Chemists"; Lewis, "Certain Organic Compounds"; Lewis, "How the American chemists"; Lewis, "Report for the Week"; May, "Early days of chemistry"; "Method for Manufacture of Lewisite"; Julius A. Nieuwland, letters to (and from) W. Lee Lewis, Sept. 28, 1922, to Sept. 7, 1923 (from University of Notre Dame Archives).

Mustard Gas and Characteristics of an Effective Poison Gas: Pechura and Rall, *Veterans at Risk;* Waitt, "No super war gas!"

Previous Research with Arsenic: BOC Gases website, "MSDS on Arsenic Trichloride"; CDC website, "International Chemical Safety Cards"; Moore, *Gas Attack!;* Prentiss, *Chemicals in War.*

Griffin's Involvement in Lewisite Development: Burrell, "Contributions"; Amos A. Fries, letter to George Bagg, Apr. 26, 1923 (from National Archives and Records Administration); Amos A. Fries, letter to William L. Sibert, Mar. 12, 1923 (from National Archives and Records Administration); Rutherford, "Julius A. Nieuwland."

Properties of L1, L2, and L3: Aldstadt et al., "Phase I Final Report"; Fries and West, *Chemical Warfare*; Lewis and Perkins, "Beta-chlorovinyl chloroarsines"; Prentiss, *Chemicals in War*; SBCCOM website, "MSDS on Lewisite."

Hazards of Working with Lewisite: Jones, "Offense Chemical Research Section"; "Lewis tells perils," *Evanston News Index*.

Credit for Lewisite Discovery: Dr. J. A. Nieuwland," *New York Times*; Amos A. Fries, letter to W. Lee Lewis, Dec. 26, 1928 (from National Archives and Records Administration); W. Lee Lewis, letter to Amos A. Fries, Dec. 11, 1928 (from National Archives and Records Administration); W. Lee Lewis, letter to Amos A. Fries, Jan. 15, 1929 (from National Archives and Records Administration); W. Lee Lewis, letter to Amos A. Fries, Jan. 22, 1929 (from National Archives and Records Administration); Lewis and Perkins, "Beta-chlorovinyl chloroarsines"; Julius A. Nieuwland, letter to Amos A. Fries, Nov. 14, 1922 (from University of Notre Dame Archives); "Notre Dame dean," *South Bend Tribune*; Shea, "Father Nieuwland"; Wood, "The chemistry."

Lewisite Credited with Helping to End the War: "Deadliest gas of war," *Washington Star*; Amos A. Fries, letter to W. Lee Lewis, Dec. 26, 1928 (from National Archives and Records Administration).

Lewis's Description of the Process He Pioneered: Lewis and Perkins, "Beta-chlorovinyl chloroarsines"; Lewis and Stiegler, "Beta-chlorovinyl-arsines."

Early German Lewisite Experiments and German Assessment of it's Potential: Büscher, *Green and Yellow Cross*; Ian MacKenzie (Ministry of Defense, London), letter to author, July 1, 2003; "Minutes of British Chemical Warfare Committee"; Meyer, *Der Gaskampf*; Wachtel, *Chemical Warfare*; Wieland and Bloemer, "Einige beiträge."

Lewis's Character: Eisenschiml, "W. Lee Lewis obituary"; Lee Harwood (daughter of W. Lee Lewis), e-mail message to author, May 26, 2003; Lewis, "Certain Organic Compounds"; Lewis, "How the American chemists"; Lewis, "Is the Elimination"; Lewis, "Why I became a chemist "; W. Lee Lewis, letter to Mr. A W. Benedict, Oct. 28, 1921 (from Phil Reiss); W. Lee Lewis, letter to Malcolm Moore, May 8, 1923 (from Phil Reiss); W. Lee Lewis, letter to Mr. Norris, Dec. 1, 1920 (from Phil Reiss).

4. The American University Experimental Station

Direct Citations

1. Hershberg, *James B. Conant*, 19.
2. Pringle, "Profiles," 24.
3. Albright, "Final Report," 6.

Sources

Conant, and Lewisite Research and Development at the AUES: Burrell, "Contributions"; Fries and West, *Chemical Warfare;* Hershberg, *James B. Conant;* Jones, "Role of Chemists."

Codes of Chemical Warfare Agents: Burn, "Chemical Warfare Agents"; Farrow, *Gas Warfare;* Reid Kirby (chemical/biological warfare expert, St. Louis, Missouri), letter to author, Apr. 21, 2004.

George Temple as Test Subject at the AUES: "Camp A.U.," *American University Eagle.*

Accidents and Casualties during Lewisite Development at the AUES: Burrell, "Contributions"; Pringle, "Profiles."

Animal Testing at the AUES: Bancroft, *Bancroft's History;* "Camp A.U.," *American University Eagle;* Gordon, Sude, and Overbeck, "Chemical testing"; Jaffe, "Spring Valley"; Vedder, *Medical Aspects.*

Lewisite Incident Involving Senator Scott: "D.C. family is gassed," *Washington Times;* George A. Burrell, letter to H. C. Newcomer, Sept. 5, 1918 (from USACE); Gordon, Sude, and Overbeck, "Chemical testing"; Lewis, "Certain Organic Compounds"; "N. B. Scott gassed," *Washington Post;* W. L. Sibert, letter to W. M. Black, Sept. 12, 1918 (from National Archives and Records Administration); West Virginia Division of Culture and History website, "West Virginia Archives."

Secrecy Surrounding Lewisite: Albright, "Final Report"; Lewis, "Certain Organic Compounds."

Life at the AUES: Albright, "American University Experimental Station"; "All to the mustard," *Retort;* Bancroft, *Bancroft's History;* Burrell, "Contributions"; Gordon, Sude, and Overbeck, "Chemical testing"; Jones, "Role of Chemists"; Tarbell and Tarbell, *Roger Adams.*

5. Willoughby

Direct Citations

1. "Then & Now in Willoughby," 27.
2. Herty, "Reserves of Chemical Warfare Service," 2.
3. Conant, *My Several Lives,* 49.
4. Lewis, "How the American chemists," 49.
5. J. W. Lyon, letter to C. H. Memory, May 27, 1927 (from National Archives and Records Administration).
6. C. H. Memory, letter to Chemical Warfare Service, June 23, 1927 (from National Archives and Records Administration).

Sources

Chemical Warfare Research and Production in Cleveland and the Role of Development Division: Dorsey, "Contributions"; *National in the World War;* USACE, "Former Cleveland Plant."

Consideration of Private Companies as Developers of Chemical Warfare Agents: Jones, "Role of Chemists."

Frank Dorsey: Cleveland Public Library website, "The Necrology File"; Dorsey, "Contributions"; *National in the World War; Official Roster of Ohio.*

Estimation of Lewisite's Potential and Feasibility: Burrell, "Contributions"; Mount, "Gas intended"; *National in the World War;* "Our super-poison gas," *New York Times.*

Dorsey's and Conant's Roles in Developing the Willoughby Plant: *National in the World War.*

Willoughby and the Choice of the Ben Hur Site for the Lewisite Plant: "Ben Hur prospect looms," *Willoughby Republican;* City of Willoughby, Ohio website, "Faith Corrigan's"; "Government takes over," *Willoughby Republican;* "Historical Willoughby"; *National in the World War;* "Then & Now in Willoughby."

Difficulties in Renovation/Construction of the Willoughby Plant: "Historical Willoughby"; "Laborer killed," *Willoughby Independent;* Lewis, "Certain Organic Compounds"; "Man killed in accident," *Willoughby Republican; National in the World War;* "Our super-poison gas," *New York Times.*

Life at Willoughby and the Reaction of Willoughby Residents to the Soldiers: "Andrews gymnasium opened," *Willoughby Republican;* "Club rooms for soldiers," *Willoughby Independent;* "Grand piano lent," *Willoughby Republican;* "Houses taken over," *Willoughby Republican; National in the World War;* "Now we know," *Willoughby Independent;* "O. E. S. again acts as hostess," *Willoughby Independent;* "Open letter," *Willoughby Independent;* "Reception for solider boys," *Willoughby Republican;* "Red Cross notes," *Willoughby Independent;* "Red Cross notes," *Willoughby Republican;* "Red Cross votes," *Willoughby Republican;* "Red Cross, Willoughby branch," *Willoughby Republican;* "Rooms for officers," *Willoughby Republican;* "Second O. E. S. party," *Willoughby Republican;* Simpson, "Nineteen-Eighteen in Willoughby"; "Soldiers entertained at supper," *Willoughby Independent;* "Willoughby entertains her soldiery," *Willoughby Independent.*

Security at Lewisite Plant: Jones, "Role of Chemists"; Mount, "Gas intended"; *National in the World War;* Stockbridge, *Yankee Ingenuity;* Michael Vickio (Society for the Historical Preservation of the Manhattan Project), e-mail message to author, Apr. 19, 2004; Waitt, *Gas Warfare.*

Safety at Lewisite Plant: *National in the World War.*

Nate Simpson, Arrival in Willoughby and Technical Questions about Lewisite: *National in the World War;* Simpson, "Nineteen-Eighteen in Willoughby."

Lewisite Manufacturing Process and Availability of Precursor Chemicals: Lewis, "Certain Organic Compounds"; Lewis and Perkins, "Beta-chlorovinyl chloroarsines"; "Method for Manufacture of Lewisite"; Mount, "Gas intended"; *National in the World War;* A. W. Smith, letters to F. M. Dorsey, Sept. 21, 1918 and Sept. 27, 1918 (from Herbert H. Dow papers, file 180002–A, Post Street Archives, Midland, Michigan); USDOJ, "Assessment of CERCLA."

Willoughby Plant Ready for Production and End of World War I: Hershberg, *James B. Conant;* Lewis, "How the American chemists"; *National in the World War.*

Closure of the Willoughby Plant and Social Activities after the War: "Ask Ben Hur boys," *Willoughby Independent;* "Ben Hur soldiers," *Willoughby Independent;* "Last of Ben Hur boys," *Willoughby Independent; National in the World War;* "Pie more important," *Willoughby Republican;* "Three-hundred and fifty," *Willoughby Republican;* USACE, "Facts on the Willoughby Plant."

True Function of the Willoughby Plant Revealed Locally: "Here is the big story," *Willoughby Republican;* "Now we know," *Willoughby Independent.*

Willoughby Plant after World War I: USACE, "Defense Environmental Restoration Program: Willoughby"; "Willoughby's war history," *Willoughby News-Herald.*

Production of Lewisite at Willoughby Plant: Bancroft, *Bancroft's History;* Conant, *My Several Lives;* "Deadly American gas," *Washington Post;* "Had deadliest gas," *New York Times;* "Here is the big story," *Willoughby Republican;* Mount, "Gas intended"; "Notre Dame dean," *South Bend Tribune;* "Our super-poison gas," *New York Times;* Pechura and Rall, *Veterans at Risk;* Shea, "Father Nieuwland"; Spiers, *Chemical Warfare;* Stockbridge, "War inventions"; Stockbridge, *Yankee Ingenuity;* Tarbell and Tarbell, *Roger Adams;* Trammell, "Toxicodynamics of organoarsenic"; "U.S. set to join," *McCook Gazette.*

Fate of Willoughby Lewisite and Equipment: Brophy, Miles, and Cochrane, *Chemical Warfare Service;* "Deadliest gas was used," *New York Times;* "Death of an inventor," *Time;* "Ex-chemical weapons site," *Willoughby News-Herald;* "Fall kills Lewis," *Chicago Daily News;* Gates, Williams, and Zapp, "Arsenicals"; "Here is Lake County, Ohio"; Hershberg, *James B. Conant;* Jones, "Chemical warfare research"; Jones, "Role of Chemists"; Mount, "Gas intended"; "Notre Dame dean," *South Bend Tribune;* "Our super-poison gas," *New York Times;* Pechura and Rall, *Veterans at Risk;* Sidell et al., "Vesicants"; Spiers, *Chemical Warfare;* Stockbridge, "War inventions"; Stockbridge, *Yankee Ingenuity;* Tarbell and Tarbell, *Roger Adams;* Trammell, "Toxicodynamics of organoarsenic"; "U.S. set to join," *McCook Gazette;* USACE, "Defense Environmental Restoration Program: Willoughby"; Waitt, *Gas Warfare;* Harrison J. Young, letter to "Commanding Officer" of the U.S. Army Chemical Corps, July 29, 1957 (from USACE, "Defense Environmental Restoration Program: Willoughby").

Memory Letters on Lewisite Production: J. W. Lyon, letter to C. H. Memory, May 27, 1927 (from National Archives and Records Administration); C. H. Memory, letters to Chemical Warfare Service, May 24, 1927, and June 23, 1927 (from National Archives and Records Administration).

Lewisite's Hypothesized Effectiveness and Battlefield Potential: Büscher, *Green and Yellow Cross; Chemical Warfare Service in World War II;* Hessel, Hessel, and Martin, *Chemistry in Warfare;* Ireland, *Medical Department;* Jarman, "Chemical Corps experience"; Mueller, *Die Chemische Waffe;* Prentiss, *Chemicals in War;* Sidell et al., "Vesicants"; Waitt, *Gas Warfare;* Watson and Griffin, "Toxicity of vesicant agents."

6. The Inter-War Years

Direct Citations

1. "Had deadliest gas," *New York Times.*
2. "'Lewisite' climax," *Chemical Bulletin,* 154.
3. Stockbridge, "War inventions," 828.
4. Warthin and Weller, *Medical Aspect,* 20.
5. Irwin, *Next War,* 37–38.
6. Fries and West, *Chemical Warfare,* 188.
7. Green and Price, "Chlorovinylchloroarsines," 453.
8. Lewis and Perkins, "Beta-chlorovinyl chloroarsines," 290–91.
9. Büscher, *Green and Yellow Cross,* 92.
10. Lewis, "Is prohibition of gas," 840.
11. Lewis, "Poison gas and pacifists," 289.
12. Lewis, "Poison gas and pacifists," 290.
13. "War gas genius," *Rochester Democrat.*
14. Lewis, "Is prohibition of gas," 836, 837, 840.
15. Lewis, "Is prohibition of gas," 837.
16. "Another chemist attacks," *Chicago Tribune.*
17. Fries, "Summary of marine piling," 14–15.
18. "Hunt fresh air," *Washington Democrat.*
19. "Deadliest gas was used," *New York Times.*
20. "Hunt fresh air," *Washington Democrat.*
21. "A Grateful Group," letter to W. Lee Lewis, May 20, 1920 (from Phil Reiss).
22. W. Lee Lewis, letter to W. C. Arsen (from Phil Reiss).
23. Büscher, preface to *Green and Yellow Cross,* vii.
24. Büscher, preface to *Green and Yellow Cross,* iii.

Sources

Lewisite in 1919 Newspapers and Magazines: "Deadly American gas," *Washington Post;* "Had deadliest gas," *New York Times;* Mount, "Gas intended"; Stockbridge, "War inventions."

Fries and the Dew of Death: Fries and West, *Chemical Warfare;* Moore, *Gas Attack!*

Disputes over Responsibility for Lewisite Development: "Controversy over poison gas," *Washington Post;* Jones, "Role of Chemists"; "'Lewisite' climax," *Chemical Bulletin.*

Kettering Bug: Leslie, "The Bug"; Stockbridge, "War inventions"; USAF Museum website, "Kettering Aerial Torpedo."

Article about Nieuwland's Role in the Development of Lewisite: "Notre Dame dean," *South Bend Tribune.*

Lewisite in 1919–21 Books: Fries and West, *Chemical Warfare;* Irwin, *Next War;* Warthin and Weller, *Medical Aspects.*

Will Irwin: Whittemore, "World War I."

Lewisite in 1920s Fiction: Chambers, "Slayer of souls"; Miller, "Poisoned light."

Lewisite in 1930s European Publications: Hanslian, *Der Chemische Krieg;* Liepmann, *Death From the Skies.*

Lewisite in 1920s Scientific Publications: Green and Price, "Chlorovinylchloroarsines"; Lewis and Perkins, "Beta-chlorovinyl chloroarsines."

American Response to the Green and Price Article and Possible Reason for Publication: Evans, *Gassed;* Fries and West, *Chemical Warfare;* Lewis, "Certain Organic Compounds"; Lewis and Perkins, "Beta-chlorovinyl chloroarsines."

German Development and Evaluation of Lewisite: Büscher, *Green and Yellow Cross;* Dafert, "Über die einwirkung"; Wieland and Bloemer, "Einige beiträge."

War Department's Intention to Abolish the CWS and Negative Public Sentiment about Chemical Weapons: Jones, "Role of Chemists"; Lewis, "Is prohibition of gas."

Rebuttal to Negative Sentiments about Lewisite, and Lewis's Defense and Justification for Its Use: "Another chemist attacks," *Chicago Tribune;* Jones, "Role of Chemists"; Lewis, "Is prohibition of gas"; Lewis, "Poison gas and pacifists"; Resume, Winford Lee Lewis (from Northwestern University Archives); "War gas genius," *Rochester Democrat;* "Who's news today," *Times Star.*

Lewis on Lewisite's Efficacy: "Lewis tells of perils," *Evanston News Index;* "Next war," *Rockford Morning Star.*

Peacetime Uses of Chemical Warfare Agents: "Army chemists use poison," *New York Times;* "Army's chlorine gas," *New York Times;* "Coolidge's cold is cured," *New York Times;* "Gas treatment taken again," *New York Times;* Russell, *War and Nature.*

Lewisite against Marine Borers: Fries, "By-products of chemical warfare"; Fries, "Summary of marine piling"; "Progress Report on the Marine Piling Investigation."

Lewisite as a Treatment for Syphilis and Loevenhart's Research: "Army chemists use poison," *New York Times;* Gasser, "Arthur S. Loevenhart"; Lewis and Hamilton, "7-chloro-7,12-dihydro-y-benzo-phenarsazin"; Lewis and Hamilton, "Arsenated benzanilide"; Swann, "Arthur Tatem, Parke Davis."

Lewisite as Bank Security Device: "Deadliest gas was used," *New York Times;* "Elnora raided," *Washington Democrat;* "Gas fumes rout yeggs," *New Orleans Times Picayune;* "Gas routs burglars," *New York Times;* "Hunt fresh air," *Washington Democrat;* Lewis, "Poison gas and pacifists"; "Mustard gas drives off," *New York Times;* "Tear gas device," *Chicago Daily News;* "Tear gas on safe," *Chicago Herald and Examiner;* "Their surprise," *New York Times;* U.S. Patent Office, "Art of Dispersing."

Lewisite as an Insecticide and Maxwell-Lefroy: "Prof. Lefroy dies," *New York Times;* Rentokil Initial website; "Savant trying lewisite," *Chicago Tribune;* "Scientist gassed on eve," *New York Times.*

Lewis's Notoriety: "A Grateful Group," letter to W. Lee Lewis, May 20, 1920 (from Phil Reiss); War gas genius," *Rochester Democrat.*

Allied Proliferation of Lewisite and British Tests: Compton, *Military Chemical and Biological;* Evans, *Gassed.*

Italian 1930s Production and Use of Lewisite: Atkinson, *Army at Dawn; Chemical Warfare Service in World War II;* Compton, *Military Chemical and Biological;*

Hanslian, *Der Chemische Krieg;* Harris and Paxman, *Higher Form of Killing;* Murphy, "Gas in the Italo-Abyssinian"; Smart, "History of chemical and biological warfare"; Spiers, *Chemical Weaponry.*

Soviet 1920s and 1930s Production and Use of Lewisite: W. C. Arsen, telegram to W. Lee Lewis, Jan. 24, 1937 (from Phil Reiss); Eudin, Fisher, and Fisher, *Life of a Chemist;* Fedorov, *Chemical Weapons in Russia;* Fedorov, *Undeclared Chemical War;* Krause and Mallory, *Chemical Weapons in Soviet Military;* Myrtilla Lewis, notes about Mr. Arsen's telephone call (from Phil Reiss); W. Lee Lewis, letter to W. C. Arsen (from Phil Reiss); Wikipedia website, "Alexsandr Solzhenitsyn."

Polish 1920s and 1930s Production of Lewisite: Stock and Lohs, *Challenge of Old Chemical.*

United States Chemical Warfare Research Between the Wars: Brophy, Miles, and Cochrane, *Chemical Warfare Service; Chemical Warfare Service in World War II;* Harris and Paxman, *Higher Form of Killing;* Kleber and Birdsell, *Chemical Warfare Service;* Smart, "History of chemical and biological warfare."

German 1930s Chemical Weapons Development and Nerve Gases: CDC website, "Facts about Sarin"; CDC website, "Facts about Tabun"; "Chemical Munitions in the Southern and Western Baltic Seas"; GeoCities website, "Nerve Gases"; "Old Chemical Weapons Reference Guide"; Russell, *War and Nature;* Sullivan, "Toxic Terrorism."

Lewisite and Mustard Experiments Between the Wars: Büscher, *Green and Yellow Cross;* Vedder, *Medical Aspects.*

7. Military Biology and BAL

Direct Citations

1. Seagrave, *Yellow Rain,* 244.

Sources

Acute Effects: SIPRI, *Problems of Chemical and Biological.*

Chemical Properties of Arsenic: Hindmarsh and McCurdy, "Clinical and environmental aspects"; Landrigan, "Arsenic"; Peters, Stocken, and Thompson, "British Anti-Lewisite"; Stocken and Thompson, "Reactions of British Anti-Lewisite."

Additional Arsenic-Based Chemical Warfare Agents: BOC Gases website, "MSDS on Arsenic Trichloride"; Jones, "Role of Chemists."

Lipophilic Properties: Augerson, *Review of Scientific Literature;* Cameron, Carleton, and Short, "Pathological changes"; Goldman and Dacre, "Lewisite"; Pechura and Rall, *Veterans at Risk.*

Hydrolysis and Consequences: Gates, Williams, and Zapp, "Arsenicals"; Munro et al., "Sources, fate, and toxicology"; "Potential Military Chemical/Biological Agents and Compounds"; Seagrave, *Yellow Rain.*

Vesicant Effects: Augerson, *Review of Scientific Literature;* Büscher, *Green and Yellow Cross;* Cameron, Courtice, and Short, "Disturbances of function"; Compton, *Military Chemical and Biological;* King, Riviere, and Monteir-Riviere, "Characterization of lewisite"; Pechura and Rall, *Veterans at Risk.*

Systemic Effects: Augerson, *Review of Scientific Literature;* Cameron, Carleton, and Short, "Pathological changes"; Cameron, Courtice, and Short, "Disturbances of function"; "Diagnosis and Treatment of Lewisite Exposures"; Goldman and Dacre, "Lewisite"; Watson and Griffin, "Toxicity of vesicant agents."

Inhalation Effects: Augerson, *Review of Scientific Literature;* Cameron, Carleton, and Short, "Pathological changes"; Cameron, Courtice, and Short, "Disturbances of function"; "Diagnosis and Treatment of Lewisite Exposures"; Goldman and Dacre, "Lewisite"; "Potential Military Chemical/Biological Agents and Compounds."

Mechanism of Action and Level of Toxicity: Inns, Bright, and Marrs, "Comparative acute systemic toxicity"; Kehe et al., "Effects of lewisite"; "Seventh Annual Report of the Chemical Warfare Research Department."

Gas Mask Efficacy: Büscher, *Green and Yellow Cross;* Hessel, Hessel, and Martin, *Chemistry in Warfare;* "Notre Dame dean," *South Bend Tribune;* "Our super-poison gas," *New York Times;* Stockbridge, "War inventions"; "War's deadliest gas," *Kansas City Star.*

Ocular Effects: Augerson, *Review of Scientific Literature;* Büscher, *Green and Yellow Cross;* "Diagnosis and Treatment of Lewisite Exposures"; Pechura and Rall, *Veterans at Risk.*

Additional Systemic Effects: Fang, *Chemical Agents Development;* Inns, Bright, and Marrs, "Comparative acute systemic toxicity."

Lethality: Augerson, *Review of Scientific Literature;* Büscher, *Green and Yellow Cross;* Cameron, Carleton, and Short, "Pathological changes"; Cameron, Courtice, and Short, "Disturbances of function"; "Diagnosis and Treatment of Lewisite Exposures"; Gates, Williams, and Zapp, "Arsenicals"; Goldman and Dacre, "Lewisite"; Karalliedde et al., "Possible immediate and long-term effects"; Potential Military Chemical/Biological Agents and Compounds"; Prentiss, *Chemicals in War;* Sollmann, *Manual of Pharmacology;* Vedder, *Medical Aspects;* Watson and Griffin, "Toxicity of vesicant agents."

Oxford University and the Development of BAL: Ord and Stocken, "Contribution to chemical defense"; Peters, Stocken, and Thompson, "British Anti-Lewisite"; Lloyd Stocken, (biochemist, Oxford), interview with author, July 9, 2003; Stocken and Thompson, "Reactions of British Anti-Lewisite"; Waters and Stock, "BAL."

Early Tests on Effectiveness of BAL: ATSDR, "Case Studies"; *Chemical Warfare Service in World War II;* Longscope and Leutscher, "Clinical uses of 2,3-dimercaptopropanol"; Ord and Stocken, "Contribution to chemical defense"; Peters, Stocken, and Thompson, "British Anti-Lewisite"; Lloyd Stocken and Margery Ord (biochemists, Oxford), letter to author, Mar. 21, 2002; Waters and Stock, "BAL."

Post-World War II Publicity about BAL: Peters, Stocken, and Thompson, "British Anti-Lewisite"; Waters and Stock, "BAL."

Adverse Reactions to BAL: Klaasen, "Heavy metals."

Derek Denny-Brown: Vilensky, Gilman, and Dunn, "Derek E. Denny-Brown"; Vilensky, Robertson, and Gilman, "Denny-Brown, Wilson's Disease."

Wilson's Disease: Cumings, "Copper and iron content"; Mandelbrote et al., "Studies on copper metabolism"; Menkes, "Disorders of metal metabolism"; Porter, "Amino acid excretion."

BAL and the Treatments of Wilson's Disease: Aposhian et al., "Mobilization of heavy metals"; Brewer, "Treatment of Wilson's Disease"; Denny-Brown and Porter, "The effect of BAL," *New England Journal of Medicine;* Denny-Brown and Porter, "The effect of BAL," *Proceedings of the American Neurological Association;* "Reverse nerve disease," *Science News Letter;* Vilensky, Gilman, and Dunn, "Derek E. Denny-Brown"; Walshe, "Penicillamine."

Additional Uses for BAL: Klaasen, "Heavy metals"; Stocken and Thompson, "Reactions of British Anti-Lewisite."

BAL as World War II Medical Discovery: Larson, "British Anti-Lewisite."

Current State of BAL: Abu Alam (Akorn Incorporated), e-mail message to author, Mar. 12, 2004; Rudolph, Kamei, and Overby, *Rudolph's Fundamentals of Pediactrics.*

Recent Army Treatment of Lewisite: "Toxic Chemical Agent Safety Standards."

Re-evaluation of BAL's Mechanism of Action: Kehe, et al., "Effects of lewisite."

8. World War II

Direct Citations

1. "Handbook of Chemical Warfare Agents."
2. "History of Rocky Mountain Arsenal," 2606.
3. "History of Rocky Mountain Arsenal," 2619.
4. "Lewisite Production and Munitions."
5. H. J. McIntyre (director, Freedom of Information and Privacy Acts Office), letter to author, June 5, 2003.
6. Gates, Williams, and Zapp, "Arsenicals," 95.
7. "Some Experiments on the Skin Burning Power of Lewisite Vapour."
8. Wachtel, foreword to *Chemical Warfare*, v.
9. "Handbook of Gas Warfare," *Newsweek*, 66.
10. Letter to William Mayer, Aug. 24, 1938 (from National Archives and Records Administration).
11. "The last weapon," *Time.*
12. "Battle of China," *Time*, 23.

Sources

NDRC History: Brophy, Miles and Cochrane, *Chemical Warfare Service;* Gates, Williams, and Zapp, "Arsenicals"; Hershberg, *James B. Conant.*

Biography of Conant: Conant, *My Several Lives;* Hershberg, *James B. Conant;* Wachtel, *Chemical Warfare.*

Conant during World War II: Hershberg, *James B. Conant;* Jarman, "Chemical Corps experience"; Vilensky, Gilman, and Dunn, "Derek E. Denny-Brown."

CWS Lewisite Production at EA between the Wars, and Controversy Over its Effectiveness: "Chemical and Physical Properties of Lewisite"; Croddy, *Chemical and Biological Warfare;* Gates, Williams, and Zapp, "Arsenicals"; "Handbook of Chemical Warfare Agents"; "Method for Manufacture of Lewisite"; Wright and Shaffer, "Development of Manufacturing Process."

CWS Budget Increase: Brophy, Miles, and Cochrane, *Chemical Warfare Service.*

Civil Defense Preparations against Chemical Weapons: Florida Memory Project website, "Sniff Kits."

Why Chemical Weapons were Not Used in World War II: Brooks, "Why Germany Did Not Use"; "Chemical-Biological-Radiological Warfare"; Haber, *Poisonous Cloud;* Harris and Paxman, *Higher Form of Killing;* Moore, *Gas Attack!;* Smart, "History of chemical and biological warfare"; "Why the delay," *Riverside Press.*

Lewisite Production at EA: Brophy, Miles, and Cochrane, *Chemical Warfare Service;* Jarman, "Chemical Corps experience"; "Report on the Preparation and Physiological Properties of Crude Lewisite"; Smart, "History of chemical and biological warfare."

Lewisite Production at PBA, HA and RMA: Brophy, Miles, and Cochrane, *Chemical Warfare Service;* "History of Rocky Mountain Arsenal"; Jarman, "Chemical Corps experience"; Pechura and Rall, *Veterans at Risk;* Smart, "History of chemical and biological warfare."

Lewisite Field Tests on Animals and Materials: "Analysis of Casualty-Producing Potentialities of Lewisite"; Gates, Williams, and Zapp, "Arsenicals"; "Lewisite Dispersion as Airplane Chemical Spray"; "Lewisite Vapor Hazard," to Cornelius P. Rhoads, letter, Aug. 6, 1943.

Lewisite Field Tests on Humans: "Analysis of Casualty-Producing Potentialities of Lewisite"; Brophy, Miles and Cochrane, *Chemical Warfare Service; Chemical Warfare Service in World War II;* Cogan, "Lewisite burns of the eye"; Gates, Williams, and Zapp, "Arsenicals"; "Officers of the 27th," *New York Times.*

Lewisite Lab Tests, and Mustard Field and Lab Tests on Humans: Pechura and Rall, *Veterans at Risk.*

End of United States Lewisite Production: "Lewisite Production and Munitions"; Alden H. Waitt, letter to W. A. Copthorne, Jan. 17, 1944.

Security Pertaining to Issues about Lewisite: Gates, Williams, and Zapp, "Arsenicals"; H. J. McIntyre (director, Freedom of Information and Privacy Acts Office), letter to author, June 5, 2003.

British Lewisite Production and Civil Preparedness from World War I to II: Gradon Carter (historian, Porton Down), letter to author, June 10, 2003; Haber, *Poisonous Cloud;* Hayward, *Shingle Street.*

British Lewisite and Mustard Testing on Humans in England: Evans, *Gassed;* "Impregnation of Underclothing to Afford Protection Against Lewisite."

British Lewisite and Mustard Testing on Humans in Australia: Freeman, "The un-
  fought chemical war"; Goodwin, *Keen as Mustard;* "Report of Chemical
  Warfare Physiological Investigations."
British Lewisite and Mustard Testing on Humans in Canada: Bryden, *Deadly Allies;*
  Gates, Williams, and Zapp, "Arsenicals."
British Lewisite Testing on Humans in India: "Some Experiments on the Skin
  Burning Power of Lewisite Vapour."
Soviet Lewisite Production: Fedorov, *Chemical Weapons in Russia;* MEDEA,
  Ocean Dumping of Chemical Munitions; Stock and Lohs, *Challenge of
  Old Chemical.*
French Lewisite Production: Manley, "The problems of old chemical weapons."
German Lewisite Production: Brophy, Miles and Cochrane, *Chemical Warfare
  Service;* "Chemical Munitions in the Southern and Western Baltic Seas";
  Büscher, *Green and Yellow Cross;* Evans, *Gassed;* Franke, *Lehrbuch der Militär-
  chemie,* vol. 1; Franke, *Lehrbuch der Militärchemie,* rev. ed., vol. 1; Gates,
  Williams, and Zapp, "Arsenicals"; "Handbook of Gas Warfare," *Newsweek;*
  Krause and Grussendorf, "Syntopie von morbus bowen"; "Lewisite is re-
  called," *New York Times;* Mueller, *Die Chemische Waffe;* "Old Chemical
  Weapons Reference Guide"; Stock and Lohs, *Challenge of Old Chemical;*
  Wachtel, *Chemical Warfare.*
German Lewisite and Mustard Testing on Humans: Evans, "German CW Experi-
  ments."
Italian Lewisite Production: Tanaka, "Poison gas."
Japanese Chemical Weapon Production: Brophy, Miles, and Cochrane, *Chemical War-
  fare Service;* "Former worker," *Daily Yomiuri;* Harris, *Factories of Death;* Har-
  ris and Paxman, *Higher Form of Killing;* Pechura and Rall, *Veterans at Risk;*
  SIPRI, *Problems of Chemical and Biological;* Tanaka, "Poison gas."
Japanese Invasion and Chemical/Biological Weapon Use in China: "American
  confirms Japanese use," *New York Times;* "Battle of China," *Time;* BICC
  website, "Historical Chemical Weapons: China"; Dangerous Legacy website,
  "Abandoned and Old Chemical Weapons"; Gates, Williams, and Zapp,
  "Arsenicals"; Harris, *Factories of Death;* "The last weapon," *Time;* NTI
  website, "Abandoned Chemical Weapons"; "Old Chemical Weapons Reference Guide"; SIPRI, *Chemical Weapons;* Smart, "History of chemical and
  biological warfare"; Tanaka, "Poison gas"; Letter to William Mayer, Aug. 24,
  1938 (from National Archives and Records Administration).

9. Lewisite Production, Use, and Sea Dumping after World War II

Direct Citations

1. Baker, "Chemical warfare in Korea," 3.
2. MEDEA, *Ocean Dumping of Chemical Munitions,* 1/7.
3. Smart, "History of chemical and biological warfare," 48.

4. "Secret diplomacy won," *New York Times.*

5. Smiley, *Arabian Assignment,* 150.

Sources

Demobilization of the CWS after World War II: *Chemical Warfare Service in World War II;* Smart, "History of chemical and biological warfare."

Renewal of the Chemical Corps during the Korean and Cold Wars: Baker, "Chemical warfare in Korea"; Smart, "History of chemical and biological warfare."

United States Decision to Obsolete Lewisite and Ocean Dump: "Disposal of Lewisite by Dumping in Deep Water"; "Obsoletion of Lewisite."

United States Dumping of Lewisite off its Coasts: ACAT website, "Superfund Site Descriptions"; "Army will dump gas," *New York Times;* Brankowitz, "Chemical Stockpile Disposal Program"; MEDEA, *Ocean Dumping of Chemical Munitions;* "Poison gas cargo," *San Francisco Chronicle;* "Poison gas will be sunk," *San Francisco Chronicle;* "Report of the Operations Involving the Disposal"; "Ship full of war gas," *New York Times;* "Survey and Analysis Report."

United States Dumping of Lewisite off Foreign Coasts: Australian Government website, Plunkett; BICC website, "Historical Chemical Weapons: India"; Brankowitz, "Chemical Stockpile Disposal Program"; OPCW website, "Chemical Weapons Convention."

United States Prohibition of Ocean Dumping and Suspension of Operation CHASE: Flamm, Kwan, and McNulty, "Chemical Stockpile Disposal Program"; MEDEA, *Ocean Dumping of Chemical Munitions;* Smart, "History of chemical and biological warfare."

United States Shipments of Lewisite Samples for Training: Brankowitz, "Chemical Stockpile Disposal Program"; Flamm, Kwan, and McNulty, "Chemical Stockpile Disposal Program."

Soviet Chemical Weapons Program after World War II: Bills, "What should be the United States position"; Fedorov, *Chemical Weapons in Russia;* Smart, "History of chemical and biological warfare."

Soviet Equipment Captured in 1973 Arab-Israeli War: Smart, "History of chemical and biological warfare."

Possible Soviet Use of Chemical Weapons in Afghanistan: "U.S. accuses Soviets," *New York Times.*

Soviet Ocean Dumping of Chemical Weapons: MEDEA, *Ocean Dumping of Chemical Munitions.*

Soviet Suspension of Chemical Weapon Production and Agreement to Dispose of Stockpiles: Averre and Khripunov, "Chemical weapons disposal."

Iraqi Use of Chemical Weapons during the Iran-Iraq War: Perera, "Lewisite"; SIPRI website, Robinson and Goldblat; Smart, "History of chemical and biological warfare."

Possible Iraqi Use of Lewisite during Operation Desert Storm: Augerson, *Review of Scientific Literature;* Eddington, *Gassed in the Gulf.*

Iraq's Suspected Possession of Chemical Weapons during Operation Iraqi Freedom: "Early tests suggest weapon," *Reuters;* "U.S. tests indicate," *Reuters.*

Libyan Chemical Weapons Program: "Secret diplomacy won," *New York Times;* Sinai, "Libya's pursuit of weapons."

Yugoslavian Production of Lewisite: FAS website, "Chemical Agents."

Japanese Ocean Dumping of Chemical Weapons: BICC website, "Historical Chemical Weapons: Japan"; "Former worker," *Daily Yomiuri;* Harris, *Factories of Death;* MEDEA, *Ocean Dumping of Chemical Munitions.*

British Production and Destruction of Lewisite: Gradon Carter (historian, Porton Down), letter to author, June 10, 2003.

Egyptian Use of Chemical Weapons in Yemen: Seagrave, *Yellow Rain;* Smiley, *Arabian Assignment;* Spiers, *Chemical Weaponry.*

Sudanese Chemical Weapons Production and Use: Barletta, "Chemical weapons in Sudan"; CSW website, "Baroness Cox's Speech"; ESPAC website, "Irresponsible Journalism"; FAS website, "House of Commons."

Chinese Lewisite Production: FAS website, "China and Weapons"; NTI website, "Country Overview: China."

North Korean Chemical Weapons Program: NTI website, "Country Profiles: North Korea"; NTI website, "Country Profiles: North Korea: Chemical."

Current Unearthing of World War I Chemical Weapons: Croddy, *Chemical and Biological Warfare.*

10. Lewisite Stockpiles and Terrestrial Residues

Direct Citations

1. "Do you know," *Deseret Dispatch,* 2.
2. USACE, "Remedial Investigation Report," 1/11.
3. Albright, "American University Experimental Station," 5.
4. *Thomas P. Loughlin v. United States of America,* 9–10.
5. USACE, "Defense Environmental Restoration Program: Willoughby," 7/1.
6. Yeoman, "Deadly dependence," 29.
7. Yeoman, "Deadly dependence," 38.
8. *Hall v. U.S. Army, Dugway Proving Grounds,* 8.
9. Stock and Lohs, *Challenge of Old Chemical,* 129.
10. Wehrfritz, Takayama, and Macleod, "In search of buried poison," 27.
11. Yahoo News website, "China, Japan Discuss War."

Sources

The CWC and OPCW: OPCW website, "Chemical Weapons Convention."

Disposal of Lewisite at the Tooele Chemical Agent Disposal Facility: Deseret Chemical Depot, e-mail message to author, Feb. 19, 2004; "Do you know," *Deseret Dispatch;* Global Security website, "Deseret Chemical Depot"; Global Security website, "Tooele Army Depot"; OPCW website, "Chemical Weapons Convention."

Loss of the Lewisite Inventory from World War I: Amos A. Fries, letter to "Adjutant General of the Army," Apr. 24, 1920 (from USACE).

History of Spring Valley: "D.C. gets update," *Washington Post;* Jaffe, "Spring Valley";
Thomas P. Loughlin v. United States of America; USACE website, "Spring Val-
ley Project Update."
Agreements between AU and the Army, and Likelihood of Munitions Buried at AU:
Jaffe, "Spring Valley"; *Thomas P. Loughlin v. United States of America.*
Health Effects, Buried Findings, Soil Testing, and Excavation in Spring Valley (1990-
95): Brooks et al., "Operation Safe Removal"; Jaffe, "Spring Valley"; *Thomas
P. Loughlin v. United States of America;* USACE, "Remedial Investigation
Report"; USACE website, "Spring Valley Project Update."
Concerns about Corps 1995 Record of Decision: Albright, "American University
Experimental Station"; Albright, "Final Report"; "Evidence of D.C. toxins,"
Washington Post; Jaffe, "Spring Valley."
Health Effects, Buried Findings, Soil Testing, and Excavation in Spring Valley (1996-
Present): Albright, "American University Experimental Station"; "Army
engineers to test," *Washington Post; Thomas P. Loughlin v. United States of
America;* USACE, "Army Corps of Engineers"; USACE website, "Spring Val-
ley Project Update."
The Loughlin Case: Albright, "American University Experimental Station"; "Resi-
dents federal lawsuit blocked," *Washington Post; Thomas P. Loughlin v.
United States of America;* "U.S. ignored high arsenic," *Washington Post.*
Soil and Human Testing at AU for Arsenic: "Arsenic, illnesses worry D.C.," *Washing-
ton Post;* Albright, "American University Experimental Station"; ATSDR,
"Exposure Investigation: Spring Valley Chemical Munitions"; ATSDR, "Pub-
lic Health Significance"; AU News website, "Army Corps Soil Removal"; AU
News website, "Statement About AU"; USACE website, "Spring Valley Proj-
ect Update."
EPA Arsenic Level Guidelines for Soil Removal: "Arsenic, illnesses worry D.C.,"
Washington Post.
Testing of Spring Valley Residents for Arsenic: ATSDR, "Exposure Investigation:
Spring Valley Neighborhood"; "Panel urges more," *Washington Post.*
Results of 2004 Soil Testing for Arsenic, and 2003 Quantities of Munitions/Laboratory
Containers Found in Spring Valley: "D.C. gets update," *Washington Post;*
USACE website, "Spring Valley Project Update."
Estimates on Quantity of Remaining Munitions and Cost/Time to Complete Reme-
diation of Spring Valley: Albright, "American University Experimental Sta-
tion"; Mark Baker (historian, USACE), e-mail message to author, Oct. 27,
2003; USACE, "Army Corps of Engineers"; USACE website, "Spring Valley
Project Update."
AU Claim against the Army: AU News website, "American University Files Claim";
AU News website, "Court Dismisses Action."
Zachary Wilnowski: Zachary Wilnowski, e-mail message to author, Aug. 28, 2003.
Removing Arsenic from Soil Using Ferns: "Toxin cleanup goes natural," *Washing-
ton Post.*
Possible Chemical Weapon Contamination at CUA: Catholic University of America
Public Affairs Office website, "D.C. Health Department"; USACE, "Defense
Environmental Restoration Program: Catholic University."

Lewisite Contamination at Willoughby and Tests by the Army Corps: "Ex-chemical weapons site," *Willoughby News-Herald;* USACE, "Defense Environmental Restoration Program: Willoughby"; "Willoughby's war history," *Willoughby News-Herald.*

Hazardous Byproducts of Lewisite Production and Contamination at RMA: Barbara Nabors (Colorado Dept. of Public Health and Environment), e-mail message to author, Feb. 13, 2004; USDOJ, "Assessment of CERCLA"; USEPA website, "From Weapons to Wildlife."

Hazardous Byproducts of Lewisite Production at PBA: Pine Bluff Arsenal Installation Action Plan."

Hazardous Byproducts of Lewisite Production at HA: Huntsville Arsenal, e-mail message to author, Feb. 2004.

Lewisite Residues in Alaska: ACAT website, "Superfund Site Descriptions"; "Survey and Analysis Report."

Lewisite Residues in South Carolina: Luca Berresford (South Carolina Dept. of Health), letter to author, Nov. 25, 2003; Yeoman, "Deadly dependence."

David W. Hall and Lewisite Residues at DPG: Global Security website, "Dugway Proving Grounds"; *Hall v. U.S. Army, Dugway Proving Grounds.*

Soviet/Russian Lewisite Production, Disposal and Environmental Consequences in Chapaevsk: "Environmental Problems in the Russian Federation"; FAS website, "Chemical Weapons"; Fedorov, *Chemical Weapons in Russia;* Fedorov, *Undeclared Chemical War;* Stock and Lohs, *Challenge of Old Chemical.*

Soviet/Russian Lewisite Production, Disposal, and Environmental Consequences in Dzerzhinsk: "Environmental Problems in the Russian Federation."

Soviet/Russian Lewisite Disposal and Environmental Consequences in Leonidovka: "Environmental Problems in the Russian Federation"; "Wastes of war," *Washington Post.*

Soviet/Russian Lewisite Disposal and Environmental Consequences in Volgograd: "Environmental Problems in the Russian Federation"; Fedorov, *Undeclared Chemical War;* Stock and Lohs, *Challenge of Old Chemical.*

Soviet/Russian Lewisite Disposal and Environmental Consequences in Moscow: "Military toxins lurk," *Boston Globe.*

Russian Signing of the CWC and the Delay of Implementation: Averre and Khripunov, "Chemical weapons disposal"; Blackwood, "Arsenic and old weapons"; Ember, "Ridding Russia of chemical weapons"; Fedorov, *Chemical Weapons in Russia;* OPCW website, "Chemical Weapons Convention."

Russian Lewisite Stockpiles: Blackwood, "Arsenic and old weapons"; Ember, "Ridding Russia of chemical weapons"; Fedorov, *Chemical Weapons in Russia;* Fedorov, *Undeclared Chemical War;* Stock and Lohs, *Challenge of Old Chemical.*

Russian Destruction and Disposal Technologies of Chemical Weapons: Ember, "Ridding Russia of chemical weapons"; NTI website, "Russia: Lewisite Destruction"; "Over 76 tonnes of lewisite," *Interfax;* "Russia starts to scrap," *Washington Post.*

European Assistance for Russian Chemical Weapons Destruction: BICC website, "Conference on Dismantlement"; Ember, "Ridding Russia of chemical weapons"; "Russia starts to scrap," *Washington Post.*

Concerns of Residents near Russian Disposal Operations: Ember, "Ridding Russia of chemical weapons"; "Russia starts to scrap," *Washington Post.*

Japanese Disposal of Chemical Weapons in Heilongjiang and Jilin Provinces in China and in Japan: Dangerous Legacy website, "Abandoned and Old Chemical Weapons"; Dangerous Legacy website, "Some Information"; Harper et al., *China;* Harris, *Factories of Death;* Japanese Disposal of Lewisite in Japan: NTI website, "Abandoned Chemical Weapons"; Wehrfritz, Takayama, and Macleod, "In search of buried poison."

Estimates of the Quantity of Chemical Weapons Remaining in China: NTI website, "Abandoned Chemical Weapons."

Agreement on Plan to Remediate Remaining Japanese Chemical Weapons in China: Dangerous Legacy website, "Abandoned and Old Chemical Weapons"; NTI website, "Abandoned Chemical Weapons"; Xinhua News Agency website, "Japanese Team Retrieves."

Injuries Caused by Japanese Chemical Weapons in China: Dangerous Legacy website, "Abandoned and Old Chemical Weapons"; NTI website, "Abandoned Chemical Weapons"; Yahoo News website, "China, Japan Discuss War."

Canadian Lewisite Procurement and Destruction: Australian EIA Network website, "International Study"; John Bryden (author of *Deadly Allies*), e-mail message to author, May 26, 2004.

Great Britain's Lewisite Production and Destruction: Gradon Carter (historian, Porton Down), letter to author, June 10, 2003.

Angela Canning Case: "Appeal court clears mother," *Guardian;* "Expert Testimony, Bad Evidence?" transcript; "Woman weeps," *Times.*

11. Human and Environmental Toxicology

Direct Citations

1. Freeman, "The VA's sorry," 41–42.
2. Freeman, "The VA's sorry," 42.
3. "Mustard Gas," transcript, 6.
4. Evans, *Gassed,* 105.
5. Pechura and Rall, preface to *Veterans at Risk,* vi.

Sources

Degradation Products of Lewisite: MEDEA, *Ocean Dumping of Chemical Munitions;* Munro et al., "Sources, fate and toxicology"; Pechura and Rall, *Veterans at Risk.*

Toxicity of Arsenic Compounds: Cullen, "Arsenic in the environment"; Klaasen, "Heavy metals"; SOS—Arsenic.net website, "Arsenic Established Carcinogen."

Nathan Schnurman Story: CDI website, "War May be Hazardous"; Freeman, "The VA's sorry"; "Mustard Gas," transcript.

Effects of Chemical Weapons Exposure on World War II Soldier Volunteers: Evans, *Gassed;* Pechura and Rall, *Veterans at Risk;* Schnurr et al., "Predictors and outcomes"; VA website, "Mustard Gas Exposure"; VAC website, "Chemical Warfare Agent Testing."

Syphilis Treatment during the 1930s and 1940s: Swann, "Arthur Tatem, Parke Davis."

ORNL and NRC Toxicology Studies on Lewisite: "Derivation of Health-Based Environmental Screening Levels"; Hackett et al., "Teratology Studies on Lewisite"; NRC, "Evaluation of Army's interim reference dose"; Sasser et al., "Toxicology Studies on Lewisite."

Charlie Bermpohl's Research in Spring Valley: Charlie Bermpohl (reporter, *Northwest Current*), letter to author, Mar. 9, 2004.

Health Effects of Chemical Weapons Production and Disposal in Russia: "Environmental Problems in the Russian Federation."

Health Effects of Japanese Chemical Weapons Disposal in China: Harris, *Factories of Death.*

Health Effects of Chemical Weapons Production Workers at Ōkunojima: Pechura and Rall, *Veterans at Risk.*

MEDEA and the Effects of Ocean Dumping of Chemical Weapons: Belt, "An Arctic breakthrough"; MEDEA, *Ocean Dumping of Chemical Munitions.*

12. Lewisite, Terrorism, and the Future

Direct Citations

1. Gur and Cole, *New Face of Terrorism,* 284.

Sources

Recent Government Policy on WMD Documents: Sherry Barnes (officer, Freedom of Information Office), letter to author, June 7, 2004; David Chuber (historian, U.S. Army Chemical School), letter to author, June 2, 2004; Database of files, Fort Leonard Wood, Missouri (from USACE); FAS website, "Memorandum for Heads."

Lewisite Use by Terrorists: Croddy, *Chemical and Biological Warfare;* Gur and Cole, *New Face of Terrorism;* Haber, *Poisonous Cloud;* Solomon, "The way we live now."

Mock Lewisite Attacks in the United States: "Firefighters tested," *Tampa Tribune;* List of mock chemical weapon exercises in the U.S. (from Michael Forgy, Branch Chief of the Office for Domestic Preparedness, U.S. Dept. of Homeland Security); "Response tested," *San Diego Union-Tribune;* Servamer Corporation website; "Weapons of Mass Destruction," videotape.

New Treatments for Lewisite Injuries and Detection: Lam, Rice, and Brown, "Treatment of lewisite burns"; Wooten, Ashley, and Calafat, "Quantitation of 2-chlorovinylarsonous acid."

Bibliography

ACAT (Alaska Community Action on Toxins) website. "Superfund Site Descriptions." http://www.akaction.net/metadata/superfund.html

Albright, Richard D. "The American University Experimental Station (AUES) Cleanup Project Debriefing Memorandum." Government of the District of Columbia, Department of Health, Environmental Health Administration, Hazardous Waste Division, Washington, D.C., 2004.

——. "Final Report on the World War I Poison Gas Production at the American University Experiment Station." Government of the District of Columbia, Department of Consumer and Regulatory Affairs, Environmental Regulation Administration, Washington, D.C., July 1996.

Aldstadt, J. H., A. F. Martin, D. C. Olson, D. K. Wolcott, and G. D. Marshall. "Phase I Final Report: A Flow Injection Trace Gas Analyzer for On-Site Determination of Organoarsenicals." U.S. Department of Energy Research Center, Argonne, Ill., May 31, 1996.

"All to the mustard." *The Retort*, October 6, 1918. Published by the Chemical Warfare Service at the American University Experiment Station.

"America had deadliest poison known that would have wiped Berlin off map." *Philadelphia Press*, May 25, 1919.

"American confirms Japanese use of gas: Army chemical officer reports effects on Chinese." *New York Times*, July 7, 1944.

"America reveals deadliest poison Hun barely escaped: Ten airplanes could have carried 'Lewisite' enough to destroy Berlin in one raid." *Shreveport (Louisiana) Times*, May 25, 1919.

"American gas was the most deadly: 'Lewisite' was ready to be used on Germans when war was brought to close." *Columbus (Ohio) Tribune*, May 25, 1919.

"Analysis of Casualty-Producing Potentialities of Lewisite, Summary." War Department, Washington, D.C., September 29, 1943.

"Andrews gymnasium opened to soldiers." *Willoughby (Ohio) Republican*, October 4, 1918.

"Another chemist attacks the gas war protocol." *Chicago Tribune*, September 20, 1925.

"Another new gas? 'Lewisite' reported from the Bureau of Mines." *Chemical Bulletin (ACS)*, 6 (June 1919): 137.

Aposhian, H. Vasken, Richard M. Maiorino, Diego Gonzalez-Ramirez, Miguel Zuniga-Charles, Zhaofa Xu, Katherine M. Hurlbut, Pablo Junco-Munoz, Richard C. Dart, and Mary M. Aposhian. "Mobilization of heavy metals by newer, therapeutically useful chelating agents." *Toxicology* 97 (1995): 23–38.

"Appeal court clears mother of killing her two babies: Fresh evidence pointed to genetic cause of deaths." *Guardian (United Kingdom)*, December 11, 2003.

Arlington National Cemetery website. "William Luther Sibert, Major General, United States Army." http://www.arlingtoncemetery.net/wlsibert.htm

"Armistice saved German people from annihilation by a new American poison: Ten airplanes in day could drop enough to destroy all life in Berlin—3,000 tons to have been at front March 1." *New York Herald,* 1919.

"Army chemists use poison gases on disease; Grip, pneumonia, paresis said to be cured." *New York Times,* May 2, 1923.

"Army engineers to test all Spring Valley sites: Arsenic search expanded after complaints." *Washington Post,* March 15, 2001.

"Army will dump gas: 10,000 tons of lewisite will be sunk off Charleston, S.C." *New York Times,* June 28, 1946.

"Army's chlorine gas helps Coolidge's cold: He spends 45 minutes in air-tight room." *New York Times,* May 21, 1924.

"Arsenic, illnesses worry D.C.: Unusual ailments near tainted sites." *Washington Post,* January 27, 2001.

"Ask Ben Hur boys to sing at union service." *Willoughby (Ohio) Independent,* January 30, 1919.

Atkinson, Rick. *An Army at Dawn: The War in North Africa, 1942–1943.* Vol. 1 of the Liberation Trilogy. New York: Henry Holt and Company, 2002.

ATSDR (Agency for Toxic Substances and Disease Registry). "Case Studies in Environmental Medicine: Arsenic Toxicity." ATSDR, U.S. Department Of Health and Human Services, Atlanta, June 1990.

———. "Exposure Investigation: Spring Valley Chemical Munitions (a/k/a American University Child Development Center), Washington, D.C." ATSDR, U.S. Department of Health and Human Services, Public Health Service, Atlanta, March 8, 2001.

———. "Exposure Investigation: Spring Valley Neighborhood (a/k/a Spring Valley Chemical Munitions/American University), Washington, D.C." ATSDR, U.S. Department of Health and Human Services, Division of Health Assessment and Consultation, Atlanta, June 28, 2002.

———. "The Public Health Significance of Arsenic in Soil at the American University Child Development Center, Washington D.C." ATSDR, U.S. Department of Health and Human Services, Atlanta, March 14, 2001.

ATSDR website. "Medical Management Guidelines (MMGs) for Blister Agents: Lewisite (L) and Mustard-Lewisite (HL)." http://www.atsdr.cdc.gov/MHMI/mmg163.html

Augerson, William S. *A Review of the Scientific Literature as It Pertains to Gulf War Illnesses: Chemical and Biological Warfare Agents.* Vol. 5. Santa Monica, Calif.: RAND Corporation, 2000.

AU News (American University News) website. "American University Files Claim against the Army," July 13, 2001. See press releases. http://www.american.edu/media

AU News website. "Army Corps Soil Removal Activities, Week of June 17, 2002." See press releases. http://www.american.edu/media

———. "Court Dismisses Action on World War I Munitions," September 26, 2003. See press releases. http://www.american.edu/media

――――. "Statement About AU Child Development Center and U.S. Army Corps of
    Engineers Project." See press releases. http://www.american.edu/media

Australian EIA Network (Environmental Impact Assessment) website. "International
    Study of the Effectiveness of Environmental Assessment—Public Participa-
    tion in Environmental Assessment for a Chemical Warfare Agent Destruc-
    tion Project, Canada." http://www.deh.gov.au/assessments/eianet/eastudy/
    casestudies/studies/cs20.html

Australian Government, Department of Defence website. Geoff Plunkett, "Chemical
    Warfare Agent Sea Dumping off Australia." Rev. ed., 2003. http://www.
    hydro.gov.au/n2m/dumping/cwa/cwa.htm

Averre, Derek, and Igor Khripunov. "Chemical weapons disposal: Russia tries again."
    Bulletin of the Atomic Scientists 57 (2001): 57–63.

Baker, E. R. "Chemical warfare in Korea." *Armed Forces Chemical Journal* 4 (1951): 3.

Bancroft, W. D. *Bancroft's History of the Chemical Warfare Service in the United
    States.* Washington, D.C.: Research Division, Chemical Warfare Service,
    American University Experiment Station, May 1919.

Barletta, Michael. "Chemical weapons in the Sudan: Allegations and evidence." *Non-
    proliferation Review* (Fall 1998): 115–36.

"Battle of China." *Time,* June 15, 1942.

Belt, Don. "An Arctic breakthrough: Heralding a new era of cooperation, the United
    States and Russia are making data from their Cold War intelligence archives
    available to science." *National Geographic* (February 1997): 36–57.

"Ben Hur prospect looms up anew." *Willoughby (Ohio) Republican,* July 12, 1918.

"Ben Hur soldiers to enjoy pie for Thanksgiving." *Willoughby (Ohio) Independent,*
    October 24, 1918.

BICC (Bonn International Center for Conversion) website. "Conference on Disman-
    tlement and Destruction of Nuclear, Chemical and Conventional Weapons,
    May 19–21, 1996." http://www.bicc.de/

――――. "Historical Chemical Weapons Sites in the Asia-Pacific Region: Australia,"
    April 16, 2002. http://www.bicc.de/

――――. "Historical Chemical Weapons Sites in the Asia-Pacific Region: China," April
    16, 2002. http://www.bicc.de/

――――. "Historical Chemical Weapons Sites in the Asia-Pacific Region: India," April
    16, 2002. http://www.bicc.de/

――――. "Historical Chemical Weapons Sites in the Asia-Pacific Region: Japan," April
    16, 2002. http://www.bicc.de/

Bills, Ray W. "What should be the United States position on chemical warfare disar-
    mament." *Military Review* 55 (May 1975): 12–23.

Blackwood, Milton E. "Arsenic and old weapons: Chemical weapons disposal in Rus-
    sia." *Nonproliferation Review* (Spring–Summer 1999): 89–97.

BOC Gases website. "MSDS on Arsenic Trichloride," 1999. http://www.boc.com/
    gases/pdf/msds/G122.pdf

――――. "MSDS on Phosgene," 1999. http://www.vngas.com/pdf/g67.pdf

Brankowitz, W. R. "Chemical Stockpile Disposal Program: Chemical Weapons Move-
    ment." Report no. SAPEO-CDE-IS-87001. Office of Program Manager, Chemi-
    cal Demilitarization, Aberdeen Proving Ground, Maryland, June 12, 1987.

Brewer, George J. "The treatment of Wilson's Disease." *Advances in Experimental Medicine & Biology* 448 (1999): 115–26.

Brooks, Jerry. "Why Germany Did Not Use Chemical Warfare in World War Two." Thesis, James Madison University, May 1990.

Brooks, Marguerite E., William T. Beaudry, Paul C. Bossie, Raymond E. Herd, J. Michael Lochner, Stephen G. Pleva, Janet H. Reeder, Dennis K. Rohrbaugh, Thomas E. Rosso, Leonard J. Szafraniec, and Linda L. Szafraniec. "Operation Safe Removal: Spring Valley, Washington D.C. Analytical Results: January–February 1993." Edgewood Research, Development & Engineering Center, U.S. Army Chemical and Biological Defense Agency, Maryland, July 1993.

Brophy, Leo P., Wyndham D. Miles, and Rexmond Cochrane. *The Chemical Warfare Service: From Laboratory to Field.* United States Army in World War II: The Technical Services. Washington, D.C.: Center of Military History Publishing, 1988.

Bryden, John. *Deadly Allies: Canada's Secret War, 1937–1947.* Toronto: McClelland & Stewart, 1989.

Burn, Walter P. "Chemical Warfare Agents." Reference and training chart. *From Phil Reiss.*

Burrell, George A. "Contributions from the Chemical Warfare Service, USA: The Research Division." *Journal of Industrial and Engineering Chemistry* 11 (February 1919): 93–104.

Büscher, Hermann. *Grün-und Gelbkeuz,* trans. Nell Conway. Ann Arbor, Mich.: Edwards Brothers, 1944.

Cameron, G. R., H. M. Carleton, and R. H. D. Short. "Pathological changes induced by lewisite and allied compounds." *Journal of Pathology and Bacteriology* 58 (1946): 411–22.

Cameron, G. R., F. C. Courtice, and R. H. D. Short. "Disturbances of function induced by lewisite (2-chlorovinyldichlorarsine)." *Quarterly Journal of Experimental Physiology* 34 (1947): 1–28.

"Camp A. U. scene of World War training trenches, drill field." *American University Eagle,* January 15, 1965.

"Capture Him with Tear Gas!" Pamphlet. Cicero, Ill.: Lewis-Hughes Company, 1921. *From Phil Reiss.*

Catholic University of America Office of Public Affairs website. "D.C. Health Department Asks Army Corps to Review its Archives on Maloney Hall," August 3, 2001. http://publicaffairs.cua.edu/news/02munitionsreview.htm

CDC (Center for Disease Control) website. "Emergency Response Card: Lewisite." http://www.bt.cdc.gov/agent/blister/ctc0020.asp

———. "Facts about Sarin." http://www.bt.cdc.gov/agent/sarin/basics/facts.asp

———. "Facts about Tabun." http://www.bt.cdc.gov/agent/tabun/basics/facts.asp

———. "International Chemical Safety Cards: Arsenic Trichloride." http://www.cdc.gov/niosh/ipcsneng/neng0221.html

CDI (Center for Defense Information) website. "War May be Hazardous to Your Health." Transcript, "America's Defense Monitor," May 9, 1993. http://www.cdi.org/adm/634/transcript.html

Chambers, Robert W. "The slayer of souls: A story of love and adventure." *Chicago Herald and Examiner,* May 31–June 4, 1922.

"Chemical-Biological-Radiological (CBR) Warfare and its Disarmament Aspects." A Study by the Subcommittee on Disarmament of the Committee on Foreign Relations, United States Senate. Washington, D.C.: Government Printing Office, 1960.

"Chemical Munitions in the Southern and Western Baltic Seas: Compilation, Assessment and Recommendations." Hamburg: Federal Maritime and Hydrographic Agency, 1993.

"Chemical and Physical Properties of Lewisite." Project A1.2-1. April 17, 1925. *From National Archives and Records Administration.*

"Chemical Warfare Agents." Edgewood Arsenal, Maryland: Chemical Warfare School, 1929. *From National Archives and Records Administration.*

The Chemical Warfare Service in World War II: A Report of Accomplishments. New York: Reinhold Publishing, 1948.

"Chicagoan finds deadliest drug: America making 'Lewisite' in quantity for war use when fighting ceased." Unidentified newspaper, 1919. *From Phil Reiss.*

City of Willoughby, Ohio, website. "Faith Corrigan's 'Willoughby Historic City.'" http://www.willoughbyohio.com/historic.htm

Clark, Edward B. *William L. Sibert: The Army Engineer.* Philadelphia: Dorrance & Company, 1930.

Cleveland Public Library website. See The Necrology File: http://www.cpl.org

"Club rooms for soldiers." *Willoughby (Ohio) Independent,* October 3, 1918.

Cogan, David G. "Lewisite burns of the eye." *Journal of the American Medical Association* 122 (1943): 435–36.

Compton, James A. F. *Military Chemical and Biological Agents: Chemical and Toxicological Properties.* Caldwell, N.J.: Teleford Press, 1987.

Conant, James B. *My Several Lives: Memoirs of a Social Inventor.* New York: Harper & Row Publishing, 1970.

"Controversy over poison gas bitter: Credit for invention given to Bureau of Mines." *Washington Post,* May 4, 1919.

Cook, Tim. *No Place to Run: The Canadian Corps and Gas Warfare in the First World War.* Vancouver: U.B.C. Press, 1999.

"Coolidge's cold is cured: President credits his quick recovery to use of chlorine gas." *New York Times,* May 24, 1924.

Croddy, Eric. *Chemical and Biological Warfare: An annotated bibliography.* London: Scarecrow Press, 1997.

CSW (Christian Solidarity Worldwide) website. "Baroness Cox's Speech to the House of Lords on Sudan and Nagorno-Karabakh." http://www.csw.org.uk/CSWnews.asp?item=57

Cullen, W. R. "Arsenic in the environment." In: *Arsenic and Old Mustard: Chemical Problems in the Destruction of Old Arsenical and 'Mustard' Munitions,* ed. J. F. Bunnett and M. Mikolajczyk, 123–34. Boston: Kluwer Academic Publisher, 1998.

Cumings, J. N. "The copper and iron content of brain and liver in the normal and in hepato-lenticular degeneration." *Brain* 71 (1948): 410–15.

"D.C. family is gassed by bomb fired in experiment." *Washington Times,* August 4, 1918.

"D.C. gets update on WWI cleanup." *Washington Post*, July 15, 2003.

Dafert, Orville A. "Über die einwirkung von acetylen auf arsenchlorid." *Monatshefte fur Chemie und verwandte teile anderer wissenschaften* 40 (1919): 313–23.

Dangerous Legacy website. "Abandoned and Old Chemical Weapons." See chronology. http://www.tcp-ip.or.jp/~e-ogawa/

———. "Some Information on Discovered Chemical Weapons Abandoned in China by a Foreign State." CD/1127 (CD/CW/W.P.384), February 18, 1992. http://www.tcp-ip.or.jp/~e-ogawa/CD1127.HTM

"The deadliest gas." *Nashville Tennessean*, May 27, 1919.

"Deadliest gas of war to be handed Germans." *Washington Star*, June 22, 1919.

"Deadliest gas was never used: Sample of 'Lewisite,' kept under guard at Washington, avoided by attendants." *Terre Haute (Indiana) Star*, May 29, 1919.

"Deadliest gas was used against burglars, and Indiana bank scheme may be copied." *New York Times*, July 9, 1925.

"Deadliest poison known." *Barber County (Kansas) Index*, (month and day unknown), 1919.

"Deadly American gas is on exhibit: Prof. Lewis' invention, planned to end war, shown in capital." *Washington Post*, May 25, 1919.

"Deadly drug ready for foe is disclosed: Germans spared from the strongest poison known, by Armistice." *Minneapolis Tribune*, May 25, 1919.

"Death of an inventor." *Time*, February 1, 1943.

Denny-Brown, Derek E., and Huntington Porter. "The effect of BAL (2,3-dimercaptopropanol) on hepatolenticular degeneration (Wilson's Disease)." *New England Journal of Medicine* 245 (December 13, 1951): 917–25.

———. "The effect of BAL (2,3-dimercaptopropanol) on hepatolenticular degeneration (Wilson's Disease)." *Proceedings of the American Neurological Association* (1951): 79–84.

"Derivation of Health-Based Environmental Screening Levels for Chemical Warfare Agents." U.S. Army Center for Health Promotion and Preventive Medicine, Aberdeen Proving Ground, Maryland; and Toxicology and Risk Analysis Section —Life Sciences Division, Oak Ridge National Laboratory, Oak Ridge, Tennessee, March 1999.

"Diagnosis and Treatment of Lewisite Exposures." Environmental Protection Agency, Salt Lake City, Utah.

"Disposal of Lewisite by Dumping in Deep Water." Report to the Deputy Chief of Staff for Logistics from H. B. Boyle, Item 3395. October 29, 1957.

Dixon, Blase R. "The Catholic University of America, 1909–1928: The Rectorship of Thomas Joseph Shahan." Ph.D. thesis, Catholic University of America, 1972.

"Do you know how to yahoo?" *Deseret (Utah) Dispatch*, December 2003.

Dorsey, Frank M. "Contributions from the Chemical Warfare Service, U.S.A.: The Development Division." *Journal of Industrial and Engineering Chemistry* 11 (April 1919): 281–91.

"Dr. J. A. Nieuwland, chemist, 58, dies." *New York Times*, June 12, 1936.

"Early tests suggest weapon 'cocktail' found in Iraq." *Reuters*, April 7, 2003.

Eddington, Patrick. *Gassed in the Gulf: The Inside Story of the Pentagon-CIA Cover-up of Gulf War Syndrome.* Lincoln, Nebraska: iUniverse.com, 2000.

Eisenschiml, Otto. "W. Lee Lewis obituary." *Chemical Bulletin (ACS)* (September 1943): 47.

"Elnora raided: 6 places entered but loot only $6: Poison gas liberated when vault handle is knocked off, drives thieves from the bank." *Washington (Indiana) Democrat*, July 7, 1925.

Ember, Lois R. "Ridding Russia of chemical weapons: The international community offers financial and technical aid to eliminate a deadly arsenal." *Chemical and Engineering News* 81 (December 1, 2003): 28–31.

Emedicine website. Noltkamper, Daniel, and Stephen Burgher. "Toxicity, phosgene," August 14, 2004. http://www.emedicine.com/emerg/topic849.htm

"Environmental Problems in the Russian Federation." London: Eastern Research Group, Foreign & Commonwealth Office, October 2000.

ESPAC (European Sudanese Public Affairs Council) website. "Irresponsible Journalism: British Media Reporting of Allegations of Chemical Warfare in Southern Sudan," January 2001. http://www.espac.org/sudan_uk/irresponsible.html

Eudin, Xenia J., Helen D. Fisher, and Harold J. Fisher, eds. *Life of a Chemist: Memoir of Vladimir N. Ipatieff*, trans. Vladimor Haensel and Ralph Lusher. Stanford, Calif.: Stanford University Press, 1946.

Evans, D. C. "German CW Experiments on Human Beings." Report no. PRO WO 195/9678. January 12, 1948. *From Public Records Office, London.*

Evans, Rob. *Gassed: British Chemical Warfare Experiments on Humans at Porton Downs.* London: House of Stratus, 2000.

Evanston (Illinois) News Index, January 8, 1918.

———. January 18, 1918.

"Evidence of D.C. toxins unheeded: New findings back '86 warning to U.S. on buried weapons." *Washington Post,* July 9, 2001.

"Ex-chemical weapons site subject of tests, sampling." *Willoughby (Ohio) News-Herald,* October 2, 2002.

"Expert Testimony, Bad Evidence?" Transcript, CBS News, *60 Minutes II,* April 21, 2004.

"Fall kills Lewis, war gas inventor." *Chicago Daily News,* January 29, 1943.

"Famed inventor former Gridleyan: Native manufactures deadly dose for boches." *Gridley (California) Herald,* (month and day unknown), 1919.

Fang, Y. *Chemical Agents Development in USSR,* trans. from Chinese. Alexandria, Va.: Defense Technical Information Center, 1983.

Farrow, Edward S. *Gas Warfare.* New York: E. P. Dutton & Company, 1920.

FAS (Federation of American Scientists) website. "Chemical Agents in the Former Yugoslavia." http://www.fas.org/nuke/guide/serbia/cw/

———. "Chemical Weapons—Russian/Soviet Nuclear Forces." http://www.fas.org/nuke/guide/russia/cbw/cw.htm

———. "China and Weapons of Mass Destruction: Implications for the United States." November 5, 1999. http://fas.org/irp/nic/china_wmd.html

———. "House of Commons Foreign Affairs: Eighth Report." July 25, 2000. http://www.fas.org/irp/threat/uk_wmd/40702.htm

———. "Memorandum for the Heads of Executive Departments and Agencies. The White House, Washington," March 19, 2002. From Andrew H. Card, Jr., "Action to Safeguard Information Regarding Weapons of Mass Destruction and

Other Sensitive Documents Related to Homeland Security." http://www.fas.
org/sgp/bush/who31902.html

Fedorov, Lev A. *Chemical Weapons in Russia: History, Ecology, Politics*. Moscow: Center for Ecological Policy of Russia, 1994.

———. *The Undeclared Chemical War in Russia: Politics versus Ecology*. Moscow: Center of Russian Ecological Policy, 1995.

"Firefighters tested on chemical attacks." *Tampa (Florida) Tribune*, February 21, 2002.

Flamm, K. J., Q. Kwan, and W. B. McNulty. "Chemical Stockpile Disposal Program: Chemical Agent and Munition Disposal. Summary of the U.S. Army's Experience." Report No. SAPEO-CDE-IS-87005. Officer of the Program Manager, Chemical Demilitarization, Aberdeen Proving Ground, Maryland, September 21, 1987.

Florida Memory Project website. "Sniff Kits: Approved and Recommended by the Office of Civilian Defense and the Chemical Warfare Service of the U.S. Army." http://www.floridamemory.com/OnlineClassroom/FloridaWWII/sniffi.cfm

"Former Oroville man invented most deadly gas: War Department announces W. Lee Lewis invented terrible weapon of war." Unidentified Newspaper, 1919. *From Phil Reiss.*

"Former University student is inventor of deadly gas." *Seattle (Washington) Post Intelligencer,* January 26, 1919.

"Former worker at toxic gas plant to publish booklet to reveal truth." *Daily Yomiuri* (Japan), August 15, 1992.

"Four alumni chemists." *Washington Alumnus* 16 (April 1925): 7, 9–10.

Franke, Siegfried. *Lehrbuch der Militärchemie*. Vol. 1. Chemie der Kampfstoffe. Berlin: Deutscher Militärverlag, 1967.

———. *Lehrbuch der Militärchemie*. Rev. ed. Vol. 1. Entwicklung der chemischen Kriegführung, Chemie der Kampfstoffe. Berlin: Deutscher Militärverlag, 1976.

———. *Lehrbuch der Militärchemie*. Rev. ed. Vol. 2. Sabotage und Phytogifte, Entgiftung und Entgiftungsmittel, Analytik Chemischer Kampfstoffe und Giftstoffe, Anhang. Berlin: Deutscher Militärverlag, 1976.

Freeman, Karen. "The unfought chemical war." *Bulletin of the Atomic Scientists* 47 (December 1991): 30–39.

———. "The VA's sorry, the Army's silent." *Bulletin of the Atomic Scientists* 49 (March 1993): 39–43.

Fries, Amos A. "By-products of chemical warfare." *Journal of Industrial and Engineering Chemistry* 20 (1928): 1079–84.

———. "Summary of marine piling investigation." *Chemical Warfare* 11 (1925): 11–15.

Fries, Amos A., and Clarence J. West. *Chemical Warfare*. New York: McGraw-Hill Book Company, 1921.

Froning, Henry B. "Father Nieuwland: Priest-scientist." *Ave Maria* 56 (September 5, 1942): 295–8 and (September 12, 1942): 327–30.

"Gas fumes rout yeggs." *New Orleans Times Picayune*, August 6, 1925.

"Gas routs burglars: Indiana bank vault had been prepared for attack." *New York Times*, July 8, 1925.

"Gas treatment taken again by Coolidge: Wife chats with him in chlorine room." *New York Times,* May 22, 1924.

Gasser, H. S. "Arthur S. Loevenhart." *Science Press* 70 (October 4, 1929): 317–21.

Gates, Marshall, Jonathan W. Williams, and John A. Zapp. "Arsenicals." In *Chemical Warfare Agents, and Related Chemical Problems: Summary Technical Report of Division 9,* Vol. 1, 83–115. Washington, D.C.: National Defense Research Committee, 1946.

GeoCities website. "Nerve Gases: A Simple Look at Chemical Warfare." http://www.geocities.com/jockoco198/Nerve.htm

Gillis, Chester. *Roman Catholicism in America.* New York: Columbia University Press, 1999.

Global Security website. "Deseret Chemical Depot, Tooele, Utah." http://www.globalsecurity.org/wmd/facility/deseret.htm

————. "Dugway Proving Grounds." http://www.globalsecurity.org/wmd/facility/dugway.htm

————. "Tooele Army Depot, Tooele, Utah." http://www.globalsecurity.org/military/facility/tooele.htm

Goldman, Max, and Jack C. Dacre. "Lewisite: Its chemistry, toxicology, and biological effects." *Reviews of Environmental Contamination & Toxicology* 110 (1989): 75–115.

Goodwin, Bridget. *Keen as Mustard: Britain's Horrific Chemical Warfare Experiments in Australia.* Queensland: University of Queensland Press, 1998.

Gordon, Martin K., Barry R. Sude, and Ruth A. Overbeck. "Chemical testing in the Great War: The American University Experiment Station." *Washington History* 6 (1994): 29–45.

"Government takes over the Ben Hur plant." *Willoughby (Ohio) Republican,* July 26, 1918.

"Grand piano lent to soldiers." *Willoughby (Ohio) Republican,* August 23, 1918.

Green, Stanley J., and Thomas S. Price. "The chlorovinylchloroarsines." *Journal of the Chemical Society* 119 (1921): 448–55.

Gur, Nadine, and Benjamin Cole. *The New Face of Terrorism: Threats from Weapons of Mass Destruction.* London: I. B. Tauris, 2002.

Haber, L. F. *The Poisonous Cloud: Chemical Warfare in the First World War.* Oxford: Clarendon Press, 1986.

Hackett, P. L., R. L. Rommereim, F. G. Burton, R. L. Buschbom, and L. B. Sasser. "Teratology Studies on Lewisite and Sulfur Mustard Agents: Effects of Sulfur Mustard in Rats and Rabbits. Final Report." Report no. AD A187495. Pacific Northwest Laboratory, Richland, Wash., 1987.

"Had deadliest gas ready for Germans: 'Lewisite' might have killed millions." *New York Times,* May 25, 1919.

Hall v. U.S. Army, Dugway Proving Grounds. Case No. 1997–SDW-5. U.S. Department of Labor, Office of Administrative Law Judges, August 8, 2002. http://www.oalj.dol.gov/PUBLIC/wblower/decsn/97sdw05a.htm

"A Handbook of Chemical Warfare Agents: Agent: Lewisite." Edgewood, Md.: U.S.A. War Office, 1936. *From Phil Reiss.*

"Handbook of gas warfare: New chemical weapons outlined by an expert on the old." *Newsweek* 17 (April 7, 1941): 66.

Hanslian, Rudolf. *Der Chemische Krieg*. Berlin: E. S. Mittler & Sohn, 1937.

Harper, Damian, Marie Cambon, Katja Gaskell, Thomas Huhti, Bradley Mayhew, Korina Miller, and Mielikki Org, eds. *China*. 8th ed. Footscray, Victoria, Australia: Lonely Planet, August 2002.

Harris, Robert, and Jeremy Paxman. *A Higher Form of Killing: The Secret of Chemical and Biological Warfare*. New York: Hill and Wang, 1982.

Harris, Sheldon H. *Factories of Death: Japanese Biological Warfare, 1932–1945, and the American Cover-up*. Rev. ed. New York: Routledge, 2002.

Hartnett, Francis J. "Father Nieuwland—The Man Who Measured the Sky." Thesis. *From University of Notre Dame Archives*.

Hayward, James. *Shingle Street: Flame, Chemical and Psychological Warfare in 1940, and the Nazi Invasion That Never Was*. Colchester, Essex, Great Britain: LTM Publishing, 1994.

Heller, Charles E. *Chemical Warfare in World War I: The American Experience, 1917–1918*. Fort Leavenworth, Kans.: Combat Studies Institute, 1984.

"Here is the big story of the great work of the soldiers who have been stationed in our midst: Gas produced in Willoughby may make future wars impossible—Armistice declared the day of its perfection." *Willoughby (Ohio) Republican*, November 29, 1918.

"Here is Lake County Ohio." Cleveland: Howard Allen Pub., 1964. *From Lake County Historical Society (Ohio)*.

Hershberg, James G. *James B. Conant: Harvard to Hiroshima and the Making of the Nuclear Age*. Stanford, Calif.: Stanford University Press, 1993.

Herty, Charles A. "Reserves of the Chemical Warfare Service." Speech, National Research Council, Washington, D.C., February 21, 1921. In Reprint and Circular Series of the National Research Council, no. 16.

Hessel, F. A., M. S. Hessel, and Wellford Martin. *Chemistry in Warfare: Its Strategic Importance*. New York: Hastings House Publishing, 1940.

Hindmarsh, J. Thomas, and Ross F. McCurdy. "Clinical and environmental aspects of arsenic toxicity." *CRC Critical Reviews in Clinical Laboratory Sciences* 23 (1986): 315–47.

"Historical Willoughby 1853–1953 Centennial Celebration." *From Lake County Historical Society (Ohio)*.

"History of Rocky Mountain Arsenal—1945. Part VIII: Production Operations. Section 9A: L Manufacturing, Distillation, and Filling." *Government document received anonymously*.

Hope, Arthur J. *Notre Dame: One Hundred Years*. Notre Dame, Indiana: Notre Dame University Press, 1943.

"Houses taken over for officers' quarters." *Willoughby (Ohio) Republican*, October 4, 1918.

"Hundreds attend tablet unveiling—Major Lewis makes plea for rational pacifism." *Gridley (California) Herald*, July 9, 1923.

"Hunt fresh air as men open gas-filled vault: First instance of new bank protection foiling robbers in this section." *Washington (Indiana) Democrat*, July 8, 1925.

Hurd, Charles D. "Development of chemical research at Northwestern from 1920 into the 1940's." August 1988. *From Northwestern University Archives*.

———. "The scientific contribution of Winford Lee Lewis." *Chemical Bulletin (ACS),* (September 30, 1943): 221.

"Impregnation of Underclothing to Afford Protection against Lewisite. Field ('Bucket') Method for the Impregnation of Service Underclothing (Army Shirts, Long Cotton Pants and Cellular Drawers) with Zinc Oxide.'" Report no. PRO WO 188/1079. January 21, 1942, and February 16, 1942. *From Public Records Office, London.*

Inns, R. H., J. E. Bright, and T. C. Marrs. "Comparative acute systemic toxicity of sodium arsenite and dichloro(2-chlorovinyl)arsine in rabbits." *Toxicology* 51 (1988): 213–22.

"The Interior Exposition." *Washington Post,* May 26, 1919.

Inventor Hall of Fame website. "Inventor Profile: Vinyl Derivatives of Acetylene and Method of Preparing the Same Synthetic Rubber." http://www.invent.org/hall_of_fame/111.html

Ireland, M. W. *The Medical Department of the U.S. Army in the World War: Medical Aspects of Gas Warfare.* Vol. 14. Washington, D.C.: Government Printing Office, 1926.

Irwin, Will. *The Next War: An Appeal to Common Sense.* New York: E. P. Dutton & Company, 1921.

"Is Chicago teacher: Captain Lewis inventor of 'lewisite' was professor at Northwestern University at Evanston." Unidentified newspaper, May 24, 1919. *From Phil Reiss.*

Jaffe, Harry. "Spring Valley as ground zero." *Washingtonian,* (December 2000): 78–83, 121–9.

Jarman, Gordon N. "Chemical Corps experience in the manufacture of lewisite." In *Metal-Organic Compounds,* 19–337. Washington, D.C.: American Chemical Society, 1959.

Jones, Daniel P. "Chemical warfare research during World War I: A Model of Cooperative Research." In *Chemistry and Modern Society,* 166–94. Washington, D.C.: American Chemical Society, 1983.

———. "The Role of Chemists in Research on War Gases in the United States during World War I." Ph.D. thesis, University of Wisconsin–Madison, 1969.

Jones, Lauder W. "Offense Chemical Research Section: Summary of Achievement, 1917–1918." Chemical Warfare Monograph no. 55. *Available at Edgewood Arsenal Technical Library.*

"Julius A. Nieuwland obituary." *Catholic World* 143 (July 1936): 492.

"Julius A. Nieuwland obituary." *Commonweal* 24 (June 26, 1936): 244.

Karalliedde, L., H. Wheeler, R. Maclehose, and V. Murray. "Possible immediate and long-term effects following exposure to chemical warfare agents." *Public Health* 114 (2000): 238–48.

Kehe, K., S. Flohe, G. Krebs, H. Kreppel, F. X. Reichl, B. Liebl, and L. Szinicz. "Effects of lewisite on cell membrane integrity and energy metabolism in human keratinocytes and SCL II cells." *Toxicology* 163 (2001): 137–44.

King, J. Randall, Jim E. Riviere, and Nancy A. Monteiro-Riviere. "Characterization of lewisite toxicity in isolated perfused skin." *Toxicology and Applied Pharmacology* 116 (1992): 189–201.

Klaasen, Curtis D. "Heavy metals and heavy-metal antagonists." In *Goodman and Gilman's: The Pharmacological Basis of Therapeutics*, 8th ed., ed. Alfred G. Gilman, Theodore W. Rall, Alan S. Nies, and Palmer Taylor. New York: Pergamon Press, 1990.

Kleber, Brooks E., and Dale Birdsell. *The Chemical Warfare Service: Chemicals in Combat*. United States Army in World War II: The Technical Services. Washington, D.C.: U.S. Army Center of Military History, 1990.

Krause, Heinrich, and Elke-Ingrid Grussendorf. "Syntopie von morbus bowen und lostnarbe." *Der Hautarzt* 29 (1978): 490–93.

Krause, Joachim, and Charles K. Mallory. *Chemical Weapons in Soviet Military Doctrine: Military and Historical Experience, 1915–1991*. Boulder: Westview Press, 1992.

"Kraybill heads research for Meat Institute." *Chicago Tribune*, April 1, 1941.

"Laborer killed at Ben Hur plant." *Willoughby (Ohio) Independent*, August 15, 1918.

Lam, D. G. K., P. Rice, and R. F. R. Brown. "The treatment of lewisite burns with laser debridement—'lasablation.'" *Burns* 28 (2002): 19–25.

Landrigan, Philip J. "Arsenic—state of the art." *American Journal of Industrial Medicine* 2 (1981): 5–14.

Larson, Edward. "British Anti-Lewisite, BAL." *Confinia Neurologica* 10 (1950): 108–26.

"Last of Ben Hur boys leave for distant homes." *Willoughby (Ohio) Independent*, February 13, 1919.

"The last weapon." *Time*, May 25, 1942.

Leslie, Stuart W. "The Bug: 'Boss' Kettering's cruise missile." *Timeline* 8 (August–September 1991).

"Lewis invents deadliest gas." *Northwestern Alumni (Illinois)*, January 1919.

"Lewis tells of perils of gas research work: Future use of gas." *Evanston (Illinois) News Index*, October 27, 1919.

Lewis, W. Lee. "Certain Organic Compounds of Arsenic." Speech, American Chemical Society Meeting, Rochester Section, November 21, 1921. *From Phil Reiss*.

———. "How the American chemists silenced Germany." *Chemical Bulletin (ACS)* 6 (January 1919): 4–6.

———. "Is the Elimination of Gas Warfare Feasible?" Speech, City Club Forum Luncheon, Chicago, March 7, 1922. *From Phil Reiss*.

———. "Is prohibition of gas warfare feasible?" *Atlantic Monthly* (June 1922): 834–40.

———. "Poison gas and pacifists: The chemist after whom lewisite is named explodes a few fallacies on the barbarity of gas warfare." *Independent*, (September 12, 1925): 289–91.

———. "Report for the Week Ending April 13, 1918 of Work at the Catholic University Annex." Available in: USACE, "Defense Environmental Restoration Program: Catholic University," March 1995 (see below).

———. "Some features of swimming pool control." *Journal of Industrial and Engineering Chemistry* 8 (October 1916): 914.

———. "Why I became a chemist, and if so, to what extent." *Chemical Bulletin (ACS)* 11 (April 1924): 100–101, 104–5.

Lewis, W. Lee, and C. S. Hamilton. "7-chloro-7,12-dihydro-y-benzo-phenarsazin and some of its derivatives." *Journal of the American Chemical Society* 43 (October 1921): 2218–23.

Lewis, W. Lee, and C. S. Hamilton. "Arsenated benzanilide and its derivatives." *Journal of the American Chemical Society* 45 (March 1923): 757–62.

Lewis, W. Lee, and G. A. Perkins. "The beta-chlorovinyl chloroarsines." *Industrial and Engineering Chemistry* 15 (March 1923): 290–95.

Lewis, W. Lee, and H. W. Stiegler. "The beta-chlorovinyl-arsines and their derivatives." *American Chemical Society* 47 (1923): 2546–56.

"Lewis-Hughes grenade does the business: Tear bomb routs seven who defied police squadrons." *Cleveland (Ohio) Plain Dealer*, February 27, 1922.

"Lewisite." *Topeka (Kansas) Capital*, June 6, 1919.

"'Lewisite' climax of lethal arts invented by Chicagoan." *Chemical Bulletin (ACS)*, July 1919.

"'Lewisite,' deadliest of poisons, ready to destroy all Germany, had Armistice not been signed." *Cincinnati (Ohio) Tribune*, May 25, 1919.

"'Lewisite' deadliest poison known, made by American chemist to kill Germans." *St. Louis Republic*, (month and day unknown), 1919.

"'Lewisite,' deadliest poison yet discovered." *Commerce and Finance*, June 1919.

"Lewisite Dispersion as Airplane Chemical Spray." Report no. TDMR 473, February 10, 1943.

"Lewisite Production and Munitions." Report to the Chief of the Control Division, November 8, 1943.

"Lewisite is recalled: Gas developed during World War has deadly, paralyzing action." *New York Times*, May 14, 1940.

"'Lewisite' is revealed as deadliest war poison: American invention which might have killed millions, was ready to use against the Germans." *New York Times*, May 25, 1919.

"'Lewisite' would have annihilated the Germans; Deadliest poison ever known was being manufactured by the ton in the United States when the Armistice was declared." *Little Rock (Arkansas) Gazette*, May 25, 1919.

Liepmann, Heinz. *Death from the Skies: A Study of Gas and Microbial Warfare*. London: Martin Secker & Warburg, 1937.

Longscope, Warfield T., and John A. Leutscher. "Clinical uses of 2,3-dimercaptopropanol (BAL). XI: The treatment of acute mercury poisoning by BAL." *Journal of Clinical Investigations* 25 (1946): 557–67.

Lyon, Marcus W. "Father Nieuwland: The Botanist." Speech, Nieuwland Memorial Exercises, Notre Dame, Ind., January 10, 1937. Reprinted in "Julius Arthur Nieuwland: Priest, Chemist, Botanist." *From University of Notre Dame Archives*.

———. "Julius Arthur Nieuwland obituary." *Science* 84 (July 3, 1936): 7–8.

"Man killed in accident at Ben Hur plant." *Willoughby (Ohio) Republican*, August 16, 1918.

"Man who found deadliest poison world ever knew." Unidentified newspaper, 1919. *From Phil Reiss*.

Mandelbrote, B. M., M. W. Stanier, R. H. S. Thompson, and M. N. Thruston. "Studies on copper metabolism in demyelinating disease of the central nervous system." *Brain* 71 (1948): 212–28.

Manley, R. G. "The problems of old chemical weapons which contain 'mustard gas' or organoarsenic compounds: An overview." In *Arsenic and Old Mustard: Chemical Problems in the Destruction of Old Arsenical and 'Mustard' Munitions,* ed. J. F. Bunnett and M. Mikolajczyk, 1–16. Boston: Kluwer Academic Publisher, 1998.

May, Leopold. "The early days of chemistry at Catholic University." *Bulletin for the History of Chemistry* 28 (2003): 18–25.

MEDEA. *Ocean Dumping of Chemical Munitions: Environmental Effects in Arctic Seas.* McLean, Va.: MEDEA, May 1997.

Menkes, John H. "Disorders of metal metabolism." In *Merritt's Neurology,* 10th ed., ed. Lewis P. Rowland, 543–8. Philadelphia: Lippincott Williams & Wilkins, 2003.

"Method for Manufacture of Lewisite." Project A1.2-6. March 25, 1925. *From National Archives and Records Administration.*

"Methyl, deadliest of gases, could have wiped out Berlin: Armistice saved Germans from 'superpoison' discovery by Professor Lewis." *Philadelphia Ledger,* May 25, 1919.

Meyer, Julius. *Der Gaskampf und die Chemischen Kampfstoffe.* Leipzig: S. Hirzel Press, 1926.

"Military toxins lurk where Muscovites swim." *Boston Globe,* July 30, 2001.

Miller, S. A. *Acetylene: Its Properties, Manufacture and Uses.* Vol. 1. New York: Academic Press, 1965.

Miller, Thorne. "Poisoned light." *Detective Story Magazine* 43 (October 1, 1921): 65–82.

"Minutes of British Chemical Warfare Committee." Report no. PRO WO 142/72. August 30, 1918. *From Public Records Office, London.*

Moore, William. *Gas Attack! Chemical Warfare 1915–18 and Afterwards.* New York: Hippocrene Books, 1987.

Mount, Harry A. "Gas intended to wipe out Hun armies dumped into the sea." *Cleveland (Ohio) Plain Dealer, Sunday Magazine,* June 15, 1919.

Mueller, Ulrich. *Die Chemische Waffe.* 2nd ed. Berlin: Verlag Chemie, 1932.

Munro, Nancy B., Sylvia S. Talmage, Guy D. Griffin, Larry C. Waters, Annetta P. Watson, Joseph F. King, and Veronique Hauschild. "The sources, fate, and toxicology of chemical warfare agent degradation products." *Environmental Health Perspectives* 107 (December 1999): 933–74.

Murphy, Paul. "Gas in the Italo-Abyssinian campaign." *Chemical Warfare Bulletin* 23 (1937): 1–8.

"Mustard Gas." Transcript, CBS News, *60 Minutes,* June 16, 1991. Produced by Charles C. Thompson II. Transcript No. 2340.

"Mustard gas drives off safe robbers who blow open a Michigan bank vault." *New York Times,* February 16, 1921.

"N. B. Scott gassed." *Washington Post,* August 4, 1918.

The National in the World War (April 6, 1917–November 11, 1918). General Electric Company, 1920.

"A new invention." *Central Christian (Missouri) Advocate,* January 9, 1919.

"New poison gas ready to make Berlin a desert." *Chicago Tribune,* May 25, 1919.

"Next war will end civilization, says Prof. Lewis." *Rockford (Illinois) Morning Star,* December 16, 1921.

Nieuwland, Julius A. "Some Reactions of Acetylene." Ph.D. thesis, University of Notre Dame, 1904.

Notre Dame website. "Congregation of the Holy Cross." See various links. http://www.nd.edu/~vocation/index.html

Notre Dame Athletics website. "Notre Dame Football Memories: Knute Rockne." http://und.collegesports.com/trads/rockne.html

"Notre Dame dean is credited with great discovery: Rev. Nieuwland shown to be first to produce 'lewisite,' deadly poison gas." *South Bend (Indiana) Tribune,* January 17, 1922.

"Now we know what those Ben Hur boys are doing: Most powerful of gas being manufactured here." *Willoughby (Ohio) Independent,* December 5, 1918.

NRC (National Research Council). "Evaluation of the Army's interim reference dose for lewisite." In *Review of the U.S. Army's Health Risk Assessments for Oral Exposure to Six Chemical-Warfare Agents,* 83–92. Washington, D.C.: National Academy Press, 1999.

NTI (Nuclear Threat Initiative) website. "Abandoned Chemical Weapons (ACW) in China." http://www.nti.org/db/china/acwpos.htm

———. "Country Overview: China." http://www.nti.org/e_research/profiles/China/

———. "Country Profiles: North Korea." http://www.nti.org/db/profiles/dprk/chem/cap/NKC_Ca_lewistnorr_bg.html

———. "Country Profiles: North Korea: Chemical." http://www.nti.org/e_research/profiles/NK/Chemical/index.html

———. "Russia Destroys 50 Tons of Lewisite." http://www.nti.org/d_newswire/issues/2004_6_1.html

"O. E. S. again acts as hostess to soldiers." *Willoughby (Ohio) Independent,* October 3, 1918.

"Obsoletion of Lewisite, L." Report to the Chairman of the Chemical Corps Technical Comm, Item 3144. October 3, 1955. *From Research, Development and Engineering Command.*

"Officers of 27th get whiff of gas: They dash through clouds of various types to learn how to fight them." *New York Times,* December 19, 1940.

Official Roster of Ohio Soldiers, Sailors and Marines in the World War, 1917–1918. Vols. 1–23. Columbus, Ohio: F. J. Heer Printing Company, 1926.

"Old Chemical Weapons Reference Guide." Aberdeen Proving Ground, Maryland, May 1998. *From Data Document Control Center, 410-436-4901.*

OPCW (Organisation for the Prohibition of Chemical Weapons) website. "Chemical Weapons Convention." See various links. http://www.opcw.org/html/db/cwc/eng/cwc_frameset.html

"An open letter: To all patriotic citizens of Willoughby." *Willoughby (Ohio) Independent,* October 17, 1918.

Ord, Margery G., and Lloyd A. Stocken. "A contribution to chemical defense in World War II." *Trends in Biomedical Sciences* 25 (May 2002): 253–6.

"Our super-poison gas: First story of compound 72 times deadlier than 'mustard' manufactured secretly by the thousands of tons." *New York Times*, April 20, 1919.

"Over 76 tonnes of lewisite disposed of in Saratov region." *Interfax*, August 23, 2004.

"Panel urges more arsenic health tests in AU area." *Washington Post*, June 10, 2001.

Pechura, Constance M., and David P. Rall, eds. *Veterans at Risk: The Health Effects of Mustard Gas and Lewisite*. Washington, D.C.: National Academy Press, 1993.

Perera, Judith. "Lewisite: New gas weapon in Gulf War." *New Scientist* 105 (1985): 8.

Peters, Rudolph A., Lloyd A. Stocken, and R. H. S. Thompson. "British Anti-Lewisite (BAL)." *Nature* 156 (November 24, 1945): 616–19.

" 'Pie more important than poetry,' Governor Willis said 'once upon a time.' " *Willoughby (Ohio) Republican*, October 23, 1918.

"Pine Bluff Arsenal Installation Action Plan." Department of Environmental Quality, Little Rock, Ark.

"Poison gas cargo sent to sea." *San Francisco Chronicle*, April 18, 1958.

"Poison gas will be sunk off coast." *San Francisco Chronicle*, March 18, 1958.

"Poison that can wipe out armies: Deadliest secret of the war—Drop on hand fatal." *Mid-Cumberland and North Westmorland (England) Herald*, May 31, 1919.

"Poison that may kill war: Single drop on the hand proves fatal." *Unidentified London (England) Newspaper*, 1919. *From Phil Reiss.*

Porter, Huntington P. "Amino acid excretion in degenerative disease of the nervous system." *Journal of Laboratory and Clinical Medicine* 34 (1949): 1623–6.

"Potential Military Chemical/Biological Agents and Compounds." Army Field Manual no. 3-9, Navy Publication no. P-467, Air Force Manual no. 355-7. Departments of Army, Navy, and Air Force, Washington, D.C., 1990.

Prentiss, Augustin M. *Chemicals in War: A Treatise on Chemical Warfare*. New York: McGraw-Hill, 1937.

"Priest on poison." *Time*, May 25, 1936.

Pringle, Henry F. "Profiles: Mr. President—I: James Bryant Conant." *New Yorker* (September 12, 1936): 20–24.

"Prof. Lefroy dies from unknown poison gas; Scientist unconscious since experiment." *New York Times*, October 15, 1925.

"Prof. Lewis honored in native city." *Alumni News* (Stanford University), July 1923.

"Progress Report on the Marine Piling Investigation: Abstract." Department of the Army, Washington, D.C., January 8, 1924.

"Reception for soldier boys." *Willoughby (Ohio) Republican*, August 30, 1918.

"Red Cross notes." *Willoughby (Ohio) Independent*, August 22, 1918.

"Red Cross notes." *Willoughby (Ohio) Republican*, October 23, 1918.

"Red Cross votes to furnish soldiers at Ben Hur plant bathing suits." *Willoughby (Ohio) Republican*, August 2, 1918.

"Red Cross, Willoughby branch: Blankets and mattresses furnished boys at Ben Hur plant." *Willoughby (Ohio) Republican*, August 16, 1918.

Rentokil Initial website. http://www.rentokil-initial.com/about_history.php

"Report on Chemical Warfare Physiological Investigations." Townsville, Queensland,

January–February 1943. Report nos. A816/1 9/301/94 and A816/1 9/301/104. *From National Archives of Australia.*

"Report of the Operations Involving the Disposal of 320 Tons of Radiological Waste and Lewisite by Dumping at Sea During the Period 6 June 1960 to 17 June 1960." Vol. 2. U.S. Army Chemical Corps, Technical Escort Unit No. 1602, Aberdeen Army Chemical Center, Maryland.

"Report on the Preparation and Physiological Properties of Crude Lewisite. Memorandum on the Production of Lewisite I by a New Process. Production of Lewisite by a New Process, Part I, Laboratory and Semi-Technical Development." Report no. PRO WO 188/463. February 20, 1934 and March 20, 1940. *From Public Records Office, London.*

"Resident's federal lawsuit blocked." *Washington Post,* September 17, 2003.

"Response tested in mock chemical attack." *San Diego Union-Tribune,* June 27, 2002.

"Reverse nerve disease: Disabling symptoms of degenerative disease of brain and liver reversed by treatment with BAL, the British antilewisite war gas." *Science News Letter,* December 29, 1951.

"Rooms for officers." *Willoughby (Ohio) Republican,* August 2, 1918.

Rudolph, Abraham M., Robert K. Kamei, and Kim J. Overby. *Rudolph's Fundamentals of Pediatrics.* 3rd ed. New York: McGraw-Hill, 2002.

Russell, Edmund. *War and Nature: Fighting Humans and Insects with Chemicals from World War I to Silent Spring.* New York: Cambridge University Press, 2001.

"Russia starts to scrap chemical weapons." *Washington Post,* April 24, 2002.

Rutherford, Richard. "Julius A. Nieuwland, CSC: The Man . . . the Priest . . . the Scientist." Thesis, Moreau Seminary, May 1960. *From University of Notre Dame Archives.*

Sasser, L. B., R. A. Miller, D. R. Kalkwarf, R. L. Buschbom, and J. A. Cushing. "Toxicology Studies on Lewisite and Sulfur Mustard Agents: Two-Generation Reproduction Study of Sulfur Mustard (HD) in Rats." Army Project Order no. 84PP4365. Pacific Northwest Laboratory, Richland, Wash., September 30, 1989.

"Savant trying lewisite on flies is gassed: Revived in hour from yank war vapor." *Chicago Tribune,* April 26, 1925.

SBCCOM (Soldier Biological and Chemical Command, U.S. Army) website. "MSDS on Lewisite," 1999. http://www.sbccom.apgea.army.mil/RDA/msds.lw.htm

Schnurr, Paula P., Julian D. Ford, Matthew J. Friedman, Bonnie L. Green, Bradley J. Dain, and Anjana Sengupta. "Predictors and outcomes of posttraumatic stress disorder in World War II veterans exposed to mustard gas." *Journal of Consulting and Clinical Psychology* 68 (2000): 258–68.

"Scientist gassed on eve of big discovery; Prof. Lefroy of London rescued by wife." *New York Times,* October 13, 1925.

Seagrave, Sterling. *Yellow Rain: A Journey through the Terror of Chemical Warfare.* New York: M. Evans and Company, 1981.

"Second O. E. S. party for soldiers has many pleasant features." *Willoughby (Ohio) Republican,* October 4, 1918.

"Secret diplomacy won Libyan pledge on arms." *New York Times,* December 21, 2003.

Servamer Corporation website. http://www.servamer.com/

"Seventh Annual Report of the Chemical Warfare Research Department." Report no. PRO WO 33/1153. March 31, 1927. *From Public Records Office, London.*

Shea, Robert D. "Father Nieuwland discoverer of 'lewisite.'" *Notre Dame Scholastic* 55 (January 14, 1922): 253.

"Ship full of war gas to be dumped in Pacific." *New York Times,* March 14, 1958.

Sidell, Frederick R., John S. Urbanetti, William J. Smith, and Charles G. Hurst. "Vesicants." In *Textbook of Military Medicine: Medical Aspects of Chemical and Biological Warfare,* ed. F. R. Sidell, E. T. Takafuji, and D. R. Franz, 197–228. Washington D.C.: Office of the Surgeon General and Borden Institute, 1997.

Simpson, Nathan A. "Nineteen-Eighteen in Willoughby, Ohio." *From Lake County Historical Society (Ohio).*

Sinai, Joshua. "Libya's pursuit of weapons of mass destruction." *Nonproliferation Review* (Spring–Summer 1997): 92–100.

SIPRI (Stockholm International Peace Research Institute). *Chemical Weapons: Destruction and Conversion.* London: Taylor & Francis, 1980.

———. *The Problems of Chemical and Biological Warfare.* Vol. 1: *The Rise of CB Weapons.* Stockholm, Sweden: SIPRI, 1971.

SIPRI website. Julian P. Robinson and J. Goldblat. "Chemical Warfare in Iraq-Iran War, May 1984." http://projects.sipri.se/cbw/research/factsheet-1984.html

Smart, Jeffrey K. "History of chemical and biological warfare: An American perspective." In *Textbook of Military Medicine: Medical Aspects of Chemical and Biological Warfare,* ed. F. R. Sidell, E. T. Takafuji, and D. R. Franz, 9–86. Washington D.C.: Office of the Surgeon General and Borden Institute, 1997.

Smiley, David. *Arabian Assignment.* London: Leo Cooper Publishing, 1975.

"Soldiers entertained at supper: Eastern Star chapter hostess at pleasant social function." *Willoughby (Ohio) Independent,* September 26, 1918.

Sollmann, Torald. *A Manual of Pharmacology and its Applications to Therapeutics and Toxicology.* Philadelphia: W. B. Saunders Company, 1957.

Solomon, Deborah. "The way we live now: Questions for Hans Blix. What weapons? The former U.N. inspector talks about Bush, Cheney and why Swedes are born diplomats." *New York Times Magazine* (March 28, 2004): 15.

"Some Experiments on the Skin Burning Power of Lewisite Vapour in a Warm Humid Climate." Report no. PRO WO 188/1441. April 19, 1946. *From Public Records Office, London.*

SOS—Arsenic.net website. "Arsenic Established Carcinogen." http://www.sos-arsenic.net/english/contamin/index.htm

Spiers, Edward M. *Chemical Warfare.* Urbana: University of Illinois Press, 1986.

———. *Chemical Weaponry.* New York: St. Martin's Press, 1989.

Stock, Thomas, and Karlheinz Lohs, eds. *The Challenge of Old Chemical Munitions and Toxic Armament Wastes.* SIPRI. New York: Oxford University Press, 1997.

Stockbridge, Frank P. "War inventions that came too late." *Harper's Magazine* 11 (September 1919): 828–35.

———. *Yankee Ingenuity in the War.* New York: Harper & Brothers Publishers, 1920.

Stocken, Lloyd A., and R. H. S. Thompson. "Reactions of British Anti-Lewisite with arsenic and other metals in living systems." *Physiological Reviews* 29 (1949): 168–92.

Sullivan, John B. "Toxic Terrorism." http://video.biocom.arizona.edu/video/ conferevents/BioTerrorism/Toxic%20Terrorism%20Hand out%209-10- 02%20Grand%20Rounds.doc

"Survey and Analysis Report." 2nd ed. U.S. Army Program Manager for Chemical Demilitarization, Project Manager for Non-Stockpile Chemical Material, 1996. *From Alaska Community Action on Toxins.*

Swann, John P. "Arthur Tatem, Parke Davis and the discovery of Mapharsen as an antisyphilitic agent." *Journal of the History of Medicine and Allied Sciences* 40 (1985): 167–87.

Tanaka, Yuki. "Poison gas: The story Japan would like to forget." *Bulletin of the Atomic Scientists* 44 (1988): 10–19.

Tarbell, D. Stanley, and Ann T. Tarbell, eds. *Roger Adams: Scientist and Statesmen.* Washington, D.C.: American Chemical Society, 1981.

"Tear gas bomb now officially police weapon: Invention of Prof. W. L. Lewis to be used by local department in bandit war." *Evanston (Illinois) News Index,* December 1, 1921.

"Tear gas device to foil bank robbers: Invention of Prof. Lewis of Northwestern gives protection to strong vaults." *Chicago Daily News,* October 14, 1921.

"Tear gas on safe doors to blind robbers." *Chicago Herald and Examiner,* February 28, 1922.

"Terrible U.S. war poison secret is bared at last." *Detroit News,* May 25, 1919.

"Their surprise must have been painful." *New York Times,* February 17, 1921.

"Then & Now in Willoughby 1835–1985 Sesquicentennial." *From Lake County (Ohio) Historical Society.*

Thomas P. Loughlin v. United States of America. Civil Action No. 02-0152 (ESH). U.S. District Court for the District of Columbia, September 2003. http://www. dcd.uscourts.gov/02-152b.pdf

"Three-hundred and fifty Willoughby soldiers to leave." *Willoughby (Ohio) Republican,* December 6, 1918.

"Toxic Chemical Agent Safety Standards." Pamphlet 385-61. Washington, D.C.: Department of the Army, 2002.

"Toxin cleanup goes natural: Army uses ferns to absorb Spring Valley arsenic." *Washington Post,* August 26, 2004.

Trammell, Gary L. "Toxicodynamics of organoarsenic chemical warfare agents." In *Chemical Warfare Agents,* ed. S. M. Somani, 255–60. San Diego: Academic Press, 1992.

"Truce saves million lives: Yankee professor produces poison which could have made Berlin city of dead." *San Francisco Examiner,* (month and day unknown), 1919.

"U.S. accuses Soviets of poisoning 3,000." *New York Times,* March 9, 1982.

"U.S. had awful preparation all ready for Huns: Ten airplanes carrying 'Lewisite' could have wiped Berlin off face of Earth." *Punxsutawney (Pennsylvania) Spirit,* May 29, 1919.

"U.S. ignored high arsenic level at NW home in mid-90's." *Washington Post,* July 25, 2001.

U.S. Patent Office. "Art of Dispersing Noxious Materials, Winford Lee Lewis of Evanston, Illinois." Patented July 3, 1928. Patent no. 1,675,940.

"U.S. set to join gas war: 'Lewisite' secret from first war to provide an effective weapon." *McCook (Nebraska) Gazette,* May 18, 1942.

"U.S. tests indicate Iraq substances not banned arms." *Reuters,* April 8, 2003.

USACE (U.S. Army Corps of Engineers). "Army Corps of Engineers Detects a Small Amount of Lewisite at Spring Valley Site." USACE, Baltimore District, September 3, 2003.

———. "A Brief History of the American University Experiment Station and U.S. Navy Bomb Disposal School, American University." USACE, Baltimore District, Office of History, 1994.

———. "Defense Environmental Restoration Program for Department of Defense Sites: Ordnance and Explosive Waste, Chemical Warfare Materials. Archives Search Report Findings: Catholic University, Washington, D.C." Project no. C03DC092001. USACE, St. Louis District, March 1995.

———. "Defense Environmental Restoration Program for Formerly Used Defense Sites: Ordnance and Explosive Waste, Chemical Warfare Materials. Archives Search Report Findings: Willoughby Plant, Willoughby, Ohio." Site no. G050HT91200. USACE, St. Louis District, December 1993.

———. "Facts on the Willoughby Plant: Willoughby, Ohio." USACE, Louisville District.

———. "The Former Cleveland Plant: Working Together for a Safer Environment." USACE, Louisville District.

———. "Remedial Investigation Report for the Operation Safe Removal Formerly Used Defense Site, Washington, D.C." USACE, Baltimore District, June 1995.

USACE website. "Spring Valley Project Update." See various links. http://www.nab.usace.army.mil/projects/WashingtonDC/springvalley.htm

USAF Museum (U.S. Air Force) website. "Kettering Aerial Torpedo Bug on Display at the U.S. Air Force Museum in Dayton, Ohio." http://www.wpafb.af.mil/museum/early_years/ey3a.htm

USDOJ (U.S. Department of Justice). "Assessment of CERCLA Hazardous Substances Released by Shell Oil Company and the United States Army at the Rocky Mountain Arsenal." Vol. 2, appendixes A–D. USDOJ, December 30, 1986. *From Rocky Mountain Arsenal library.*

USEPA (U.S. Environmental Protection Agency) website. "From Weapons to Wildlife, Rocky Mountain Arsenal." http://www.epa.gov/superfund/accomp/success/pdf/rma.pdf

VA (Veterans Affairs) website. "Mustard Gas Exposure and Long-Term Health Effects." http://www.va.gov/pressrel/99mustd.htm

VAC (Veterans Affairs Canada) website. "Chemical Warfare Agent Testing Recognition Program," February 19, 2004. http://www.vac-acc.gc.ca/general/sub.cfm?source=department/press/chem_dnd_back

Vedder, Edward B. *The Medical Aspects of Chemical Warfare.* Baltimore: Williams and Wilkins, 1925.

Vilensky, Joel A., Sid Gilman, and Elizabeth Dunn. "Derek E. Denny-Brown (1901–1981): His life and influence on American neurology." *Journal of Medical Biography* 6 (1998): 73–78.

Vilensky, Joel A., Wendy M. Robertson, and Sid Gilman. "Denny-Brown, Wilson's Disease, and BAL (British antilewisite [2,3-dimercaptopropanol])." *Neurology* 59 (2002): 914–16.

"W. Lee Lewis inventor of a deadly gas: Peace prevents use." *Evanston (Illinois) News Index,* January 9, 1919.

"W. Lee Lewis, the new chairman." *Chemical Bulletin (ACS)* 7 (June 1920): 166–67.

Wachtel, Curt. *Chemical Warfare.* Brooklyn, N.Y.: Chemical Publishing Company, 1941.

Waitt, Alden H. *Gas Warfare: The Chemical Weapon, Its Use, and Protection Against It.* New York: Duell, Sloan & Pearce, 1942.

———. "No super war gas! Ideal war gas may never be found . . . requirements and limitations . . . nations still rely on wartime combat chemicals." *Scientific American* 153 (December 1935): 293–97.

Walch, Timothy. *Catholicism in America.* Malabar, Fla.: Robert E. Krieger Publishing, 1989.

Walshe, J. M. "Penicillamine: A new oral therapy for Wilson's Disease." *American Journal of Medicine* 21 (1956): 487–95.

"War gas genius is guest here: Dr. W. Lee Lewis, creator of 'lewisite' at University." *Rochester (New York) Democrat,* April 1921.

"The war's deadliest gas: 'Lewisite' would have smothered German army by divisions." *Kansas City (Missouri) Star,* May 17, 1920.

Warthin, Aldred S., and Carl V. Weller. *The Medical Aspects of Mustard Gas Poisoning.* St. Louis: C. V. Mosby Company, 1919.

"Wastes of war: Russia's forgotten chemical weapons." *Washington Post,* August 16, 1998.

Waters, L. L., and Chester Stock. "BAL (British Anti-Lewisite)." *Science* 102 (December 14, 1945): 601–606.

Watson, A. P., and G. D. Griffin. "Toxicity of vesicant agents scheduled for destruction by the chemical stockpile disposal program." *Environmental Health Perspectives* 98 (1992): 259–80.

"Weapons of Mass Destruction." Videotape showing full-scale chemical weapons exercise, St. Petersburg, Florida, March 20, 2002.

Wehrfritz, George, Hideko Takayama, and Lijia Macleod. "In search of buried poison: Japanese chemical weapons from the war years can still sicken and kill." *Newsweek* 132 (July 20, 1998): 27.

West Virginia Division of Culture and History website. "West Virginia Archives and History: Time Trail, West Virginia, December 1997 Programs." http://www.wvculture.org/history/timetrl/ttdec.html

Whittemore, Gilbert F. "World War I, poison gas research, and the ideals of American chemists." *Social Studies of Science* 8 (May 1975): 135–63.

"Who's news today." *Times Star* (Alameda, California), May 15, 1940.

"Why the delay in using gas warfare: Inventor of lewisite, deadliest war gas, says world prejudice, lack of chemical industrialization and military tactics provide answers." *Riverside (California) Press,* October 28, 1939.

Wieland, Heinrich, and A. Bloemer. "Einige beiträge zur kenntnis der organischen arsenverbindungen. II: Arsentrichlorid und acetylen." *Justus Liebigs Annalen der Chemie* 431 (1923): 30–39.

Wikipedia website. "Alexsandr Solzhenitsyn." http://en2.wikipedia.org/wiki/Aleksandr_Isaevich_Solzhenitsyn

"Willoughby entertains her soldiery: Evening reception tendered to officers and men at Ben Hur plant by Red Cross." *Willoughby (Ohio) Independent,* September 5, 1918.

"Willoughby's war history coming into focus." *Willoughby (Ohio) News-Herald,* February 17, 2002.

"Winford Lee Lewis." In *The National Cyclopaedia of American Biography: Being the History of the U.S.,* vol. A, 369. New York: James T. White & Company, 1930.

"Winford Lee Lewis obituary." Unidentified newspaper, 1943. *From Phil Reiss.*

"Woman weeps as she denies family murders." *Times* (London), March 13, 2002.

Wood, Cyrus B. "The chemistry of the chemical warfare agents and of protection against them." *Military Surgeon* 62 (March 1928): 322–38.

Wooten, Joe V., David L. Ashley, and Antonia M. Calafat. "Quantitation of 2-chlorovinylarsonous acid in human urine by automated solid-phase microextraction—gas chromatography—mass spectrometry. *Journal of Chromatography B* 772 (2002): 147–53.

Wright, H. V., and H. G. Shaffer. "Development of Manufacturing Process for M-1." Report no. EACD 367. March 1, 1926.

Xinhua News Agency website. "Japanese Team Retrieves Chemical Weapons," September 28, 2002. http://www.china.org.cn/english/2002/Sep/44546.htm

Yahoo News website. "China, Japan Discuss War, Chemical Weapons," September 3, 2003. http://sg.news.yahoo.com/030903/1/3dwbc.html

"Yankee gas would have wiped Huns from globe." *Salt Lake City Herald,* May 25, 1919.

Yeoman, Barry. "Deadly dependence: The South's economic reliance on military bases has left a toxic legacy throughout the region." *Creative Loafing* (Charlotte, S.C.) (August 25, 2004): 29, 31, 33–35, 37–38.

Index

43, 45–47, 50; during World War II, xxi,
86–88
copper chloride, 98

Denny-Brown, Derek E., 83–85; at Boston
City Hospital, 83; British Anti-Lewisite
and, xx, 83–85; Wilson's disease and, xx,
83–85; during World War II, 83, 87
Deseret Chemical Depot, 120
Dorsey, Frank M., 37–42, 47–48, 51, 53
Dow Chemical Company, 47
Dugway Proving Ground, 120, 133–134

Eddington, Patrick, 113
Edgewood Arsenal, 32, 88–89, 92, 95–96, 102,
109, 122–123, 145–146
Egypt, 115–116
Elnora, Indiana, 65
England: Chemical Defense Research Es-
tablishment (Sutton Oaks), 115; lewisite
disposal/destruction in, 115, 141; lewisite
manufacture in, 67, 87, 98, 115, 141; lewis-
ite testing in, 67, 97–100, 147, 149; Porton
Down, 67, 80, 87, 98–100, 141–142, 149; War
Department Factory (Randle), 141. *See also*
under World War I; World War II
Environmental Protection Agency, 124, 127,
132–133, 150
Ethiopia, 67, 104
Evans, D. C., 103–104
Evans, Rob, 97, 99–100

Fort Leonard Wood, 154
France, lewisite manufacture in, 67, 101, 142.
See also under World War I; World War II
Franke, Siegfried, 155
Fries, Amos A., 22, 25–27, 56, 60–62, 64, 108

gas masks, 14–16, 20, 28–29, 37–39, 48, 73, 76,
93, 99, 133
Germany: chemical weapons and, 61, 67,
69, 138; Kaiser-Wilhelm Institut für Physikalische Chemie, 13, 27, 86; lewisite discoveries in, 27–28, 61; lewisite manufacture in,
101–103; lewisite testing in, 103–104. *See also*
under World War I; World War II
Goodwin, Bridget, 99–100
Green, Stanley, 60–61
Gulf War, 113

Haber, Fritz, 13, 86
Hague Treaties, xxi, 13
Hall, David, 133–134
Huntsville (Redstone) Arsenal, 92–93, 95,
109, 120, 131–132
hydrochloric acid, 14, 19, 23, 47, 74, 143, 165
hydrocyanic acid, xxi

India, 101, 110, 119, 144, 149
Iran, 112–113
Iraq, xix–xx, 112–114, 116, 142, 156
Ireland, M. W., 55
Italy: lewisite disposal in, 110, 142; lewisite
manufacture in, 67, 104, 142; lewisite use in
Ethiopia by, 67, 104. *See also under* World
War II

Japan: chemical weapon cleanup by, 139–
141; invasion of Manchuria/China by,
105; lewisite disposal by, 114–115, 138–141;
lewisite manufacture in, 69, 104, 107, 118;
lewisite testing by, 105–106; lewisite use in
China by, xxi, 69, 105–107; Ōkunojima,
104, 107, 114, 151; Unit 516, 105–106. *See also*
under World War II

Kettering Bug, 57–58
Korean War, 108–109

Lewis, Winford Lee, 7–12, 19–28; at Catholic
University of America, 17, 19–25; as a chemist, 7–8, 10, 19–25, 68; discovery of lewisite
by, xix, 19–27; at Institute of American
Meat Packers, 10; Lewis-Hughes Police Grenade, 10; Lewis Plaque, 11; at Morningside
College, 7; at Northwestern University, 8–
10; personal life of, 8, 10–12, 28, 66; as a professor, 7–9; at Stanford University, 7; thesis
of, 8; at University of Chicago, 7–8; at University of Washington, 7; at U.S. Department of Agriculture, 8; views of, on poison
gas, 11, 62–63; during World War I, 8–9, 17,
19–26, 28, 35; writings of, 7–8, 10–12, 24, 27,
34, 50, 57, 60–63, 65, 90–91
lewisite: battle use of, xxi, 67, 69, 104–107,
111–113, 115–116; chemistry of, 4, 23–24, 165;
classified documents about, xx, 54, 97–98,
154–155; credit for discovery of, 5, 25–28, 56–
58, 60; degradation products of, 55, 74–75,
123–124, 133–135, 143, 158, 165–166; discovery

JOEL A. VILENSKY is Professor of Anatomy and Cell Biology at Indiana University School of Medicine. He has taught Medical Gross Anatomy at its Fort Wayne campus for the past twenty-five years. His interest in the history of lewisite stems from research on the history of Wilson's disease, which was first successfully treated using British Anti-Lewisite in 1951.